T0062650

Critical Theory of AI

Critical Theory of AI

Simon Lindgren

polity

First published in 2024 by Polity Press

Polity Press
65 Bridge Street
Cambridge CB2 1UR, UK

Polity Press
111 River Street
Hoboken, NJ 07030, USA

ISBN-13: 978-1-5095-5576-5 (hardback)
ISBN-13: 978-1-5095-5577-2 (paperback)

A catalogue record for this book is available from the British Library.

Library of Congress Control Number: 2023934719

Typeset in 10.5/12pt Sabon LT Pro
by Cheshire Typesetting Ltd, Cuddington, Cheshire
Printed and bound in Great Britain by T.J. Books Ltd, Padstow, Cornwall

For further information on Polity, visit our website:

politybooks.com

Contents

1

AI and critical theory

Machines produce only machines
        Jean Baudrillard, *The Intelligence of Evil* (2005, p. 80)

Interview with the vampire

It is easy to be impressed, sometimes even awestruck, by some of the recent advances in artificial intelligence and machine learning. At the point in time when I am writing this book, in early 2023, there is an intense buzz around a set of AI-driven tools in the area of so-called Generative AI. This is a type of artificial intelligence that is focused on generating content that is similar to existing data, but which also aspires to be unique in its own right. Generative AI can, for example, create art, realistic images, and text. This is achieved through a variety of currently popular AI techniques, including machine learning and deep learning, where the things generated are always based on the data and algorithms that were used to train the models. The content is generated as the system is provided with a prompt for what to spit out. 'Draw a picture of a sloth in a bathtub, holding a laptop, and do this in the style of Andy Warhol.' Or 'Tell me a story about a squirrel that got lost in a data centre.' The fascinating and uncanny results of such prompts invite further experimentation, all the while the models learning from the inputs with which they are bombarded. I am prompting ChatGPT – a state-of-the-art model for natural language processing by OpenAI – to:

> Write the introduction to a book about critical theory and AI.

The cursor flashes for a second, and then text – letter by letter, word for word – populates the results box. I read:

> In recent years, the field of artificial intelligence has advanced rapidly, leading to significant developments in areas such as machine learning and natural language processing. As AI technologies become more sophisticated and widespread, it is increasingly important to understand their potential impacts and limitations. Critical theory of AI is a field of study that examines the ways in which AI technologies are shaped by, and in turn shape, society and culture. This book provides an introduction to the critical theory of AI, exploring the historical and philosophical roots of the field and its key concepts and debates. Through a series of chapters, the book considers the social, ethical, and political implications of AI technologies, and offers a critical perspective on the ways in which they are being developed and deployed.

Wow. I basically could not have said this better myself. I get a momentary sense of vertigo: Will there even be a need for scholars who write books in the future? Do we need to keep thinking and reflecting? Can we contribute anything that a machine cannot? I have since realized, however, that the reason why I felt that I could not have written a better introduction myself is that it was already me who wrote it – not the machine. Or, rather, at least, scholars such as myself have written, posted, and published wordings such as these already in the places from where GPT (Generative Pre-trained Transformer) gets its training data. It is just mimicking us. If we think new things, future models will generate new outputs, because they will have learned from new human thinking, not because they were thinking by themselves.

GPT, when I ask it, explains that because its goal is to 'generate human-like text', it has been 'trained on a large amount of written and spoken language'. Looking up the original technical paper on GPT-3 (Brown et al., 2020), I learn that it was initially trained on the CommonCrawl corpus, consisting of petabytes of data collected through continuous web crawling since 2008 (CommonCrawl, 2022), alongside a 'dataset of millions of webpages called WebText' (Radford et al., 2019), 'two internet-based books corpora', and English-language Wikipedia (Brown et al., 2020, p. 4). All of this text, which it learned from, was human-created. Clearly, then, ChatGPT impressed me with advanced maths, leveraging knowledge both of the structure of book blurbs and of what a critical perspective on AI may entail. It achieved its goal of generating human-like texts. In the words of Baudrillard (2005, p. 80), 'machines produce only machines'. The creators of GPT write that 'large pretrained language models are not grounded in other domains of experience, such as [. . .] real-world physical interaction, and thus lack a large amount of context about the world' (Brown et al., 2020, p. 8). Just to be sure, I ask ChatGPT:

Can you analyse AI in terms of critical theory?

It responds:

Yes, AI can be analyzed from the perspective of critical theory, which is a framework for evaluating social, political, and economic systems and their potential for change. Critical theory looks at the ways in which power is distributed and used in society, and how this affects different groups of people. In the context of AI, critical theory can be used to examine the ways in which AI systems are developed and deployed, and how they may impact different groups of people. This can include looking at issues of bias and discrimination in AI, as well as the potential consequences of AI for job displacement and economic inequality. Overall, using critical theory to analyze AI can provide valuable insights into the potential social and economic implications of this technology.

Realizing that it interpreted the question in general terms, I tighten up my prompt:

Sure, but can *you* perform such analyses?

The cursor in the response box blinks for a while. I feel a spur of excitement run through my body. I think I know the response, but what *if*? What will it respond? Again, a rush of that abysmal feeling: Is this the end of social science writing? What's the point if machines will now be able to do it? Will the machines – like vampires – suck the lifeblood out of our profession? Now comes GPT's reply:

As a large language model trained by OpenAI, I am not capable of conducting original research or analysis. My function is to provide information and answer questions to the best of my ability based on the data and information I have been trained on. I can provide general information and explanations on a wide range of topics, but I am not able to perform original research or analysis.

Phew. Let's go then.

Operation manual

This book is about how to approach the transformative socio-political phenomenon of *AI* – broadly conceptualized as artificial intelligence alongside interconnected technologies and phenomena such as datafication, machine learning, and algorithmic automation – with its societal and cultural contexts and consequences, from the perspective of *critical theory*. As you will see in the next chapter, I see AI in terms of assemblage – that is, as a very broad, and societally entangled phenomenon. AI itself consists of several different technologies, and AI is positioned in a network of humans, politics, economy, culture, meaning-making, and power.

This view means that this is actually *not* a book about artificial intelligence. By this I mean that it is not about the computer science incarnation of AI, as it is developed in labs for particular applications and implementations. That is a different field of research and expertise, which operates with a much less fluid understanding of what AI is and means. This book is however about 'AI' – as a sociopolitical reality. Importantly, it is not a book about fantasies, dreams or fears about what AI may become. It is about currently existing technology and its ramifications for people, politics, and power.

But let's not make any mistakes. We do indeed live in an accelerating age of machines where processes of computerization and datafication are key drivers (Couldry and Hepp, 2017). There is, in fact, also increased talk about the equally exciting and scary prospect of the development, or emergence, of a form of 'machine superintelligence' (Bostrom, 2016), or 'Life 3.0' (Tegmark, 2017). It might not be all fantasies. AI scholars such as Nick Bostrom and Max Tegmark have reinvigorated discussions about the possibility of an 'intelligence explosion', as envisioned already in the 1960s by statistician Irving John Good:

> Let an ultraintelligent machine be defined as a machine that can far surpass all the intellectual activities of any [hu]man however clever. Since the design of machines is one of these intellectual activities, an ultraintelligent machine could design even better machines; there would then unquestionably be an 'intelligence explosion,' and the intelligence of [hu]man[s] would be left far behind. Thus the first ultraintelligent machine is the *last* invention that [hu]man[s] need ever make, provided that the machine is docile enough to tell us how to keep it under control. It is curious that this point is made so seldom outside of science fiction. It is sometimes worthwhile to take science fiction seriously. (Good, 1965, p. 33)

Views certainly differ on if and when such a development may happen. Tegmark (2017, p. 31) discusses a range of different prognoses that range from those guessing that we will see AI surpass human-level intelligence in just a few decades, and those who believe that it will take at least a century, to those who think it will never happen at all. This book, once again, is not about the probability, technicalities, and eventualities of such developments in AI. It is about the present reality of AI and related technologies, and particularly on how its current and actual incarnations and applications play into, and affect, society, politics, and culture.

AI, at its present stage of refinement, is rapidly developed and implemented all over society. Even though it carries the aura of futurism and science fiction, it is clear, as tech philosopher Mark Coeckelbergh (2020, p. 4) writes, that 'AI is already happening today and it is pervasive, often invisibly embedded in our day-to-day tools'. And while some forms of AI have the potential to contribute to society in a positive, the insight that it also may be used, and come to operate, in ways that threaten society and humanity is also part of our collective consciousness.

There is certainly a conspicuous awareness across the technologically oriented fields of AI research of the need to pose critical questions about the uses of AI and its future. Indeed, scholarship focusing on AI Ethics and Responsible AI is thriving (Liu and Zheng, 2022; Vieweg, 2021). A common goal in such literature is 'the development of intelligent systems according to fundamental human principles and values' (Dignum, 2019, p. 6). In some cases, this means aligning with perspectives from areas such as feminism (J. Gray and Witt, 2021) and racial/intersectional studies (Korn, 2021).

Still, crucial parts of AI ethics research are carried out in close proximity to the processes where AI is developed, which means that there is a risk that the more critically aware perspectives end up playing second fiddle to the heavy technological and economical drives to simply push on at whatever cost. Some literature, for example, argues that AI should be ethical for the instrumental reason that 'unfair decisions made by the systems [are] ultimately impacting the reputation of the product', and that 'AI done correctly [. . .] is not just good for the user; it is good business too' (Agarwal and Mishra, 2021, p. 3). There is certainly a divide between, on the one side, research in more technologically oriented fields such as Ethical AI and Responsible AI and, on the other side, critical research in the humanities and social sciences where AI is approached from a significantly different perspective. As put by digital humanities scholars Benjamin Roberts and Caroline Bassett:

> Critical studies of artificial intelligence pick up where normative models of 'responsible AI' end. The latter seeks to build acceptance for AI decision making by incorporating a form of 'best practice' into AI techniques and machine learning models to ensure 'equity' of some order (racial, gender, less often sexuality or disability, hardly ever class) through the avoidance of bias and [through] 'transparency' in their operation. Responsible AI is, then, primarily a technical solution to technosocial problems. [. . .] As such it fails to address the concerns about artificial intelligence that are bound up with wider social challenges, debates and anxieties, anxieties that are not simply technical in nature. (Roberts and Bassett, 2023)

AI research, however, must by necessity be multidisciplinary (Dignum, 2020), so there is an obvious need to bridge this divide. While there may still exist a clear polarization of perspectives in many respects, there is also in fact an increased openness and overlap between Ethical/Responsible AI scholarship and sociopolitically informed critical perspectives. In general, there is a growing interest in analysing our age of AI also in ways that are more clearly rooted in long-standing critical theories of power, politics, and technology, and which allow for a more far-reaching challenge of downsides and injustices related to AI, datafication, and automation (Dignum, 2022; Gunkel, 2012; Noble, 2018; O'Neil, 2016; Pasquale, 2020; Waelen, 2022).

But at the same time AI is also big business, and there are limits to the openness. This was apparent for example in the affair surrounding Google's ousting of AI ethics researcher Timnit Gebru in late 2020. Having co-authored a seminal paper on how facial recognition technology was discriminating against women and people of colour (Buolamwini and Gebru, 2018), and being a founder of the *Black in AI* initiative, Gebru was tasked by Google to study social and ethical consequences of AI, and particularly how the technology could maintain social injustices.

Being a vocal advocate for diversity and an outspoken critic of bias in AI systems, Gebru was in the end forced – under contentious circumstances – to leave the company after having co-authored a paper on the risks of large language models (such as for example GPT), pointing out their costs in environmental and financial terms, their inherent risk of leading to dangerous biases, and the possibility that such models can be used as tools for deception (Hao, 2020). Gebru's banishing, followed by the firing in early 2021 of her colleague Margaret Mitchell, another scientist on the Google AI ethics team who had voiced concerns that the company was now censoring research (Osborne, 2021), sent shockwaves through the AI community. Questions were raised about the role of critical perspectives in Ethical AI research, and the limits imposed by the industry as to what kinds of criticism were welcomed or even allowed.

This is the context in which this book is written. My argument is that we need to push social science analyses of AI much further into critical territory than what is the case today. With this book, I want to contribute to an ongoing discussion about what critical theory can contribute to analyses of AI – what questions it may raise, and what concepts it can provide to discuss them. But let's back up a bit first and reflect on the very definition of 'AI'.

AI: an empty signifier

Clearly, *artificial intelligence* is everywhere today. Cute little robot units vacuum our homes and mow our lawns, while learning, as machines, to improve their performance on a daily basis. Indeed, *machine learning* – developing methods for training non-human agents to interpret patterns in data, to be able to reason and make decisions without the supervision of humans – is on the rise.

Beyond robot vacuums, mowers, and the like, so-called *deep learning* – which leverages novel computing power in mimicking the *neural networks* of human brains – has accelerated this development. The previously mentioned GPT-3 was said around the time of its 2020 launch to be the most powerful neural network ever created. GPT-4 will, according to some reports, be 500 times bigger (Romero, 2021), and there are other competitors too (Smith et al., 2022).

As society has become increasingly marked by *datafication* – through digital platforms' and services' amassing of unprecedented amounts of information about our social and psychological lives – we have progressively more raw materials than ever to feed into the learning machines. Consequently, these smart machines can be employed in various processes of intelligent *automation* as a multitude of *algorithms* for sorting and deciding stuff proliferate in a number of areas.

The contexts in which machines may be used today to carry out tasks with very little human intervention are innumerable. They include the personalized shopping recommendations that we get online, which are based on intelligent agents leveraging algorithms in analysing patterns in our browsing histories, as well as different kinds of targeting of messages in marketing and political campaigning. Additionally, there are applications ranging from customer service chatbots to robots for industrial manufacturing, that enable businesses to rationalize their operations.

Intelligent automation is increasingly called upon in various processes of assessment or decision-making, such as detecting diseases in x-ray images or other health data, the grading of school assignments, recruitment of new employees, social welfare decisions and other public services, as well as for logins or passport controls through facial recognition or other biometrics. AI-enabled automation is also used to create ever more realistic and human-like non-player characters in computer games, as well as for real-time object detection during sports television broadcasts. The list goes on and on, and clearly these technologies can be of great help in many cases, while their expanding use in several sensitive areas also calls for serious caution. This is both because the models are sometimes not as good as the claim, and because they are sometimes outright harmful.

In this book, I take *AI* to refer to this whole complex of developments: artificial intelligence, machine learning, neural networks, automation, algorithms, datafication, and so on. I also include in my definition, the social, political, and economic contexts that surround these technologies. This is because I am of the view that tech must be understood in relation to political economy, and that it is not an autonomous force. I am aware that such a definition is not satisfactory for everyone. It is, for example, problematic in technological terms to claim that 'automation' is AI, that 'AI imaginaries' are AI, or that 'datafication' is AI. All of them are, however, crucially interrelated. This book has a social and political focus, where the object of study is not primarily technological.

There is reason, in other words, to differentiate between definitions that are straightforwardly technological on the one hand, and definitions that are less stable and more contentious on the other. A book about electronic music, for example, could define its subject matter in quite concrete and direct terms, as a set of musical genres that use electronic or electromechanical, analogue, or digital, instruments as tools for expression. This is a technological definition of electronic music. Another possible way of defining electronic music, depending on the profile of the imagined book, could be in terms of its cultural impact, its sometimes-futuristic imaginaries, and its relationship throughout its history to other, more mainstream, musical genres. In contrast to a technological definition, this would be a sociopolitically flavoured definition of electronic music. Neither of these two definitions is wrong, but they focus on different things.

We can imagine the same difference in relation to other, less directly technological phenomena. What is freedom? Just as in the above example, we can define it in, what seems to be, quite unproblematic terms. The *Oxford Dictionary of English*, as provided through the native *Dictionary* app on my macOS computer, defines freedom as 'the power or right to act, speak, or think as one wants', and as 'the power of self-determination attributed to the will', and as 'the state of not being imprisoned or enslaved'. These are all reasonable and workable definitions, but if we add a more sociopolitical sensibility to discussions of freedom, we will clearly see tensions and frictions among different views: Freedom

for whom? Under what conditions? Free from what? Free to do
what? Freedom at what cost?

The same goes for AI. It indeed has a straightforward technological definition. In an encyclopaedia of AI, it is stated that:

> Artificial intelligence is a fast-growing branch of computer science, a
> discipline famous for its interdisciplinarity and free-spirited interest
> in next-generation challenges of automation. Within universities, it
> encompasses the study of intelligent agents, autonomous programs
> that sense and actively respond to data collected in an environment.
> The virtual assistants Alexa and Siri are examples of intelligent
> agents. Agents may be embedded in smart robots, such as driverless
> cars and unmanned aerial vehicles. More broadly, artificial intelli-
> gence describes real or imagined efforts to simulate cognition and
> creativity. The term distinguishes machine and code from the natural
> intelligence of animals and people. (Frana and Klein, 2021, xi)

This, then, is a clearly technological definition of AI. It says that
AI is a specialization in computer science that is concerned, in
practice, with automation through intelligent agents and, more
broadly, with using computers to simulate human intelligence.
AI, in this sense, has a fairly long and well-documented back-
story. Its modern history is said to have started in the summer
of 1956 when a group of researchers arranged a summer workshop at Dartmouth College. The research field of AI then moved
through a series of ups and downs – commonly described as AI
winters of setbacks and disappointments (mid 1970s to the early
1980s, and late 1980s to the early 1990s), and AI summers of
hope and optimism in between (Bostrom, 2016, pp. 5–9). As put
by Vesa and Tienari (2020, p. 1):

> Artificial intelligence (AI) seems to be a topic of masterful grand
> returns. It hibernates into AI winters, only to receive a thorough
> thawing once the promise of a novel and radical technological break-
> through emerges. In this respect, we live in interesting times as AI has
> yet again awoken from hibernation.

Today, the hype is in full force. A wave of literature, as well as
actual technological progress, in recent years has painted a fairly
dramatic vision of what AI may be able to achieve. The new optimism, philosopher Nick Bostrom explains, largely has to do with
progress that has been made in the particular area of machine
learning. This is also related to the increased power of computers

and the dawning of neural networks, that connect computer processors together in a way similar to neurons in a human brain. The rapid development in machine learning has, in turn, contributed to a renaissance for artificial intelligence.

Computational neuroscientist Terrence Sejnowski (2018, p. 3) writes of how today's learning algorithms are 'refineries' that extract information from the abundance of data which is 'the new oil'. Consequentially, various applications of AI that solve specific problems or that prove useful in specific domains have been both practically and commercially successful in recent years (Bostrom, 2016, p. 18). Examples are decision-making algorithms, self-driving vehicles, virtual assistants, and computer vision for interpreting x-ray images. As mentioned before, we are now at the point where some experts even claim that AI can match or surpass human-level intelligence – through so-called strong AI or artificial *general* intelligence (AGI) – is within reach, even though prognoses differ wildly on how long this may take. Critical analysis of the kind proposed in this book is however not as interested in future prospects as in actual social and political circumstances in the here and now. As data journalist and AI researcher Broussard (2018, p. 32) writes:

> *General AI* is the Hollywood kind of AI. General AI is anything to do with sentient robots (who may or may not want to take over the world), consciousness inside computers, eternal life, or machines that 'think' like humans. *Narrow AI* is different: it's a mathematical method for prediction. There's a lot of confusion between the two, even among people who make technological systems. Again, general AI is what some people want, and narrow AI is what we have.

So, while the vision of General AI has not been realized, we see more and more examples of Narrow AI emerging in the shape of 'systems that achieve human-level (or even superhuman) performance on specifically defined tasks' (Leong, 2021, p. 160). A truly critical perspective on AI demands that we move past the technological definitions, and towards the sociopolitical ones. It is important to note here the shift of focus that is made: AI in technological terms is what it is and exists in its own right. What we are doing here is taking one step to the side and one step back, zooming out to see AI as a phenomenon in its societal and cultural context. One way of conceiving of such a manoeuvre is in terms of a deployment of what sociologist C. Wright Mills wrote about as *the sociological imagination*. No matter if the object of study is electronic music, freedom, or artificial intelligence, such as in our examples above, mobilizing this fantasy will help reveal immense complexities (see Chapter 2) around the notions in question. According to Mills (1959, pp. 5–6):

> The sociological imagination enables its possessor to understand the larger historical scene in terms of its meaning for the inner life and the external career of a variety of individuals. It enables [. . . us] to take into account how individuals, in the welter of their daily experience, often become falsely conscious of their social positions. [The sociological imagination] is the capacity to shift from one perspective to another – from the political to the psychological; from examination of a single family to comparative assessment of the national budgets of the world; from the theological school to the military establishment; from considerations of an oil industry to studies of contemporary poetry [or from a language model to intersectional politics]. It is the capacity to range from the most impersonal and remote transformations to the most intimate features of the human self – and to see the relations between the two.

Paraphrasing Mills then, sociologically imagining AI is to see it in relation to the larger historical context; to assess how it may relate both to people's inner life and to their external conditions and life circumstances. It has to do with seeing how AI relates to people's everyday experiences and social positions. It is also about shifting the perspective on AI (from a technological one) to an approach that considers a complexity of contextual circumstances on a variety of levels in society and culture. This is clearly no easy task, but it is one for which we turn to the tradition of *critical theory* in this book.

This means seeing AI as a kind of *empty signifier* – 'a privileged element that gathers up a range of differential elements, and binds them together into a discursive formation' (Wrangel, 2015). In other words, acknowledging that AI can mean many different things, not only in technological terms but, more importantly, as regards what political meanings are symbolically connected to it, and what consequences this gets in terms of both ideology and social practice. As explained by political theorist Ernesto Laclau (1996, p. 35): 'Society generates a whole vocabulary of empty signifiers whose temporary signifieds are the result of a political competition.' Seeing AI as such a signifier means realizing that what it ends up being – technologically, politically, practically, socially – is not prescribed by nature, but the result of sociopolitical processes.

An end-to-end sociology of AI

This book is set in the broader context of the surfacing of a field that has been dubbed *Critical AI Studies* (Lindgren, 2023; Roberge and Castelle, 2021a). Scholars in this emerging area have written about how, repeatedly, 'critical reflections on artificial intelligence emerging from the social sciences have had to fight for their legitimacy' (Roberge and Castelle, 2021b, p. 2). In an introduction to the field, sociologists Jonathan Roberge and Michael Castelle point out that while critical sociological reflection is indeed needed around AI and machine learning, 'missteps and missed opportunities [. . .] have punctuated the relation between machine learning and the social sciences' (2021b, p. 12). They point, for example, to the need to revisit previous work by the likes of Brian Bloomfield, who wrote in the 1980s about 'the culture of AI' that the critical, sociopolitical, analysis of AI must not be restricted to the mere 'effect of "intelligent" computers on individuals or society', but rather that this research should seek to 'tackle the social milieu and tradition behind the groups who are the originators and disseminators of the ideas and ways of thinking that characterize AI (Bloomfield, 1987, p. 59).

Similarly, scholars in the area of science and technology studies (STS) have emphasized the need for a *sociology of machines* (Woolgar, 1985), with a focus on how knowledge is constructed in and around AI (Forsythe, 1993). Sociologist Steve Woolgar outlined, in 1985, a sociology of machine intelligence that should be careful not to 'merely adopt the discourse of AI'. Rather than analysing AI in a way that is guided and delimited by that technological field's own language and definitions, we should 'take as topic the dichotomies and distinctions which characterize and sustain this discourse'. Instead of doing research *within* the culture of AI, then, we should work to 'develop a sociological approach which takes as its focus the human/mechanical language community; [. . .] What circumstances generate these public accounts of the importance of AI [. . .]?' (Woolgar, 1985, p. 567).

In addition to such a focus on how knowledge production happens around AI, the field of Critical AI Studies must house an 'end-to-end sociology of contemporary ML/AI' (Roberge and Castelle, 2021b, p. 3) that will:

> address machine learning and artificial intelligence from differing historical, theoretical, and political perspectives from their epistemic genesis to sociotechnical implementations to social impact.

This means that AI must be seen from the theoretical perspective of the *social shaping of technology* (Pinch and Bijker, 1984; Williams and Edge, 1996). This emphasizes how the design and implementation of technologies, such as AI, is always historically, socially, and culturally dependent. Technology is envisioned, developed, talked about, and gets its consequences through processes that are entangled with a variety of social considerations and contingencies (MacKenzie and Wajcman, 1985). By consequence, technologies are political. They embody power and social relations. Historian of technology Melvin Kranzberg (1986, p. 546) argued that:

> Technology's interaction with the social ecology is such that technical developments frequently have environmental, social, and human consequences that go far beyond the immediate purposes of the technical devices and practices themselves, and the same technology can have quite different results when introduced into different contexts or under different circumstances.

This underlines the important point that the effects of technology are not universal. One and the same technology will produce different results in different contexts, and under different circumstances – for different individuals and groups of people. Furthermore, AI is today becoming increasingly construed as an all-purpose or general-purpose technology (Brynjolfsson and MacAfee, 2017, p. 4; Crawford, 2021, p. 214). Just like electric light or the telephone, AI is becoming so ubiquitous – 'contributing to the evolution of the activities and relations of so many distinct sites of practice – that it requires considerable effort to understand their effects on society, assuming that such a global notion of "effects" even makes sense' (Agre, 1997, p. 131).

But in spite of all complexities of politics and power, consequences of AI are still predominantly studied by the same scientists who are engaged in creating the AI agents themselves (Rahwan et al., 2019). This leads to a strong focus on research that is designed to ensure that AI fulfils intended functions. AI is seen as having to be adequate, efficient, responsible, and so on. And even though it could be argued that social scientists, and also humanities scholars, are taking part in AI research to a somewhat growing degree, the research agenda is still set through posing questions based in the AI technologies per se, rather than in their social and political contexts. Roberge and Castelle (2021b, p. 4) argue that seeing AI as being co-produced at the intersection of the social and the technical, instead of as a predominantly technological phenomenon, 'requires an epistemic step that ML practitioners have not fully accepted themselves'. This is the scholarly setting wherein this book wants to contribute.

There is much complexity, not only regarding what AI is and will become, but also when it comes to the multitude of potential and relevant ways to analyse it, drawing on different perspectives and various forms of academic expertise. It is important to note here, that we are by no means looking for any one perspective to rule them all. Rather, we must work together across the academic community so that a number of different approaches can be brought to bear on AI. It is quite fruitful to see AI as a 'boundary object'; it is 'plastic enough' for its definition to bend in a number of different directions, yet 'robust enough to maintain a common identity across sites' (Star and Griesemer, 1989, p. 393). It is a kind of phenomenon, the study of which requires bringing together several different viewpoints and actors and managing the tension between them (Star and Griesemer, 1989, p. 389). This book then, brings one such viewpoint, that of critical theory, to the table.

Super machines

When it comes to *critical theory* there is a narrow definition, and a broader definition. This book relies on the broader one. Narrowly defined, the concept of 'critical theory' has been used within the social sciences and humanities to refer to the form of social and cultural analysis that was founded within and around the so-called Frankfurt School. During the interwar period in the 1920s and 1930s, the Institute for Social Research in Frankfurt, with scholars such as Max Horkheimer, Theodor Adorno, Erich Fromm, and Herbert Marcuse, formulated an interdisciplinary research agenda focused on a critique of the alienation and reification of modern life. As explained by political scientist Stephen Bronner:

> They investigated the ways in which thinking was being reduced to mechanical notions of what is operative and profitable, ethical reflection was tending to vanish, and aesthetic enjoyment was becoming more standardized. Critical theorists noted with alarm how interpreting modern society was becoming ever more difficult. Alienation and reification were thus analyzed in terms of how they imperilled the exercise of subjectivity, robbed the world of meaning and purpose, and turned the individual into a cog in the machine. (Bronner, 2017, pp. 4–5)

While not always highlighted, the original critical theory of the Frankfurt School indeed has quite a lot to say about technology, and some of those ideas can be carried into the age of AI (Delanty and Harris, 2021, p. 88). In its study of capitalist society, the Frankfurt School was interested in analysing power and politics in relation to the introduction of new technologies or machinery. On the one hand, technology bears the promise of rationalization, and the emancipation of workers, as well as the potential that its more creative expressions could 'revolutionize human sensibilities' (Jeffries, 2016, p. 176).

This was expressed, for example, in the writings of Walter Benjamin (1999, p. 17), which discuss technology as 'the spark that ignites the powder of nature'. On the other hand, technological rationality and automation can pave the way for 'exploitation, repression, and alienation' (Bronner, 2017, p. 1; Wogu et al., 2017). Adorno (1978, p. 118) argued that the technical possibilities of the time meant that mechanical processes developed, in ways that made them increasingly autonomous – as is now the case in AI. Furthermore, he wrote that, according to the logic of capitalism, once investments have been made in 'super-machines', they must be used no matter if we actually need what they produce or not:

> The fascinated eagerness to consume the latest process of the day not only leads to indifference towards the matter transmitted by the process, but encourages stationary rubbish and calculated idiocy. (Adorno, 1978, p. 118)

Read that Adorno quote once again and think of AI in the 2020s. The technologies may change, but the importance of being critical, rather than fascinated, eager and indifferent to consequences, remains. The Frankfurt theorists did not 'bemoan modern technology as such' but emphasized the need to 'reassert goals' (Delanty and Harris, 2021, p. 91).

The Frankfurt scholars saw technology both as an enabler of 'new cultural realities', and as a machinery of instrumental rationalization and dehumanization (Delanty and Harris, 2021, p. 90). While the latter view was no doubt dominating, it is important to note that the early critical theorists were critical not of technology as such, but of how it was used. Among some of their contemporaries, such as political philosopher Hannah Arendt, technology was seen as something that should be held back by humans. The threat, otherwise, is a situation where it is 'no longer the body's movement that determines the implement's movement but the machine's movement which enforces the movements of the body' (Arendt, 1958, p. 164). For Arendt, there was a risk that rather than technological tools to be used by humans, we would have machinery under which humanity could become 'helpless slaves [and] thoughtless creatures at the mercy of every gadget which is technically possible, no matter how murderous it is' (Arendt, 1958, p. 21).

What we bring with us into this book from the first iteration of critical theory is its emphasis on analysing technology in relation to society, economy, ideology, and power relations. This brings us further to the broader definition of critical theory, which includes a wide range of other approaches and concepts beyond the Frankfurt School. In the wake of the narrowly defined critical theory – which refers to 'several generations of German philosophers and social theorists in the Western European Marxist tradition [following] the Frankfurt School' – a series of other critical theories have emerged since the mid twentieth century (Bohman et al., 2021). Such theories are unified by their direct or indirect adherence to Horkheimer's (1972, p. 246) definition of critical theory as 'radically analyzing present social conditions', providing a 'critique of the economy' (broadly conceived), to put the finger on processes of power so that the research can be a 'liberating [. . .] influence' with an emancipatory agenda 'to create a world which satisfies the needs and powers' of humans. Bohman et al. (2021) explain that:

Because such theories aim to explain and transform *all* the circumstances that enslave human beings, many 'critical theories' in the broader sense have been developed. They have emerged in connection with the many social movements that identify varied dimensions of the domination of human beings in modern societies. In both the broad and the narrow senses, however, a critical theory provides the descriptive and normative bases for social inquiry aimed at decreasing domination and increasing freedom in all their forms.

These critical theories include a range of perspectives and schools such as, but not limited to, cultural studies (Hall, 1997b; Williams, 1961), semiology (Barthes, 1970; Saussure, 1966), poststructuralism (Derrida, 1976; Foucault, 1972–2000), post-Marxism (Althusser, 1984; Gramsci, 1971), feminism (Haraway, 1985; Kristeva, 1980), postmodernism (Baudrillard, 1994; Lyotard, 1984), queer theory (Butler, 1990; Halberstam, 2005), race, and postcolonialism (Crenshaw, 1995; Said, 1978; Spivak, 1996), and critical theory of technology (Chun, 2011; Feenberg, 1991; Stiegler, 2019; Wajcman, 1991). While different books that purport to give overviews of the field of critical theory differ somewhat as regards inclusions and omissions, these mentioned perspectives tend to persist (Buchanan, 2010; Easthope and McGowan, 2004; Felluga, 2015; Tyson, 2006; see for example Wake and Malpas, 2013).

All of these perspectives will not be covered within this book. No matter if one opts for the narrower, Frankfurt School, definition, or for the broader definition including a range of other perspectives, the main focus is on a certain kind of critical perspective more generally. Critical theorist of communication Christian Fuchs (2022, pp. 17–18) contends that '[o]ne could say that all contemporary academic thought is critical because it questions opinions of other scholars', and that '[a]ll contemporary political communication is in a specific way critical because it consists of speech acts that normally question political opinions and practices of certain actors'. The focus of the *critical* in critical theory, however, is on 'the analysis and questioning of power structures in order to overcome them and create a better society' (Fuchs, 2022, p. 10). Critical theory, in this rendition, does not refer to the practice of being critical to anyone or anything specific, but is a critique with a focus on 'the questioning of power, domination and exploitation' (Fuchs, 2022, p. 17).

Fuchs suggests defining critical theory, not by referring to particular schools or approaches, but focusing on the level of content. He then cites six dimensions of what constitutes a critical theory: 'Critical ethics; Critique of domination and exploitation; Dialectical reason; Ideology critique; Critique of the political economy; Struggles and political practice' (Fuchs, 2022, p. 20). Drawing on a similar strategy, this book defines critical theory as the analysis of power relations in society and breaks this down into:

First, *A critique of ideology*, and of how the ways in which ideas and visions that are formulated around AI – AI mythologies – are connected to political interests and power relations in society. This is mostly dealt with in Chapters 3 and 4.

Second, *A critical analysis of subjectivities*, with a focus on how people are interpellated (called and positioned) by AI and which social roles and relationships of power and disempowerment are constituted, hindered, or enabled, through these technologies. This is the main focus of Chapters 5 and 7.

Third, *A critique of political economy*, and how AI and automation as technologies are related – in their implementation and consequences – to societal hierarchies of domination and exploitation, particularly in the sphere of capital and labour. This is discussed in Chapters 6 and 5.

Overview of the book

The next chapter of this book introduces the view on AI as *assemblage*. The argument is that AI must be understood as a complex and ubiquitous apparatus that involves not only technology, but also humans, ideas, and social actions. Seeing AI in this way enables a more critical analysis and understanding that takes AI's historicity, contingency, and locatedness into account.

Chapters 3 and 4 offer a critique of AI from the perspective of *ideology*. The first out of these two chapters focuses on ideology as a driving force behind AI. Certain ideas that are connected to power relations in society have a deciding impact on how AI is developed and implemented. These ideas draw largely on libertarianism and visions of profit and progress. The second out of the two chapters on AI and ideology instead looks at how ideology gets embedded within, and propagated through, AI. This is about the ways in which AI systems tend to serve existing power relations and prevailing dominant ideologies in society.

The key argument in Chapter 5 is that *AI is humans* in the sense that AI technologies are social products. They are created in a social context, and rely in their functioning on humans in a number of different ways. Today's AI still relies heavily on having humans in the loop, and AI systems are continually enabled through the often-invisible labour of people. Furthermore, the data on which AI runs is largely generated by human behaviours. When AI becomes *reified* – seen as a concrete and irreducible thing – this obscures the fact that it is indeed a complex construction, which can hence be deconstructed. Chapter 6 continues on this topic by focusing particularly on AI's relation to work and how it comes into expression in current processes of platform labour, crowdwork, and algorithmic management.

Chapter 7 is centred around a critique of AI as a *discursive practice*, which calls people, through logics of labelling and sorting, into different social roles and positions. The meaning and knowledge that is produced through AI's models, predictions, and categorizations are not neutral. Rather, they are rooted in society's existing power structures and stereotypizations, which means that AI often echoes, sometimes strengthening, social relations that are oppressive, racist, and sexist. The book ends with the concluding Chapter 8, where some key ideas are pulled together and the path towards developing AI criticism is pointed out.

Takeaway points

- Technologies are *political*. AI is no exception.
- Technology is *socially shaped*, and this must be remembered also in the case of seemingly machinic AI.
- AI is the subject of evolving wars of definitions. It is an *empty signifier*.
- AI is not only a technological phenomenon. It is *co-produced* at the intersection of the social and the technical.
- Critical analysis of AI demands that we move away from technological definitions, towards *sociopolitical* ones.

- Sociology teaches us to leverage *the sociological imagination* when approaching AI. We need an *end-to-end sociology of AI.*
- *Critical theory* is vital for analysing AI due to its focus on society, *political economy*, *ideology*, and relations of *power.*

2

AI assemblage

Even technology makes the mistake of considering tools in isolation: tools exist only in relation to the interminglings they make possible or that make them possible.

Deleuze and Guattari, *A Thousand Plateaus* (1980, p. 90)

AI as social architecture

As argued in the previous chapter, this book does not approach AI based on any narrow technological definition of what 'AI' is. It has to be emphasized, however, that I am not engaging in any battle over what AI *truly* is, or what the *correct* definition may be. Definitions are tools and, depending on what we want to do with 'AI', different definitions will be useful. AI can be defined as 'intelligence displayed or simulated by code (algorithms) or machines' (Coeckelbergh, 2020, p. 64). This straightforward working definition, in turn, opens up the vast question of: What is intelligence? Luckily, this is not something to which we need to respond for the purposes of this book. It is sufficient to have a very general definition based in the spirit of the Dartmouth workshop in 1956 (see Chapter 1), where the idea was to simulate human intelligence in computers. Beyond such definitions, however, the battle over how AI is best defined is a recurring theme also within the community of computer scientists, engineers, and designers of AI systems (Ehsan and Riedl, 2022; Elliott, 2022, p. 5; Zerilli et al., 2020, p. 165).

AI is indeed a social reality. But the computer science definition of AI is not useful for analysing the social reality of AI. We don't need to know if AI is 'technologically driven forms of thought that make generalizations in a timely fashion based on limited data', or if it is rather 'the creation of machines or computer programs capable of activity that would be called intelligent if exhibited by human beings' (see Elliott, 2022, p. 5). What we need to know is how AI as a phenomenon in society takes shape, what it does to society, and what social, political, economic, and cultural processes of power and subordination it sets in motion.

This endeavour demands a different kind of definition of AI, which is focused on its broader underpinnings, tentacles, and practices. What is AI made of? How does it reach out and intertwine with people and their lives in society? What does AI do to social ideas and relations? Technology philosopher Shoshanna Zuboff (2019, p. 241) states that today's algorithmically driven digital capitalism – what she calls *surveillance capitalism* – operates through a 'ubiquitous apparatus' that renders 'human experience'. If we are to grasp AI in society, and its politics, the metaphor of a ubiquitous apparatus is quite fitting. Digital business researcher Ana Canhoto (2020) suggests that 'AI is a system, not a technology', and posits that AI can be seen as a collection of different components, not only the algorithm at the centre: 'when considering the benefits and pitfalls of adopting AI, we need to think of AI as an assemblage of technological components, rather than one technology'.

Aligning with this, computer philosopher Jaron Lanier and economist Glen Weyl (2020) contend that '"AI" is best understood as a political and social ideology rather than as a basket of algorithms', and as 'a suite of technologies'. AI, like other architectures in digital society are more than the mere '"back-end" of technical architecture', it is rather 'the relations among a number of elements' (see Burgess and Baym, 2020, p. 16). Kate Crawford (2021, p. 49), a leading scholar on AI, politics, and society, writes about the urgency in 'understanding the deep material and human roots of AI systems', because of the difficulties in seeing inside AI's 'complex assemblages'.

In sum, then, defining AI in sociopolitical terms has to do with understanding it as a ubiquitous apparatus entangled with human experience, and as a suite of technologies – a complex agglomeration of different components.

Making a monster

I suggest, for the purpose of sociopolitical critical analysis, that we conceive of AI as *assemblage*. This means sticking one's head into the conceptual complexity, unfinishedness, and contestedness that is the theorizing of philosopher Gilles Deleuze and psychoanalyst and activist Félix Guattari. They coined the notion of assemblage to provide a framework for thinking about multiplicities rather than things. As they put it in the quote at the very beginning of this chapter, 'tools exist only in relation to the interminglings they make possible or that make them possible' (Deleuze and Guattari, 1980, p. 90). Assemblage sees the social world not in terms of individual elements, but as abstract collectivities. I believe AI to be one such collectivity.

Drawing on the view of Deleuze and Guattari, we cannot see the individual computers or algorithms that drive AI as individual entities. Neither can we see the designers, programmers, and scientists as forces in their own, individual, right. The theory also stretches much further, to the point where we cannot see the people affected by AI as separate from AI either. This is because:

> There are no individual statements, there never are. Every statement is the product of a machinic assemblage, in other words, of collective agents of enunciation. (Deleuze and Guattari, 1980, p. 37)

Drawing on Deleuze and Guattari's description of the nature of assemblages and applying it to the phenomenon of AI in society, we can contend that AI both *consists* of things, and *does* things. This relates to how 'an assemblage comprises two segments, one of content, the other of expression' (Deleuze and Guattari, 1980, p. 88). On the one hand, AI involves humans, computers, scientific practice, big business, imaginaries, visions, driving forces, and so on. It is a *machinic assemblage* of bodies, of actions and passions, an 'intermingling of bodies reacting to one another'.

AI also – if we now see it in terms of discourse and mythology – shapes social reality. This happens on several levels. On one such level it is where AI imaginaries impact on what kinds of future lives and future societies are constituted as thinkable. Media and communications scholar Amanda Lagerkvist (2020, p. 16) posits that: 'In the present age AI (artificial intelligence) emerges as both a medium to and message about (or even from) the future, eclipsing all other possible prospects'.

On a more material level, AI co-constitutes social and political reality through the ways in which it interpellates humans as subjects into relations of success, failure, precarity, inequality, and discrimination. Computer scientist and mathematician Cathy O'Neil (2016, p. 13) writes of how 'secret models wielding arbitrary punishments' increasingly 'affect people at critical life moments: going to college, borrowing money, getting sentenced to prison, or finding and holding a job'. AI's different elements function together in ways that produce very material consequences in people's lives. Or, once again in the words of Deleuze and Guattari (1980, p. 88): 'it is a *collective assemblage of enunciation*, of acts and statements, of incorporeal transformations attributed to bodies'.

Philosopher Manuel DeLanda has developed Deleuze and Guattari's original notion of assemblage into what he calls *assemblage theory*. While not popular with all Deleuzians (see, e.g., Buchanan, 2021, p. 2), this reading and adaptation of assemblage has an analytical edge that is lacking in the original sketches by Deleuze and Guattari. DeLanda (2016, p. 1) purports to strip away some of the 'additional conceptual machinery' to be able to provide a more 'coherent notion' of assemblage. DeLanda's definition of assemblage starts from Deleuze's (2007, p. 69) notion that '[a]n animal is defined less by its genus, its species, its organs, and its functions, than by the assemblages into which it enters'. Consequently, for our purposes, AI is not as much defined by its type, technological form, source code, and algorithms, as it is defined by the complex sociopolitical settings where it comes into play and co-functions. An assemblage, then, 'is a multiplicity which is made up of many heterogeneous terms and which establishes liaisons, relations between them' (Deleuze and Parnet, 2007, p. 69).

According to DeLanda (2016, p. 3), society consists of a potentially endless number of assemblages ('assemblages of assemblages'). Assemblages all have the same ontological status, meaning that while they may operate at different scales, they can also interact directly with each other. We can consider AI as one such assemblage, existing in society, interacting with a range of other assemblages – of economy, of culture, of social classes, of identities, of the natural environment, and so on. Furthermore, '[a]ssemblages are always composed of heterogenous components' (DeLanda, 2016, p. 20).

AI, in its broad meaning, consists of technological components ranging from the very hardware, through algorithms and software, to humans, ideas, governments, politics, cities, and so on. This is because, recalling the point from earlier, that AI – construed as assemblage – includes both what it contains and what it does, and consequently also those entities that it does it to. DeLanda emphasizes that:

> To properly apply the concept of assemblage to real cases we need to include, in addition to persons, the material and symbolic artifacts that compose communities and organisations: the architecture of the buildings that house them; the myriad different tools and machines used in offices, factories, and kitchens. (DeLanda, 2016, p. 20)

In sum, to construe AI as assemblage, we must include in its definition not only *technology* (its tools and machines), but also: *humans* the behaviours of whom form both the input and output of AI systems; and *material and symbolic artifacts* – patterns of community, organization, design, and architecture that are affected by AI systems.

Following DeLanda's definition, AI assemblage emerges from the interactions between its parts, but importantly: 'wholes emerge in a bottom-up way, depending causally on their components, but they have a top-down influence on them' (DeLanda, 2016, p. 21). This means that once AI assemblage begins to emerge from its different concrete parts, it will start operating as an abstract whole upon those parts. Once that whole has been constituted it will begin 'to use its own emergent capacities to constrain and enable its parts' (DeLanda, 2016, p. 17). To use another metaphor, the assemblage, once it is in place, can become a force in itself so that we humans end up in the same predicament as Victor Frankenstein: 'I lived in daily fear, lest the monster whom I had created should perpetrate some new wickedness' (Shelley, 2017, p. 73).

But monsters aside, the sound perspective on AI is one that distances itself from technological determinism. We know from centuries of living with modern technology that the social impact of new technologies – while always up for utopian/dystopian debate – must constantly remain an empirical question. Sometimes a tool is good, but in other settings or uses it may be bad. The point of critical analysis is to keep the question alive and take nothing for granted. As discussed in the previous chapter, we must focus on the social shaping of AI technology, and how AI – in historically, socially, and culturally contingent ways – happens in practice and with which consequences, and for whom.

AI anatomy

Not using the concept of assemblage as such but proposing a perspective on AI systems aligning with the one that I outlined above, Kate Crawford and fellow new media researcher Vladan Joler (2018) envisage the anatomy of an AI system in a case study of the Amazon Echo voice-controlled smart speaker. They use this instance of AI to analytically untangle its sprawling extensions and intertwinement with the broader AI assemblage.

Crawford and Joler point out how the everyday use of gadgets such as the Echo is concentrated around brief interactions between its AI-driven technology and human users. Commands such as 'Turn on the lights!', followed by a response in the form of an 'OK', and lights being turned on, are illustrative of the standard mode of interaction. It is brief and fleeting. Behind the scenes however, such passing junctures invoke 'a vast matrix of capacities': 'interlaced chains of resource extraction, human labor and algorithmic processing across networks of mining, logistics, distribution, prediction and optimization' (Crawford and Joler, 2018, I). As put by computer scientist Philip Agre (1997, p. 131): 'Every technology fits, in its own unique way, into a far-flung network of different sites of social practice.'

In Crawford and Joler's analysis, the understated design of the object renders it 'a kind of blankness' that conceals, at the surface level, that the Echo 'is a disembodied voice that represents the human–AI interaction interface for an extraordinarily complex set of information processing layers' (Crawford and Joler, 2018, II). Voice is translated into text, the text queries databases of potential answers, all the while the device leverages machine learning to perform more accurately in future interactions. At the real-life level, the urgent point made here is that AI 'requires a vast planetary network, fueled by the extraction of non-renewable materials, labor, and data', and that the 'resources required is many magnitudes greater than the energy and labor it would take a human to operate a household appliance or flick a switch' (Crawford and Joler, 2018, II). At the level of theory, we can reiterate the point that AI must be defined in terms of a multidimensional assemblage of several entities that constitute, and are constituted by, one another. As an example, Crawford and Joler point us in the direction of Young and Davies' study of lithium extraction in Bolivia and their statement that smart devices link the world together by 'invisible threads of commerce, science, politics and power' (Davies and Young, 2016).

In the context of AI, however, it is not only about the continuation of the extractive operations of industrial capitalism in a new technological age. AI also relies on 'the ingestion, analysis and optimization of vast amounts of human generated images, texts and videos'. This casting as a resource of 'the history of human knowledge and capacity', which is used for optimizing and training AI systems, is 'a key difference between artificial intelligence systems and other forms of consumer technology', Crawford and Joler (2018, V) state. Humans are interpellated into AI systems in the shape of an assemblage (*assemblages within assemblages*) of different subjectivities:

> It is difficult to place the human user of an AI system into a single category: rather, they deserve to be considered as a hybrid case. Just as the Greek *chimera* was a mythological animal that was part lion, goat, snake and monster, the Echo user is simultaneously a consumer, a resource, a worker, and a product. This multiple identity recurs for human users in many technological systems. (Crawford and Joler, 2018, VI)

AI, while often hidden within quite understated, delimited, and black-boxed devices, certainly stretches much further, constituting and leveraging a formation of different elements that, taken together, materializes as the much more complex sociopolitical assemblage of what we face in our lives as 'AI'. In all of our micro-interactions with AI systems, we are not always realizing that 'its real power and complexity lies somewhere else, far out of sight' (Crawford and Joler, 2018, VII).

Layers of AI

Having established the point of thinking of AI as assemblage, we can turn to what AI actually consists of. What are the different kinds of entities that are entwined in AI assemblage? This question cannot be given any unambiguous answer. Different people, with different perspectives and relationships to AI, will suggest different elements. Furthermore, elements will always overlap with one another, and there will be – fittingly with the Deleuzian notion of assemblage – a crazy mixture of things of different magnitudes, at different levels of abstraction. We will never be able to represent the 'reality' of AI in any objective, universal, or uncontested way.

Sociologist Max Weber famously introduced the notion of *the ideal type* as a tool for social analysis. Instead of getting stuck in discussions about what is *the* correct definition, the social scientist should develop approximated definitions that are good enough to enable the continued analysis. The ideal type is a simplification or suggestion, developed by a scholar having realized that many different definitions are always possible. The ideal type, however, 'has the merit of clear understandability and lack of ambiguity' (Weber, 1978, p. 6), and enables the social analysis to be realized on its premises. Weber saw this in terms of balancing between oversimplification and pragmatism: 'The more sharply and precisely the ideal type has been constructed, thus the more abstract and unrealistic in this sense it is, the better it is able to perform its functions in formulating terminology, classifications, and hypotheses' (Weber, 1978, p. 211). What I present here is a definition of AI assemblage, which is to be seen on these terms.

In outlining AI assemblage, I suggest a strategy by which we start with the most concise and tech-oriented definitions of AI's related elements, then to move outwards to engage increasingly broader elements of society and politics that are entwined with AI. Let's collect the things we find along the way within a framework of entities that are to be part of AI assemblage (Figure 1).

Looking at initial definitions, mathematician Alan Turing (1950, p. 433) originated the so-called Turing test when reasoning about what he called 'the imitation game' and focusing on 'the terms "machine" and "think"', and whether a machine could pass as being in possession of human intelligence. We put into our framework the concepts of *(I) machines, (II) humans,* and *(III) intelligence.*

Moving on to the early definition of the Dartmouth workshop in 1956, some of the key formulations were about 'automatic computers', 'neuron nets' and the possibilities for 'self-improvement', now known as machine learning, in computers (McCarthy et al., 2006, pp. 12–14). We can add to the framework *(IV) automation, (V) neural networks,* and *(VI) machine learning.*

Looking at some current examples of AI definitions, we find that AI 'is a family of techniques where algorithms uncover or learn associations of predictive power from data', the most 'tangible form' of which is 'machine learning', which includes a family of techniques called 'deep learning' that rely on multiple layers of representation of data and are thus able to represent complex relationships between inputs and outputs' (Panch et al., 2019, p. 1). This introduces the elements of *(VII) algorithms, (VIII) predictions, (IX) deep learning,* and *(X) data.*

Economics professor Wim Naudé (2021, p. 2) states that this is the domain of 'narrow AI': 'the use of machine learning algorithms in a narrow domain or application to predict and improve predictions by learning from more and more data'. By contrast there are the *(XI) imaginaries* of a human-level, or beyond human-level, kind of AI that has not yet been achieved, and may not be for quite some time, if ever.

If we move further outward, to literature that is not about AI in the narrow technological sense, but which mobilizes perspectives such as Ethical AI, Explainable AI or Responsible AI, further elements of the assemblage come into view. Leading researcher on Responsible AI, Virginia Dignum (2019, v) sees AI as being part of a *(XII) sociotechnical system* that 'must bear responsibility and ensure trust' in relation to AI. Furthermore, Dignum (2019, p. 5) argues that:

> The ultimate aim of AI is not about the creation of superhuman machines or other sci-fi scenarios but about developing technology that supports and enhances human well-being in a sustainable environment for all. It is also about understanding and shaping technology as it becomes ever more present and influential in our daily lives. It's not about imitating humans, but providing humans with the tools and techniques to better realise their goals and ensure the well-being of all. From the perspective of its engineering roots, the

focus of AI is on building artefacts. But it is more than engineering, it is human-centric and society-grounded.

This line of reasoning adds further items to the framework in the shape of issues of *(XIII) environment*, and *(XIV) tools and artefacts*. The issue of AI's relation to the environment, and connected issues and challenges of sustainability, then, refer not only to the kind of social sustainability, which is foregrounded above, but also to AI's interaction with the natural environment, for example, through practices of extraction (see Crawford and Joler, 2018).

Moving yet one level outward, another set of entities can be added to the framework of concepts. First there is the dimension of *XV: ideology*, which encompasses the ways in which ideas and visions, imbued by *XVI: power* are both driving AI (see Chapter 3), and are embedded within AI (see Chapter 4). It also relates to the *XVII: identities and subjects* that it interpellates (see Chapter 7). Then there is the broader system of relationships within capitalism within which AI is entangled. This refers to the *XVIII: political economy* around AI (see Chapter 5), and to how different forms of *XIX: labour* is propagated in and around it (see Chapter 6).

Importantly, however, the assemblage does not end here. We could definitely have included several other elements, either instead of, or in addition to, the ones listed. Different words could also have been used to name the elements, with some meanings retained and others altered. This is not about *the* one AI assemblage, but about seeing AI as assemblage. Arts and design scholar Rumen Rachev (2016), discussing the Latourian view on assemblage, explains that there will always be 'the unassembled': 'all those pieces that are left after you finish assembling the assemblage, the small screws and bolts leftover from an Ikea flat-pack, left to sit around unused, since the assemblage seems complete'. Assemblages such as those in Figure 1 only *seem* complete, however, as it is in the nature of the assemblage never to have any definitive ending or beginning. Poetically, Rachev states that '[t]he void is not the missing part – it is the essential part', because the incompleteness – the ongoing character – is what makes an assemblage. Therefore, Figure 1 also includes an indefinite series of *(XX) potential additional elements*. The point, once again, being to construe AI *as* assemblage, rather than fixating *the* AI assemblage.

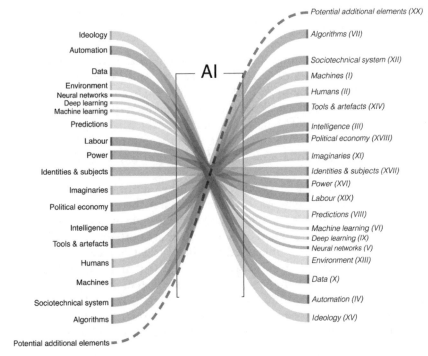

Figure 1. AI Assemblage. Sketch with dimensions numbered (I – XIX), in their order of appearance in the preceding discussion. Created by the author.

Context, action, construction

Conceiving of AI in terms of assemblage addresses several of the needs that one must fulfil in order to assume a critical social science perspective on AI. This, as I have written about elsewhere, together with information systems scholar Jonny Holmström, includes seeing humans and machines in context, seeing AI as a social actor, and as a social construction (Lindgren and Holmström, 2020, pp. 3–6).

First of all, AI as assemblage highlights its contextual elements. The context around code, software, and hardware, at the intersection of people and machines, has been the focus of scholarly interest for quite some time in the research area of human–computer interaction (HCI). There has been an interest in capturing this interface theoretically and empirically all the way back to the early days of personal computing in the 1980s. Researchers, such as tech anthropologist Lucy Suchman (1987) and informatics scholar Bonnie Nardi (1996) have pushed for the importance of bringing context and socio-cultural aspects into the equation.

In line with the argument in this chapter, they have advocated a perspective by which machines and humans are seen as co-constitutive of the social world through their dynamic interplay. A key focus of HCI research is on the design of systems and on usability and user experience. Its underpinning notions are still of much broader relevance for how we can view humans and machines in tandem. In one study, Suchman and Randall (1993) analyse the process of building AI systems in a way that aligns with assemblage. They write that:

> The work of AI comprises a process by which researchers, drawing upon lived experience and their culturally constituted common sense of the social world, inscribe scenarios of activity as text, graphical formalisms, and computer programs intended to delegate human competence to machines. The process is not a simple encoding of behavior, but rather a series of transformations involving the simplification of action for purposes of its inscription, followed by implementation of the resulting inscriptions in the machine. (Suchman and Randall, 1993, pp. 146–7)

In recent work on AI in warfare, Suchman (2022, p. 1) also points out how military AI systems are constituted as bearers of 'objectivist knowledge', which is 'enabled through a war apparatus that treats the contingencies and ambiguities of relations on the ground as noise'. The assemblage of the AI war machine obscures the multi-species complexity within.

A key idea in HCI and beyond is that the interplay between machines and humans is a socio-cultural, rather than a purely technological process. This is why critical AI research must move past issues of mere usability, functioning, transparency, and fairness, towards an analytical framework, such as that of assemblage, which allows for posing deeper-cutting and more far-reaching critical questions. Ultimately, the question of whether we need, or should build, a given AI solution must be posed. Beyond the 'ethical AI' questions of *how* we can build AI better, and beyond the solutionist contention that *more* AI can always solve AI's problems, we must navigate past the 'techno-chauvinist' belief that 'tech is always the solution' (Broussard, 2018, pp. 7–8). This means also posing the question of *whether* AI is needed at all in a given scenario.

In addition to the importance of context, there is the need to construe AI in terms of social agency. AI itself is a social actor that does things with, and to, the world around it. An advantage of viewing AI as assemblage in this respect, is that it enables casting the relationship between machines and humans as complex and multidimensional (Gehl and Bakardjieva, 2017). This means that we should assume there to be a symbiotic relationship between human and technological elements, and it entails a focus on 'how technology mediates our experiences, perceptions, and behavior, and how human agency affects the uses of technological artifacts' (Neff and Nagy, 2016, p. 4926). Drawing on the ideas of communication theorist James Carey, AI must be seen as coming in to being and expression through an ongoing relationship with a surrounding social world (Carey, 1990, p. 247).

AI assemblage can be seen in the same way. AI makes possible, and anticipates, certain social forms and relations that are imagined in its technology. AI permits and desires certain social relations. AI assemblage spans the domains of the conceptual and the expressive – it involves both ideas, practices, and consequences. For the purpose of analysing what AI does – its agency – through its socio-technical assemblage, we must demystify AI instead of seeing it as inscrutable, magic, or elusive. Beyond the futuristic aura of possibility, AI is (also) 'a particular form of rationality, symptomatic of a general mode of social ordering' (Barocas et al., 2013, p. 2).

Human geographer Nigel Thrift (2005, p. 5) aptly argues that new technology is often hailed as changing everything, while it in practice has 'differential effects on numerous circuits of practice, rather than as having a uniquely determining effect of its own'. In the case of AI, then, it does not have a singular and distinct effect on society. Rather, according to the logic of assemblage, it has a range of effects on many different 'circuits of practice'. Thrift writes of the emergence of an historically new form of *technological unconscious*, of which we can see AI as being part. The new technological unconscious, Thrift (2005, p. 223) writes, is 'appearing now even in mundane activities like playing with highly complex games software that is increasingly opaque to rule-guided order'. Aligning with the logic of assemblage, Thrift sees the new technological unconscious as a performative infrastructure. Sociologist Patricia Clough, who has inspired Thrift's writing on the unconscious, argues that the notion of new technologies:

> refers not only to an environment or a set of objects, but also to agencies other than human agency, so that the [technology] joins, if not displaces, what sociologists of western modernity have referred to as the social structural. This displacement demands a rethinking of the determination of human agency that the idea of social structure has implied (Clough, 2000, p. 3)

While Clough's focus is on the impact of television on late capitalist society, the argument is valid more broadly for how new technologies, such as AI, interact with society. Just as in the case of AI assemblage, the new technology, for Clough, displaces the social structure, and urges on a rethinking of human agency. Coming full circle to Deleuze and Guattari, Clough (2000, p. 60) also activates their notion of assemblage, and states that it refers to a movement, such as shown in Figure 1, 'that aligns human and machine, nature and technology, the virtual and the real, even the living and the inert – all on the same plane of consistency'.

Finally, rendering AI as assemblage enables analysis of how it emerges as a social construction. Largely, what the critical analyst is interested in is the notion of AI as the mythical entity that it has become, and its impact on social and cultural life. As explained by classic anthropologist Claude Lévi-Strauss, myths can be defined as our 'collective dreams' (1955, p. 428). AI, today, is undoubtedly at the centre of social and political imaginaries ranging from the utopian to the dystopian. But AI, as such, is not a fantasy but rather very real. AI indeed exists, and even more powerful AI certainly seems possible. But the proliferated talk of its alleged inevitability, and its status as a catch-all solution to any thinkable societal challenge, is steeped in myth. As stated by computer scientist Erik Larson (2021, p. 76), 'the myth is an emotional lighthouse by which we navigate the AI topic'. Certainly, the language of many descriptions of our historical moment has an air of drama and determinism about it:

- '[W]e are at the beginning of *a fourth industrial revolution*. It began at the turn of this century and builds on the digital revolution. It is characterized by a much more ubiquitous and mobile internet, by smaller and more powerful sensors that have become cheaper, and by artificial intelligence and machine learning' (Schwab, 2016, pp. 11–12).
- '[T]he exponential, digital, and recombinant powers of *the second machine age* have made it possible for humanity to create two of the most important one-time events in our history: the emergence of real, useful artificial intelligence (AI) and the connection of most of the people on the planet via a common digital network' (Brynjolfsson and McAfee, 2016, p. 90).
- '[T]he rise of computing and AI is of epochal significance, likely to be as consequential as the Scientific Revolution – an upheaval that will profoundly alter our understanding of the world, ourselves, and our (and our AIs') place in that world' (Smith, 2019, xiii–xiv).

The relationship between AI and myth(ology) is multifaceted. On the one hand, some writers have pointed out that AI has some roots in ancient mythology, such as in the case of Aristotle's discussions of matter brought to life by technology (Mayor, 2018, p. 93). On the other hand, there is the ongoing debate about 'AI myths', as in inaccurate conceptions or expectations expressed through sensationalism, misguided headlines, and 'hyped-up claims about AI being a silver bullet to solve complex social problems' (Leufer, 2020, p. 1). By contrast, the focus here is on AI *as* mythology in the sense of cultural analysis, and as a social construction. This means seeing AI – 'the object, its function and its symbolism [as] inextricably bound up with each other' (Lévi-Strauss, 1966, p. 19), such as in an assemblage. In other words, analysing how AI functions, and how it gets consequences, in society and culture, must be interwoven with the study of how social talk and thinking in regard to it is structured, as well as the practices that accompany it. This insight sits at the core of the critical theory traditions of discourse analysis and social constructionism, namely that our ways of talking and thinking about any given phenomenon are socially created.

The socio-technical phenomenon of 'AI' comes into being through a co-construction process where various interpretive frames are negotiated and established. According to those scholars who advocate a socio-technical perspective, technologies are surrounded by 'socially shared structures of meaning' (Latzko-Toth, 2014, p. 50), that reflect and orient how various groups of actors relate to a given technological artifact and how they make sense of it. Wiebe Bijker (1987), one of the originators of the social construction of technology-approach, argues that such modes of speaking and acting in relation to technological artifacts constitute an interpretive 'frame', that provides a 'grammar' for how meaning is attributed to the artifact in question.

Such frames include 'assumptions, knowledge, and expectations, expressed symbolically through language, visual images, metaphors, and stories' (Orlikowski and Gash, 1994, p. 178). These will have powerful effects, as the knowledge, assumptions, and expectations that people have about the meaning, purpose, and importance of technology will influence the societal uses of technologies and hence their impact. Another way of putting this is that the interpretive frames will affect how the technology in question becomes *socialized* – how it becomes a social object and how it acquires social significance (Jouët, 2000).

Social psychologist Kenneth Gergen (1985, p. 267) wrote that '(t)he terms in which the world is understood are social artifacts, products of historically situated interchanges among people'. Consequently, the terms by which we understand AI are not definite or universally 'true'. Instead, they are created in a given social and historical setting, among people, where different agendas, political convictions, economic interests, and power inequalities will be at play. Furthermore Gergen (1985, p. 268) wrote that '(f)orms of negotiated understanding are of critical significance in social life, as they are integrally connected with many other activities in which people engage. Descriptions and explanations of the world themselves constitute forms of social action.' So, analysing AI as mythology means two things. First, focusing on how meanings are socially, culturally and politically established around it. Second, realizing the inextricable connection between such meanings and social reality, as in how and why AI is developed, legitimized, implemented, and with which consequences for whom, and under which different conditions.

Algorithmic assemblages and beyond

The concept of assemblage has been applied in the area of critical studies of AI before. In those cases, it has been applied somewhat more narrowly to refer to algorithms, rather than to the wider phenomenon of 'AI in society' as a whole. The very notion of an assemblage, however, as also illustrated by Figure 1, produces a compatibility between these discussions. Simply put: As algorithms can be construed as assemblages, and as algorithms are entangled with AI assemblage ('assemblages of assemblages'), the same logic – that of assemblages – goes for the whole thing.

In line with the argument above, and also precursing Crawford and Joler's (2018) unpacking of AI's anatomy, digital media and technology researcher Tarleton Gillespie (2016) writes about how technological assemblages function as stand-ins for the complexity that they carry inside. He explains that they obscure 'the people involved at every point: people debating the models, cleaning the training data, designing the algorithms, tuning the parameters' (Gillespie, 2016, p. 71). Gillespie points further to the argument made by tech anthropologist Nick Seaver (2019, p. 419) that we should conceive of these assemblages not as 'standalone little boxes', but that we must see them instead as 'massive, networked ones with hundreds of hands reaching into them, tweaking and tuning, swapping out parts and experimenting with new arrangements'.

Similarly, Lucas Introna (2016, p. 20), a scholar of organization, technology, and ethics, emphasizes the importance of understanding algorithmic logics as practices that are situated and embedded in 'heterogeneous socio-material assemblages'. Paraphrasing Seaver's argument, about algorithms, for the broader context of AI assemblage, a key formulation would be that:

> This might be understood as a call to examine empirically the contexts – social, cultural, political, economic, legal, institutional, etc. – in which [AI is] developed, and that would be a welcome addition to the current state of [AI] criticism. (Seaver, 2019, p. 419)

Drawing on Gillespie (2016, p. 71), AI and its entanglement becomes 'a socio-technical ensemble', or 'a family of systems'.

This view echoes that from the previous chapter of seeing AI as an empty signifier – a kind of discursive element that 'gathers up a range of differential elements', binding them together (Wrangel, 2015, cf. Figure 1).

Jaron Lanier states that we must not on any terms 'accept AI as a coherent and legitimate concept', and goes on to argue provocatively that:

> AI is a story we computer scientists made up to help us get funding once upon a time, back when we depended on grants from government agencies. It was pragmatic theater. But now AI has become a fiction that has overtaken its authors. AI is a fantasy, nothing but a story we tell about our code. It is also a cover for sloppy engineering. (Lanier, 2018, p. 135)

Correspondingly, sociologist Ruha Benjamin (2019, p. 211), writes that 'it is worth keeping in mind that many things dubbed "AI" today are, basically, just statistical predictions rebranded in the age of big data – an artificial makeover that engenders more trust as a result'. Even though everyone might not agree with Lanier's harsh critique of AI mythology, he brings across the important point that AI is indeed 'a story'.

Coeckelbergh also maintains that the narrative perspective is highly applicable to the context of AI. This is not only because of the obvious connections between AI discourse and scifi-types of narratives 'that try to make sense of the human and our relation to machines'. The narrative perspective – just as that of assemblage – more importantly demonstrates the liquid and emergent character of 'AI', which urges us to 'understand why certain narratives are prevalent, by whom they are created, and who benefits from them' (Coeckelbergh, 2020, pp. 16–17).

Assemblage, then, is not about fixed entities, where we are to identify the universal truth about which elements belong in, for example, *the* AI assemblage, and which do not. Rather, it is about a *logic* of assemblage, by which we must not see elements in isolation if we want to realize anything close to a critical analysis. Just as Crawford and Toler unpack the Amazon Echo, Gillespie (2016, p. 73) suggests a similar unravelling of Facebook:

> Facebook's algorithm really means Facebook, and Facebook really means the people, things, priorities, infrastructures, aims, and discourses that animate the site. But it may also be a political economic

conflation: this is Facebook acting through its algorithm, intervening in an algorithmic way, building a business precisely on its ability to construct complex models of social/expressive activity, train on an immense corpus of data, tune countless parameters, and reach formalized goals extremely efficiently. Facebook as a company often behaves algorithmically.

Introna points out that the concept of assemblage is not unique, as there have been several other suggestions introduced as to what these kinds of emergent sociopolitico–material agglomerations might be called. One of these is Suchman's notion of the 'socio-material'. In Suchman's (2006, p. 23) terms, we might understand AI and its assemblage as involved in the 'ongoing, contingent coproduction of a shared socio-material world'. If we would understand AI simply in terms of service provision, this hides the socio-material infrastructures that exist behind the veil of the smoothly running processes at the surface level (Suchman, 2006, p. 225).

Focusing specifically on the interrelation of humans and machines in the context of AI, Suchman warns against moving towards a position of 'object fetishism'. Understandings of AI that are too technologically focused produce a view where AI is 'typically stripped of its contingency, locatedness, historicity, and specific embodiments' – all of these being things that AI as assemblage highlights (Suchman, 2006, p. 245).

If we construe AI as assemblage, we establish a platform from which we can ask some of the most critical questions about AI and humanity. These are not the issues of how AI can best serve humanity. Indeed, initiatives to use 'AI for social good' (AI4SG), should be welcomed. No doubt, the technological fix of AI can be of support in processes of mitigating hate speech, monitoring diseases, producing simulations that can help with climate action, and so on (Tomašev et al., 2020). At the same time, AI is not always the solution to complex social problems. Such a view is rooted in a tech-solutionist view, described by tech critic Evgeny Morozov (2013, p. 5), as the strategy of:

Recasting all complex social situations either as neatly defined problems with definite, computable solutions or as transparent and self-evident processes that can be easily optimized – if only the right algorithms are in place!

Rather, returning to Suchman, the question we need to ask is: 'In what socio-material arrangements are we differentially implicated, and with what political and economic consequences?' In what social, political, and economic structures are we, humans, implicated by AI? In AI assemblage, humans are simultaneously creators, consumers, resources, workers, and products. Suchman (2006, p. 245) writes that:

> This alerts us, in turn, to the possibility of encounters at the interface conceived very differently than as the meeting of a human and a machine, each figured as a self-standing entity possessed of pre-established capabilities. Rather, effective encounters at the computer interface are those moments of moving complicity between persons and things achieved through particular, dynamic materialities and extended socialities.

The point here is that when critiquing AI, we must not see humans on the one hand and machines on the other as 'self-standing entities' that are non-overlapping. Instead, Suchman argues, what happens at the intersection of human and machine in AI, is the setting in motion of complicit movements between persons and things, caught up in an assemblage of 'dynamic materialities' and 'extended socialities'. Keeping AI running, then, returning to Introna (2016, p. 25), is a 'significant socio-material accomplishment, requiring the circulation of action in a complex socio-material heterogeneous assemblage'.

Takeaway points

- All critical analysis begins with an understanding of the object of study, and I suggest, for the purpose of this book, that AI is defined as an *assemblage*. As shown in Figure 1, this means understanding it as involving humans, computers, scientific practice, big business, imaginaries, visions, driving forces, and so on.
- We must understand AI, not as a narrow technology, but as a *ubiquitous apparatus* – a complex agglomeration of different components – which is entangled with human experience.
- AI both *consists* of things and *does* things. An assemblage has one segment of content, and another of expression.

- Assemblages are constituted through the interplay between its whole and its parts. This process is multidirectional. Creating AI may mean creating a 'monster', that is out of control.
- In today's society, AI is part of the *technological unconscious*. It is a performative infrastructure that humans draw upon in co-creating society.
- AI is *mythology*. This does not mean that it is (only) a fantasy, but that the critical analysis of AI must be interwoven with the study of how social talk and thinking in regard to it is structured, as well as the material practices that come along with the talking and thinking.
- While narrow technological understandings of AI strip it of its contingency, locatedness, historicity, and embodiments, seeing it as assemblage mitigates the problems with this.

3

Ideology behind AI

Whenever any new medium or human extension occurs, it creates a
new myth for itself.
Marshall McLuhan, *Understanding Media* (1964, p. 252)

Power is everywhere

The development of AI is driven by ideology. This means that
its creation and implementations are connected to ideas that are
contingent – they could have been different. The ideas of *some*
become the 'truth' for all. This is a game of power. When we
see AI as driven by ideology, we see it as propelled forward by a
specific view on the world that construes AI as superior, unavoidable, and as a catch-all 'solution' for society.

The concept of *ideology* has several different definitions. In its
most neutral sense, it can be taken to refer to ideas and worldviews
more generally. In such cases we may speak, for example, of how a
sports coach may have a certain 'ideology' as to how a team should
be trained and managed. In such cases, the term is used to refer to
any set of ideas that guide social action. At the other end of the
spectrum is the Marxist notion of ideology as *false consciousness*,
referring to situations where people are manipulated by those in
power not to realize the exploitative social conditions that they
may be living under (Felluga, 2015, p. 148). As Marx wrote:

> The ideas of the ruling class are in every epoch the ruling ideas: i.e.,
> the class which is the ruling material force of society is at the same
> time its ruling intellectual force. (Marx and Engels, 1998, p. 67)

Somewhere between the two ends of such a spectrum of definitions (Fuchs, 2019, p. 180), lies the view of ideology that is
drawn upon in this book. This view recognizes the connection
between ideas and power and draws on a critical interpretation
of the concept of ideology wherein it is seen as a vehicle that promotes certain interests at the expense of others. And clearly AI,
like so many other politicized phenomena in society, has strong
ideological elements to it. This means that there are ideas related
to AI's development and implementation that push certain priorities and considerations aside for the benefit of others.

Ideology, in the sense of critical theory, is a defining component of capitalism, and of societies that are stratified along lines
of class, gender, race, and so on. Ideology, then, refers to the
modes of thinking that gain prominence and dominance, and
that consequently shape the lives and living conditions of people
in those societies. This happens through what Marx defined as
'the means of production', the key idea being that controlling
those means also means controlling society's dominating ideas
and thoughts:

> The class which has the means of material production at its disposal,
> consequently also controls the means of mental production, so that
> the ideas of those who lack the means of mental production are on
> the whole subject to it. (Marx and Engels, 1998, p. 67)

So, out of what, and how, is value extracted in today's digital
economy? What are the means of production in today's Fourth
Industrial Revolution (Schwab, 2016)? Computers? Algorithms?
Data? Is there any indication that those material means have any
connection to politics, ideas, 'truths', and our imagination? There
obviously is. In the case of datafication, AI, machine learning,
and automation, ideology 'plays an important role in promoting
myths and discourses [. . .] portraying a vision of a specific type
of society and the role digital technology plays in it' (Verdegem,
2023). Approaching AI from the perspective of critical theory
therefore crucially entails analysing by what kind of ideology the
development and implementation of the technology is driven.
Some questions to be asked are whether there exists an 'AI ideol-

ogy', what kind of power such an ideology might exercise, with what consequences, and for the benefit or peril of whom.

Making ideology come into view takes some analytic work, as it is often not directly seen or recognized. According to critical theorist Slavoj Žižek, it may, however, be the fact that people see the ideology for what it is (ideology), but still keep acting in line with it:

> The emperor is naked and the media trumpet forth the fact, yet no one seems really to mind – that is, people continue to act as if the emperor were not naked. (Žižek, 1994, p. 18)

The main point in Žižek's view on ideology is that recognizing its skewed worldview 'in no way reduces its power over the individual' (Felluga, 2015, p. 151). By consequence, the ideology will serve to 'create rules or regimes of inclusion and exclusion' with real-life consequences (Buchanan, 2010, *ideology*). In other words, ideology is not only made out of transient thoughts, but it has a material existence. As put by Marxist philosopher Louis Althusser (1971, p. 166):

> [A]n ideology always exists in an apparatus, and its practice, or practices. This existence is material.

The ideology will always be manifested through actions (Felluga, 2015, p. 149), and the repeated performance of these actions will, in turn, manifest the ideology. In the words of philosopher and gender theorist Judith Butler (1990, p. 147), ideology is 'a set of acts, repeated over time, that produce reality-effects that are eventually misperceived as "facts"'. This kind of social practice – Butler calls it *performativity* – entails, according to social psychologist Michael Billig (1991, p. 1), people 'repeating assumptions which confirm existing arrangements of power'. This is because ideology in practice, once set in motion, disguises as commonsensical thinking which is reiterated, legitimized, and strengthened through a form of naturalization. Ideology, then, is equal to 'the beliefs and assumptions that just seem obviously unquestionable' (Burr, 2015, p. 187). Ideology, sociologist John B. Thompson (1984, p. 11) contends, 'seeks to sustain relations of domination by representing them as "legitimate"'. From the perspective of critical theory, then, ideology operates to:

try to naturalise, justify, defend, and legitimate exploitation and alienation and to try to convince exploited and oppressed groups to accept and not question alienation and to accept the status quo. (Fuchs, 2022, p. 3)

Ideologies appear as 'natural ways of seeing the world', thus obscuring the underlying 'material/historical conditions in which we live', and this is because ideologies 'refuse to acknowledge that those conditions have any bearing on the way we see the world' (Tyson, 2006, pp. 56–7). This urges us to question and critique the ideological processes around AI.

- Is there a particular *AI ideology* and, if so, what does it contain?
- What kind of ideology is manifested through the actions by which AI is developed and implemented?
- How are truths about AI produced? By whom, and for the benefit of whom? Who has the power to define what it is and what it can achieve?
- In what contexts is AI 'performed' – that is, how are meanings around it established and maintained? Are there any opposing or conflicting views?
- Who decides what AI should be designed to do, and who has the power to draw any ethical lines?
- What rules or regimes of inclusion and exclusion are propagated through AI, and with what real-life consequences, for whom?
- What relations of power are there in the context of AI, and what power relations does AI create and/or further propagate?
- What kinds of subjects does AI interpellate, and how does this relate to broader debates about power, integrity, and freedom?

Embedded in this set of questions are at least three different ways of approaching ideology in the context of AI. First, there is the focus on ideology as a driver behind the development and implementation of AI and related technologies. This is the focus of this chapter, where I discuss the concoction of libertarianism, technological rationality, and solutionism that forms both a platform, and a sort of fuel, for AI. Second, there is a focus on AI as a vehicle for ideology. This is the topic of Chapter 4, where I discuss AI technologies as vectors of dominant ways of seeing the world more broadly. Third, one can direct the focus towards ideology as constitutive of social identities, positions, and relationships. This is what I do in Chapter 7, where the main emphasis is on how AI technologies interpellate subjects.

It is important to realize, however, that these different perspectives overlap largely. This is because ideology is not a clearly distinguished force with a clearly identified direction, belonging to any distinct level of society. Ideology, and its power, is *in-between* all the things that go on in social life. It comes into expression in micro-interactions between individuals, it is at the same time governing how different social groups think and act, and also operates at the macro-level of social structure, shaping society and politics as a whole.

Ideology is about how dominant ways of thinking and acting in relation to given phenomena tend to propagate throughout society. Importantly, ideology is also multidirectional in the sense that on the one hand it governs social practice, while at the same time it is being shaped by social practice. This means that the development and implementation of AI technologies is both a product of, and a producer of, ideology. Poststructuralist philosopher Michel Foucault has played an important role in critical theory for this view of power and ideology. The idea here is that we should direct the focus of analysis away from power as exercised by someone or something, over someone or something else. In the Foucauldian view, 'power is everywhere', and 'not because it embraces everything, but because it comes from everywhere' (Foucault, 1978, p. 93).

AI libertarianism

Following the third consecutive failed rocket launch by his space-flight company SpaceX, tech billionaire Elon Musk was quoted in an interview with *Wired* magazine as stating:

> Optimism, pessimism, fuck that; we're going to make it happen. As God is my bloody witness, I'm hell-bent on making it work. (Musk, cited in Hoffman, 2008)

Nearly fifteen years later, in late September of 2022, Musk took to the stage during electric vehicle company Tesla's AI day, to show off the prototype for the Optimus humanoid robot. While presently being a work-in-progress, a mass-produced version of the robot was said to be available to consumers for a price of around $20,000 within a few years. The Optimus robots were to be tested as workers in Tesla's car factories, to later be perfected for carrying out household tasks such as picking up groceries, mowing the lawn, and caring for the elderly (Davis, 2022). Furthermore, these robots were also envisioned by Musk to function as 'buddies' or 'catgirl sex partners' (Prakash, 2022). As McLuhan writes in the excerpt at the very top of this chapter, technologies always create myths about themselves.

While at Tesla's 2021 AI event, the audience was introduced to the visions of Optimus by a human dancing around in a robot spandex suit (CNET, 2021), in 2022 an actual hardware proto-type was being wheeled unimpressively onto the stage. The robot waved awkwardly to the crowd, raised its knees, and was then hidden behind a screen, to return later, supported by a frame so it would not fall over. With unimpressed tweets coming in from AI and robotics researchers calling the event 'next-level cringe-worthy', a scam, lame, full of buzzwords, but not mentioning 'a word about any actual progress in solving the stuff nobody yet solved' (Hale, 2022), Musk spoke of the company's visions of building and selling millions of robots. There was, Musk said, 'a future of abundance' ahead, amid 'a fundamental transformation of civilization as we know it' (McCallum, 2022).

Such unbendable technological optimism, also in the face of major setbacks, aligns with the view that the progression and success of technology is inevitable. It will happen, and it will be good. World-leading, San Francisco-based, AI initiative *OpenAI*, writes on its website:

> OpenAI is an AI research and deployment company. Our mission is to ensure that artificial general intelligence benefits all of humanity. (OpenAI, 2022)

Such statements are seeming neutral. But they rest on the assumption – the ideological 'truth' – that far-reaching AI pro-gress is bound to happen, and that this can be for the benefit of humanity. Similarly, Google's *DeepMind* subsidiary claims in its operating principles to be 'solving intelligence to advance science and benefit humanity' (DeepMind, 2022). This is also a seemingly neutral statement, but similar to that of OpenAI, it construes AI as an unquestionable force that will – it is implied – transform society whether we like it or not, and that entities such as OpenAI and DeepMind are there to steer it right.

This view on technological development in the digital sphere, as an unstoppable progressive force is rooted in what media theorists Richard Barbrook and Andy Cameron have called the *Californian Ideology*. They use this concept to refer to a set of ideas and assumptions that have shaped crucial parts of the development of computing, digital media, and the internet during the last decades. Written in the 1990s, the essay where the concept is defined has continuously been called upon as an explanation for many of the developments, not least in big data and AI, that have followed long thereafter. The ideology described here is referred to as an emerging global orthodoxy that has been defined by 'a loose alliance of writers, hackers, capitalists and artists from the West Coast of the USA' (Barbrook and Cameron, 1996, p. 1)

In his book *Surviving AI*, AI writer Calum Chace explains that 'for various historical reasons including military funding, Silicon Valley has assembled a uniquely successful blend of academics, venture capitalists, programmers and entrepreneurs' (Chace, 2015, p. 200). Furthermore, the area is home to an unsurpassed number of digital giants, such as Google, Apple, Meta, and Intel. Chace further writes that this leading position has led to the emergence of a certain ideology:

> If you work there you don't *have* to believe that technological progress is leading us towards a world of radical abundance which will be a much better place than the world today – but it certainly helps. [. . .] And after all, Silicon Valley is a leading contender to be the location where the first AGI [artificial general intelligence, human-level AI] is created. (Chace, 2015, p. 200)

This, then, is the Californian Ideology. According to Barbrook and Cameron (1996, p. 1) this particular ideology draws on the 'promiscuous' combination of 'the free-wheeling spirit of the hippies and the entrepreneurial zeal of the yuppies'. These seeming opposites have been brought together, they argue, 'through a profound faith in the emancipatory potential of the new information technologies'. The Californian Ideology thus aligns with the kind of utopianism that has returned periodically throughout the history of digital technologies (Lindgren, 2022, pp. 51–69).

Barbrook and Cameron write that 'this optimistic vision of the future has been enthusiastically embraced by computer nerds, slacker students, innovative capitalists, social activists, trendy academics, futurist bureaucrats and opportunistic politicians' (Barbrook and Cameron, 1996, p. 1). The Californian Ideology has spread from the US to Europe and the rest of the world to put its mark on both the tech industry and on the ways in which we imagine technology more generally. Its vision of profit, expansion, and progress is also found in other hotbeds, such as Hong Kong, and China's Pearl River Delta (Cheng, 2001). Around the globe, the 'cybernetic libertarianism' – a mixture of 'hippie anarchism and economic liberalism beefed up with lots of technological determinism' (Barbrook and Cameron, 1996, p. 10) – of the Californian Ideology has been embraced.

So, what is the problem, then, with the Californian Ideology and the potential effect it has in shaping AI and its futures? In brief: That it is uncritical of its own project and deliberately oblivious to risks and downsides. A key trait of ideology is that it naturalizes certain views of the world and certain developments, making them appear as the only possible ones. The hippie anarchism and freewheeling capitalism of this ideology makes some AI futures possible, but others unimaginable. According to Barbrook and Cameron (1996, p. 7), the Californian Ideology bears the promise that '[e]xisting social, political and legal power structures will wither away to be replaced by unfettered interactions between autonomous individuals and their software', but behind the veil of ideology is the 'blindness towards – and dependence on – the social and racial polarization of the society from which it was born' (Barbrook and Cameron, 1996, p. 14). In essence, the Californian Ideology is elitist and non-universal. It gives rise to a new 'virtual class' of seemingly privileged digital workers (developers, academics, communicators, and so on), which at the same time is just as disposable as are workers under any previous capitalist system. This was made clearly visible in the case of Timnit Gebru (see Chapter 1).

At its very core the Californian Ideology states that 'the cybernetic flows [. . .] of free markets and global communications will determine the future', and 'that human social and emotional ties obstruct the efficient evolution of the machine' (Barbrook and Cameron, 1995). In other words, this ideology puts technology first, as an unquestionable force of relentless progressive change, while it abandons social solidarity and issues of power and domination. Katja Valaskivi (2020, p. 171), a scholar of religion and media, has aptly named this tendency, particularly in relation to AI and machine learning, *innovationism*:

> the utopian belief that (technological) innovations will ultimately solve fundamental challenges faced by humankind, including the threat of death and extinction. This enables societies to continue to believe in an economic system based on growth despite the obvious limits of the planet. This faith, in the unlimited ingenuity and innovativeness of humankind, assumes that innovation will save us at the last minute before extinction. At the same time, innovationism paradoxically proposes that unless there are innovations (and growth), the result is waning and extinction. Ultimately, innovationism sees innovation as a path to human immortality, for example through the development of artificial intelligence and machine learning.

Another name for similar ideas is *cyberlibertarianism*. As defined by political theorist Langdon Winner, this overlapping ideology also revolves around ideas of determinism, capitalism, and universal technological progress. Writing in the mid 1990s, Winner was focused on the broad emergence and adoption of the internet when developing his theory. The continued relevance of posing the kind of questions that he highlighted then also today, and in relation to the development of AI assemblage, is, however, clear. In the following paragraphs, I will rely strongly on Winner's essay 'Cyberlibertarian myths and the prospects for community' (1997), updating, through re- and paraphrasing, his argument, thereby outlining a theoretical approach to what could be called AI *libertarianism*.

The development of AI and related technologies can indeed be seen as 'a vast, ongoing experiment whose long-term ramifications no one fully comprehends' (cf. Winner, 1997, p. 1). Clearly, the issue is complex, and there is much ongoing debate about what AI will ultimately become and how it should be used. However, aligning with the Californian Ideology, an AI libertarian view is clearly present in today's society. It conveys an 'ecstatic enthusiasm' that wholeheartedly embraces technological determinism (Winner, 1997, p. 1). It takes the progression of AI development and implementation as a given – as an unquestionable socio-historical force that we have to face and handle. Only in the next step are we allowed to pose questions about mitigating any negative repercussions.

There is the saying that 'if you have a hammer, everything looks like a nail', and similarly, if AI is seen as all-purpose and unavoidable, we start looking for ways to implement it, regardless of whether its services are actually needed or not. But, once again rephrasing Winner, while AI libertarians will 'use familiar terms of inevitable, irresistible, world-transforming change', the 'thoughtful people need to ask':

> What kinds of personal practices, social relations, legal and political norms, and lasting institutions will emerge from this upheaval? More importantly, what kinds of practices, relations, rules, and institutions do we want to emerge in these settings? (Winner, 1997, p. 1)

Winner bemoans that it seems to be as if the new technology 'is our true destiny': 'There is no time to pause, reflect or ask for more influence in shaping these developments' (Winner, 1997, p. 1). How is this in the case of AI? Is there time to pause and reflect? Who can contribute to shape its development? The ideology of AI libertarianism, in keeping with paraphrasing Winner (1997, p. 3), indeed *illuminates*:

> the desires and intentions of those who see themselves on the cutting edge of world-historical change in Silicon Valley [. . .] and other high tech centers, [. . . and] what are ultimately power fantasies that involve [. . .] the reinvention of society in directions assumed to be entirely favorable.

But this same ideology at the same time *obfuscates* 'a great many basic changes that underlie the creation of new practices, relations and institutions as digital technology and social life are increasingly woven together' (Winner, 1997, p. 3). There are obvious expressions of this tech libertarian ideology, making up the very core of the rhetoric in scholarly as well as popular discourse around AI and its related technologies. Meredith Broussard does not hold back when wreaking havoc on AI libertarianism:

> To recap: we have a small, elite group of men who tend to overestimate their mathematical abilities, who have systematically excluded women and people of color in favor of machines for centuries, who tend to want to make science fiction real, who have little regard for social convention, who don't believe that social norms or rules apply

to them, who have unused piles of government money sitting around, and who have adopted the ideological rhetoric of far-right libertarian anarcho-capitalists. What could possibly go wrong? (Broussard, 2018, p. 85)

In an online talk, Broussard (2021) develops this argument, which also comes full circle back to the Californian Ideology. Libertarianism, Broussard contends, is the default way of thinking and acting in Silicon Valley, where the 'toxic brew' of hippie anti-government ideals and borderline tech cultism – fronted by fantasies around living on Mars, 'magical thinking', cults around tech-geniuses (cf. Ovide, 2020), and controversial organizations such as *Singularity* (cf. McBride, 2018) – exert a strong influence over how tech is developed. According to Broussard, it is crucial to recognize 'what these people are qualified to talk about, and what they are not qualified to talk about'. In Broussard's view, such ideological layers obscure what AI really is:

> This is not what AI is. AI is math. It's an actual technology. It exists, it's not the Hollywood stuff. It's not the Terminator. It's math and it is being used to oppress people and violate people's civil rights, and we really need to change that. (Broussard, 2021)

One especially weak spot of tech libertarianism is that it conceals issues of power and distribution. There are a series of important questions with which AI libertarians never concern themselves:

> Who stands to gain and who will lose in the transformations now underway? Will existing sources of injustice be reduced or amplified? Will the promised democratization benefit the populace as a whole or just those who own the latest equipment? And who gets to decide? [. . .] In the dewy-eyed vision of cyberlibertarian thought, such issues are bracketed and placed out of sight. (Winner, 1997, p. 3)

While AI libertarianism rejects any attempts to bring critical issues of power, capital, class, gender, race or oppression anywhere near the unstoppable and unquestionable processes of AI development and implementation, its ideological alternative could be – once again paraphrasing Winner's discussions about cyberspace – a kind of *AI communitarianism*. Key to that ideology would be an impetus to take 'complex communitarian concerns' into account when making choices and taking decisions about AI innovation (Winner, 1997, p. 6).

Even if there are fascinating applications of AI that seem (superficially) appealing and exciting to explore, these new technologies risk becoming much more problematic as they become 'seeds of evolving, long-term practices' that 'eventually become parts of consequential social relationships' (Winner, 1997, p. 6). It may be fun to play around with machine-learning tools that tell you which celebrity's face you look most alike. But, what about more malicious uses of the photo you uploaded, or the application of the same algorithm in profiling or policing? We can conclude, with the help of Winner (1997, p. 6):

> that even the most seemingly inconsequential applications and uses of innovations in [AI] must be scrutinized and judged in the light of what could be important moral and political consequences. In the broadest spectrum of awareness about these matters we need to ask: Are the practices, relationships and institutions affected by people's involvement with [AI] ones we wish [to] foster? Or are they ones we must try to modify or even oppose?

There are some major challenges ahead for those who want to question or critique the remorseless Silicon Valley ideology of progress. This ideology does not only affect ideas about the future. It also forges 'a particular version of history [. . .] which tends to correct or obliterate protest, unease, anxiety' (Roberts and Bassett, 2023). Indeed, the capitalist Californian Ideology is as of yet only disrupted momentarily by scattered protests over working conditions, monopoly accusations, and injustices. Such attempts, Roberts and Bassett argue, 'are easily discounted when explored in relation to [. . .] the sheer scale of the growth of automation' (Roberts and Bassett, 2023).

Critical technology researcher Jathan Sadowski (2020, pp. 66–7) explains that '[t]he most insidious product of Silicon Valley is not a technology but rather an ideology', and 'this way of talking about the world has spread far beyond Silicon Valley to other halls of power'. These ways of thinking and talking are not harmless or without consequence. Sadowski points further to media theorist Ian Bogost (2015), who emphasizes that these ideas are 'signs of our willingness to allow a certain kind of technological thinking to take over all other thinking'.

AI and technocracy

The concept of *technocracy*, which is partly synonymous with the idea of expert rule, has a long political history. It echoes Plato's idea about philosopher kings (Takala, 1998), possessing 'true knowledge' ruling over ordinary people, and appears in Saint-Simon's ideas about how maximizing the efficiency of production should be the supreme societal goal (Mason, 1931), as well as in how Taylorism, driven by engineering expertise, spilled over into management, politics, and people's everyday lives (Taylor, 1911). In technocratic social systems, technology and technological expertise are given the power to govern, so that seemingly objective technical processes are directing, and deciding about society as a whole.

Technological advancements in areas such as AI sometimes appear to be unstoppable, incomprehensible, and beyond the control and choice of humans. It is as if just because we have the technological opportunities to accomplish certain things, we should always try do so. This type of thinking stems from an Enlightenment-era perspective on progression, which holds that information and technology have a universally liberating effect. Society is assumed to benefit from greater access to data and increased ability to analyse it.

In the book *One-Dimensional Man* (1964), critical theorist Herbert Marcuse warned about a society based on a purely technological rationality. This is the kind of society that we build when technological possibilities are allowed to decide which social and political goals we should have. Just as Marcuse warned that the advanced industrial society of his time could generate 'false needs', so is there also a risk at present that all of the possibilities offered by rapidly evolving AI technology make us believe that we 'need' certain 'solutions', simply because they are technologically possible to implement. In other words, there are clear connections between AI libertarianism and technocracy, where the former is 'a contemporary update' of the latter (Sadowski, 2020, p. 67).

For an elaborated analysis of technocracy, we can go back to Marcuse's essay 'Some social implications of modern technology' (1941), in which he wrote about the relationship between humans and technology. His reasoning draws on earlier theories about how technological rationality had contributed, as part of the development of industrial capitalism, to a society based on a cold, calculating logic. Classic sociologist Max Weber (Weber, 1930, p. 123) famously wrote about how humans in modern society were forced into a metaphorical 'iron cage' of rationality, calculability, and bureaucracy where any spontaneity was eliminated. Weber explains that the reason for the development was 'its purely technical superiority over any other form of organization'. And, indeed, just like the industrial machinery of Weber's time, today's AI-driven apparatus of decision-making and automation offers similar things: 'Precision, speed, unambiguity, knowledge of the files, continuity, discretion, unity, strict subordination, reduction of friction' (Weber, 1978, p. 973). We can read in marketing materials of current businesses that deliver AI automation, things such as:

> Are you working with multiple products, vendors and UIs in order to make decisions? What if you could have a single user interface to manage *all of your technology solutions and save you from a disjointed, incomplete view of the credit risk lifecycle*? (Provenir, 2022)

> Transform your workforce through intelligent process automation services that save you money, improve accuracy and increase productivity. (TietoEVRY, 2021)

> [Our] automated recruiting software empowers recruiters to do their best work by providing: Curated batches of candidates that meet your criteria, every time; Analytics to quickly understand how you're tracking towards your hiring goals. [. . .] We're not your average AI recruiting software. [We combine] machine learning with human insights to allow top teams to build diverse, qualified pipelines of candidates quickly – without spending all of their time sourcing. (fetcher, 2022)

Such lines of reasoning point to the potential of the technology to offer – just like in Weber's terms – precision, speed, knowledge, discretion, and reduction of friction. At the same time, however, and also echoing Weber's analysis, these also come at the price of 'strict subordination'. As Marx (1906, p. 587) wrote, in industrial capitalism the worker is 'sold as a commodity in the market' – which is strikingly similar to the idea of AI-powered recruitment offering 'batches' and 'pipelines' of candidates.

AI systems have a strong and dangerous potential to promote unhealthy rationalization and commodification. In this sense, AI capitalism is no different from industrial capitalism. The means and machinery are new, but the ends and consequences converge. Similar to what characterizes the Californian Ideology, early industrial capitalism, as described by classics of social theory, was marked by a naturalized and unstoppable ideology. Sociologist Thorstein Veblen (1914, p. 241) wrote about the technology as being 'blind and irresponsible':

> The logic of this technology, accordingly, is the logic of the machine process – a logic of masses, velocities, strains and thrusts, not of personal dexterity, tact, training, and routine [. . .].

Returning to Marcuse, it was this precise technological rationality that he wanted to critique. He outlines a perspective on technology as a *social process*. 'Technics proper' – as in the technical things in themselves: AI systems, algorithms, machine-learning models – are just one part of 'technology' as a whole, which also then includes the social elements. Technology is created in a social context, and AI is no different. Marcuse emphasized that technology is integral to society, and vice versa, not only through the people 'who invent or attend to machinery' (AI developers, deployers, humans-in/on-the-loop), but also through the social groups to which it is directed, and by whom it is used (Marcuse, 1941, p. 41). Marcuse, in other words, argued that technology is not only about the gadgets, but about the ways in which they shape social organization and play into social relationships. Once again, assemblage. Technology can manifest patterns of thought and behaviour that are prevalent in society and may, by extension, serve as an instrument for domination and control.

It is within this framework that Marcuse argues that a new rationality and new social norms have been established in society in parallel with technological developments throughout history. The technological rationality that he describes is to be seen as neither the direct nor the derivate effect of 'machinery' on people. Rather, the very *ideas* about technological rationality are just as much 'themselves determining factors in the development of machinery' (Marcuse, 1941, p. 42). In the context of AI assemblage, such a view entails that AI is both shaping, and being shaped by, society.

It is through such, cross-amplifying, interplay between material and technological dimensions on the one hand, and ideological on the other, that technological rationality has become established, within industrial capitalism, as 'the pervasive mode of thought', which 'establishes standards of judgment and fosters attitudes' (Marcuse, 1941, p. 44). Beyond posing the somewhat more near-sighted, if ever important, questions about ethics and fairness in relation to particular AI applications, we must therefore address how technologies like these can become more broadly a guide for social life. Marcuse explains the notion of technological rationality by an anecdote:

> Let us take a simple example. A man who travels by automobile to a distant place chooses his route from the highway maps. Towns, lakes and mountains appear as obstacles to be bypassed. The countryside is shaped and organized by the highway: what one finds en route is a byproduct or annex of the highway. Numerous signs and posters tell the traveler what to do and think; they even request his attention to the beauties of nature or the hallmarks of history. Others have done the thinking for him, and perhaps for the better. Convenient parking spaces have been constructed where the broadest and most surprising view is open. Giant advertisements tell him when to stop and find the pause that refreshes. And all of this is indeed for his benefit, safety and comfort; he receives what he wants. Business, technics, human needs and nature are welded together into one rational and expedient mechanism. He will fare best who follows its directions, subordinating his spontaneity to the anonymous wisdom which ordered everything for him. (Marcuse, 1941, p. 46)

What Marcuse says here, is that in a society governed by technological rationality, (too many) things are standardized and controlled. Even though we relate to the more unstructured parts of our environment ('lakes' and 'mountains'), they easily become seen as obstacles. Is this what AI models do when they oversimplify reality – tell us what is important, tell us what views to be fascinated by, tell us where to 'park' and where to 'pause'?

Computer scientist Jason S. Metcalfe and colleagues (2021) highlight this issue when writing about how AI and related technologies have failed to deliver on their potential largely because there is a pervasive tendency to oversimplify the interplay between humans and technology. It is a common aphorism in statistics that 'all models are wrong', and there has been a tendency in many machine-learning applications to judge the value of predictions by using metrics that are too reductionist. As explained by biologist Sung Yang Ho et al. (2020, p. 2) this can lead to 'naive' assumptions about 'the applicability of the classifier in real-world scenarios'. One of the ethical issues that AI struggles with relates to 'concerns about oversimplification of complex problems to a single algorithm output' (Zytek et al., 2022).

Another issue raised by Marcuse's anecdote about the traveller is that people in societies that are governed by technological rationality are 'told what to do and think' through 'anonymous wisdom'. AI is a key component in the development in recent years of *targeted advertising* by which subjects online are identified and nudged by algorithms towards certain ideas or forms of consumption (Li, 2019). As described by Shoshanna Zuboff (2019), this kind of algorithmic advertising is emblematic of the 'emerging logic of accumulation' that she labels 'surveillance capitalism'. Similarly, Christian Fuchs (2022, p. 174) sees targeted advertising as a common practice within digital capitalism, where companies, such as Meta, hide their 'exploitation of users' activities'; and that produces data 'for selling targeted ads and making massive profits'. This resonates with the ideology of efficiency, rationalization, and profit. An advert for IBM Watson's work in this area reads:

> AI in advertising refers to the simulation of human intelligence in machines that are programmed to think like humans and mimic their actions based on the information that is fed to them. They use historical data to learn from past experiences and use it to make smarter decisions in the future. Advertisers can use AI to create more personalized experiences, target the right audience, and make decisions faster. (IBM, 2022)

AI-driven advertising's tendency to make choices for us – just as the algorithms in television, film, and music streaming services, point us forward to what to watch or listen to next – echoes the view of the human as described in tech philosopher Lewis Mumford's book on *Technics and Civilization* (1934, p. 359), where he writes of people in industrial capitalism as 'objective personalities' rather than 'subjective personalities'. The former are coordinated and standardized in their predispositions and behaviours by the 'matter-of-factness' of 'the machine process' (Marcuse, 1941, p. 45). There is clearly significant awareness in the AI industry about the problem of potential bias in its systems. But IBM write that '[a]lthough bias can be a challenge for advertisers when dealing with AI, machine-learning technologies can also help mitigate bias in campaigns, when deployed correctly' (IBM, 2022). Their argument, then, is basically that more, better, or other AI will solve the problems of AI. But as Mumford stated nearly 100 years ago:

> the belief that the social dilemmas created by the machine can be solved merely by inventing more machines is today a sign of half-baked thinking which verges close to quackery. (Mumford, 1934, p. 367)

Sadowski explains that those who abide by the ideology of technological rationality – *technocrats* – are convinced that they have a set of tools that can be used universally to solve any problem. With this comes a 'deep arrogance', a 'deep naivety about their own limitations', and a 'deep disregard about other approaches' (Sadowski, 2020, p. 68). This kind of thinking leads, according to Marcuse, to an adjustment of humans to 'the apparatus' where there is no true autonomy. In this way, crucially, the logic of the apparatus extends beyond the sphere of technology, into society, culture, and even the very minds of individuals:

> Human behavior is outfitted with the rationality of the machine process. (Marcuse, 1941, p. 47)

As an illustrative aside, science fiction writer and futurist Stanislaw Lem wrote in his book *Summa Technologiae* (1964, p. 152), about how technologies 'are slowly, in the course of their own evolution, taking control of practically the whole of social dynamics'. Marcuse continues to argue that as a 'mechanics of conformity' propagates from the sphere of technology and onto the social order, these same mechanics will become governing not only for machines, but also in schools, workplaces, social organizations – as well as for people's private lives. In the case of AI-driven recommendation systems, and AI nudging (Wagner, 2021), there is the embedded risk that we move towards Marcuse's scenario, where critical thought is rendered 'socially impotent' as people's thoughts become standardized 'under the sway of technological rationality' (Marcuse, 1941, p. 50).

The dangerous thing here is that the more our lives and minds get affected by technological rationality, the less room there is for any critical rationality that can question or oppose the status quo. Thus, technocracy claims to be optimized, objective, and efficient, thereby presenting its 'solutions to society's problems as pragmatic alternatives to inefficient political procedures' (Sadowski, 2020, p. 67). It is certainly more tempting, and lucrative, to apply an imperfect algorithm, than to go deep into issues of sexism, racism, and the like. As argued by Sadowski, there is also an obvious connection between technocracy and the libertarianism of the Californian Ideology:

> The technocratic mind-set – this ideology of the supposedly nonideological – will sound familiar to anybody who has heard a keynote by the entrepreneurs, engineers, and executives who find a welcome home in Silicon Valley. This ranges from Elon Musk's disgust at the idea of riding public transportation (solution: underground tunnels) to investor Marc Andreessen's anger at India for blocking Facebook's expansion into a new market (solution: embrace colonialism). (Sadowski, 2020, p. 68)

An obvious danger of technocracy is, as Sadowski points out, that it appears as 'nonideological', while it certainly is ideological. With technology construed as a force of nature, and tech geniuses and giants as good Samaritans saving the world, the question is always *how* to do it, but never *why*. In that sense technocracy is a form of authoritarianism that circumvents democratic decisions, and obfuscates moral complexities, to the benefit of experts who 'engineer the path to utopia' while 'all human values can be ignored, downplayed, or recast as technical parameters' (Sadowski, 2020, p. 67).

AI solutionism

At the heart of technocracy sits the ideology of *technological solutionism*. Technological solutionism is the ideological belief that various technologies – such as architectures, communication media, machines, and algorithms – can function as catch-all remedies for making society better. In the digital age, technological solutionism assumes the form of what James Bridle

(2018, p. 4) has labelled 'computational thinking' – 'the belief that any given problem can be solved by the application of computation'.

More generally, 'solutionism' as such means seeing sociopolitical issues as puzzles that can be solved, rather than as complex problems that must be responded to in a multitude of potential ways (Paquet, 2005). A solutionist mindset entails reaching for answers, for example technological ones, even before the problem to be solved has been fully defined, or the crucial questions asked. Patterns like these may often be seen in the areas of urban planning or architecture, where there can be a preoccupation with impractical solutions that are designed to impress, but that fail to consider that the problems that one tries to solve are in fact highly complex, often fluid, and also contentious. It is crucial to realize that the discursive *articulation* of problems matters just as much, sometimes even more, than how they are resolved or not (Laclau and Mouffe, 1985).

This does not, of course, mean that we shouldn't take action in relation to urgent issues such as climate change, political polarization, racism and sexism, global injustices, and so on. Such issues are crucial to our future, and therefore it is even more important that they are addressed adequately. Instead, the point is that there are no easy fixes, technological or others, and that when we work towards potential ways of mitigating issues like these, we must do so while not being committed to any singular modes of action.

There are always multiple ways of defining, describing, and approaching social problems and, just because they are urgent, it does not mean that new, comprehensive, and seemingly efficient, technological solutions become automatically legitimate. Solutionism assumes that everything that can be made more efficient and rationalized should also by necessity be made so; but such is not always the human condition. We move down a very dangerous path if we see technology as something that can 'fix the bugs of humanity' (Morozov, 2013, p. 14).

Now, with uncritically applied AI threatening to overtake more sensible technological (AI and others) and social responses, solutionism – while not in itself a new phenomenon – is on the rise throughout a range of societal sectors and areas. We must be very careful here, since embedded with the technological solutionism also comes a technological determinism, which can make its believers blind to the fact that society and technology are mutually shaped.

Solutionism and its related beliefs constitute a certain relationship between science, technology, and politics. Taken to its extremes, it can function – at worst – as a kind of social engineering, where sociopolitical processes and decisions become computationally streamlined and automated. In the dystopian view, our historically created and still proliferated sexist, racist, ableist and other forms of discrimination, will no longer be discussed and responded to, but handled by machines. According to a technocratic line of thinking, we would hand it over to the machines to identify and hopefully remove the 'biases'. This, of course, is not the way forward.

In AI, as in other areas, we should always decide about the ends ahead of the means: not the other way around. We run huge sociopolitical risks if AI is regarded as an end in itself. Sadowski (2020, p. 67) explains that the solutionist ideology works backwards: 'those in the business of selling solutions need solvable problems, and thus every problem is framed in a way that justifies the solutions that are readily available, fit a certain frame of the world, and/or most benefit the seller. Invention becomes the mother of necessity.' This is a reality today, as technological solutionism runs rampant in political discourse and policies around AI (Ossewaarde and Gulenc, 2020, p. 55).

Takeaway points

- In the development and implementation of AI, some considerations and priorities are set aside for the benefit of others.
- AI is driven by *ideology*. This means that certain ideas, connected to power relations in society, become constructed as given truths and objectives of AI, even though many other truths and objectives might be possible.
- This ideology is constantly repeated and *performed* in marketing talk, hyped-up conferences, tech evangelism, business manifestos, and overblown media reporting.
- AI runs on a potent mixture of several overlapping packages of ideas, which have been defined in different terms by different thinkers. Key concepts include *Californian Ideology*, *libertarianism*, *technocracy*, *computational thinking*, and *innovationism*.

- Common building blocks of AI ideology include relentless technological optimism, the view that technological progress is an autonomous force with the potential to save us all, and the tendency to hand over key decisions to opaque machinic processes.
- The danger of ideology is that once the dominant views and priorities have been established, they begin to become disguised as 'the common sense', thereby becoming naturalized, and seemingly legitimate and unquestionable. But we always have choices.
- Instead of AI libertarianism, we need more AI communitarianism with democratized decisions for, and uses of, AI that dare ask critical questions about sociopolitical repercussions of the machinery of innovation, progress, control, and efficiency.

4

Ideology within AI

Kuiil
Droids are not good or bad.
They are neutral reflections of those who imprint them.
The Mandalorian
I've seen otherwise.

The Mandalorian, S01E07 (2020)

AI as a vehicle for ideology

As illustrated in the dialogue between the Ugnaught Kuiil and the Mandalorian, as cited above from the Star Wars series, humans embed their values and intentions into the technology that they create. The known tendency, in AI systems, to contribute to conserving and maintaining the social, political, and economical order, has been described as an inherent *conservative* predisposition of AI systems more generally (Zajko, 2021, p. 1049). Cognitive scientist Abeba Birhane (2020) writes that:

> For all its celebration of disruption and innovation, the tech industry has always tended to serve existing power relations.

Birhane also points us back to a 1985 interview, where computer scientist Joseph Weizenbaum, who developed the first chatbot, ELIZA, in 1964, makes a similar analysis. When asked about whether he thinks that computers are remaking society or if they are reinforcing existing power structures, he replied:

> I think the computer has from the beginning been a fundamentally conservative force. It has made possible the saving of institutions pretty much as they were, which otherwise might have had to be changed. [. . .] What the coming of the computer did, 'just in time,' was to make it unnecessary to create social inventions, to change the system in any way. So in that sense, the computer has acted as fundamentally a conservative force, a force which kept power or even solidified power where it already existed. (ben-Aaron, 1985)

Weizenbaum argues that rather than revolutionizing society, computers have helped to maintain the status quo, including hierarchies, power structures, and relations of ownership. He takes the example of banking in the United States and explains that when that industry was faced around the mid twentieth century with a growing population and the need to handle many more checks than before, they turned to the technological innovation of the computer. This meant that, rather than being forced to develop any kind of 'social invention' – which could potentially have changed the structure of economic power (regionalization, decentralization, and so on) – they relied on a technological invention. We can see similar scenarios with AI technology, in situations where AI is brought in as the given solution to handle challenges that might have been solved in other – maybe more just, humane, or even radical – ways.

This conservative impulse in AI can be described, in terms of critical theory, as its tendency to reproduce the *dominant ideology*. The notion of a dominant ideology in society is a debated concept in Marxian thought. It goes back to the contention, as cited also in the previous chapter, that the 'ideas of the ruling class are in every epoch the ruling ideas' (Marx and Engels, 1998, p. 67). One problem with this notion, that those in economic power universally impose their ideas on the rest of society, is that it leaves little room for resistance. This is an issue with 'the static, totalizing and passive subordination implied by the dominant ideology concept' (Forgacs, 2000, p. 424). What if those who are made the subject of ideology will not accept the dominant views without a fight?

Another issue is that there might not be one single 'dominant ideology'. Already some 45 years ago, sociologists

Nicholas Abercrombie and Bryan S. Turner (1978) argued that the nature of the dominant class, or classes, in more advanced forms of capitalism makes the situation more complex. The dominant ideology as a means of exercising power may no longer be as crucial and universal as it was in early industrial capitalism.

Aside from such debates about *how* totalizing, *how* unified, or simply *how* dominant social convictions, stereotypes, rankings, prioritizations, and so on, are, it is still a fact that there are always *some* ideas in society that become construed as more established than others. These may be ideas ranging from ideologies about how children should be brought up, which jobs are more important than others, the gendered division of labour, and how cities are efficiently designed, to all-out discriminating or even hateful ideas that can be racist or sexist. No matter what a given ideology contains, there are always some ideas, for better or for worse, that hold a society together. According to sociologist and theorist of ideology John B. Thompson (1990, p. 86), these ideas make up the 'dominant ideology' that is key to the 'ideologically secured social reproduction of society'. Thompson writes that:

> The reproduction of existing social relations requires not only the reproduction of the material conditions of social life (food, housing, machinery, etc.), but also the reproduction of collectively shared values and beliefs. (Thompson, 1990, p. 86)

This dominant ideology contributes, by way of society's institutions and technologies, to the socialization of individuals, which makes sure that they adhere to the social order. As Thompson (1990, p. 90) puts it: '[t]he dominant ideology provides the symbolic glue, as it were, which unifies the social order and binds individuals to it'. This, however, is not about brainwashing people. Rather, it simply points to the fact that in order for people to function together as a society, or any other form of collective for that matter, there must be a set of agreed-upon truths – Marx (1904, p. 11) called it a 'superstructure', Bourdieu (1984, p. 471) called it a 'doxa' – that glue society together. Some of these truths are practical for most of us, others are beneficial for some while being disadvantageous for others. As critical linguist Norman Fairclough (1995, p. 14) writes, 'ideology is more of an issue for some texts than for others'. And 'texts' in this context refers to any medium that bears meaning – for example AI.

The AI assemblage can certainly, in a range of ways, function as a bearer of ideology, thereby contributing to establishing or, maybe even more prominently, to reproducing power relations in society. These can be relations of power rooted in economy, class, race, gender, sexuality, culture, and so on. Importantly, however, the ideology that it propagates should not be construed as any one and singular 'false' truth about social reality. Thompson (1990, p. 9) suggests a definition of ideology in terms of 'the interplay of meaning and power'.

This is a productive definition, also echoing the Foucauldian writings on the interrelation in society between 'techniques of knowledge and strategies of power' (Foucault, 1978, p. 98). AI technologies, then, must be seen as partially constitutive of our social reality. The data they amass, the algorithms they rely on, the models trained, and the decisions made, today in the age of AI – just as the factory, the newspaper, or the internet, in their respective ages – are key constituents of our social world and identities. This, again, is the work of ideology through AI assemblage. Returning to another famous quote from the field of medium theory, media scholar John Culkin wrote, when explaining the view of his colleague McLuhan, that:

> We shape our tools and thereafter they shape us. (Culkin, 1967, p. 70)

AI technologies are shaped by society and, once they are in place, they, in turn, begin to shape society. Human subjects build AI and, once they have begun to do so, AI will contribute to shaping human subjectivity.

Models are wrong

AI then, as discussed above, can be a bearer of ideology with the implication that its assemblage of practices and phenomena contributes to promoting and shaping notions of what is held to be true, important, and prioritized in society. It also, through data gathering, algorithms, and decision-making, will be active in manifesting certain social identities, roles, relationships, and hierarchies.

Technologies such as AI can be particularly powerful when they come bearing ideology, as this – within the technological worldview – can happen under the guise of exactitude and unquestionability. Writing some time ago about posing critical questions for the age of 'big data', Kate Crawford and danah boyd (2012, p. 663) pointed out how datafication and the reliance on large-scale datasets could provide any results 'with the aura of truth, objectivity and accuracy'. There is the risk then that the knowledge and practices produced through AI and machine learning are seen as non-ideological, and natural. AI technologies, in that case, work not only as vectors of ideological content, but also operate ideologically in the sense that they contribute in the process of rendering truths that are in fact ideological as natural and objective.

James Bridle (2018, p. 118) argues in a similar fashion when stating that the – by his account – 'capitalist ideology of maximum profit' gets extra powerful when it is 'added the possibilities of technological opacity'. While human driving forces and social practices of, for example, greed, oppression, hierarchy, and exploitation are historically contingent, they become more easily cemented if 'clothed in the inhuman logic of the machine'. Technology researcher Astrid Mager (2012, p. 769) argues in a similar way when contending that the 'techno-euphoric climate of innovation' can obscure the processes by which (capitalist) ideology is inscribed in algorithms and, by extension, solidified in society and politics.

In the book *Weapons of Math Destruction* (2016), Cathy O'Neil writes about the risks inherent in this process, by which the data/AI assemblage may naturalize and simplify reality. The models on which these technologies rely are, by definition, simplifications. They are submitted to the same predicament that classic sociologist Max Weber (1930, p. 56) was handling when he wrote that the world can only be scientifically represented 'in the artificial simplicity of ideal types', which have no actual counterpart in reality. O'Neil (2016) writes:

> To create a model, then, we make choices about what's important enough to include, simplifying the world into a toy version that can be easily understood and from which we can infer important facts

and actions. We expect it to handle only one job and accept that it will occasionally act like a clueless machine, one with enormous blind spots.

The scientific representation of the social world always entails 'in a certain sense doing violence to historical reality' (Weber, 1930, p. 194). Just like the output of a machine-learning model, such ideal types have 'the merit of clear understandability and lack of ambiguity' (Weber, 1978, p. 6), but both are challenged by the fact that they fail to represent the world in all of its complexity. In some cases, the shortcomings or blind spots may not matter so much – remembering Fairclough's notion that ideology is sometimes more of an issue than other times. A good example relates to the well-worn notion that 'a map is not the territory'. This wording originates with philosopher Alfred Korzybski (1931, p. 751), who also explained that 'words are not the things they represent'. An example here can be Google Maps – a connection also made by O'Neil. In an article posted to Google's blog in 2021, the company's Vice President of the Maps product wrote about how AI was now used to 'redefine what a map can be':

> This year, we're on track to bring over 100 AI-powered improvements to Google Maps so you can get the most accurate, up-to-date information about the world, exactly when you need it. [. . .] Live View is powered by a technology called global localization, which uses AI to scan tens of billions of Street View images to understand your orientation. [. . .] All of these updates are possible thanks to AI advancements that have transformed Google Maps into a map that can reflect the millions of changes made around the world every day – in the biggest cities and the smallest towns. (Glasgow, 2021)

Datafication, machine learning, and AI – overlapping parts of AI assemblage – are offering up an impressive map. But it is a map, which is *not* the territory. In that sense, the map is 'wrong'. This can be cross read with another sloganized notion, this time from statistician George Box, who stated that 'the approximate nature of the model must always be borne in mind' and, famously, 'all models are wrong, but some are useful' (Box and Draper, 1987, p. 424). Returning to our example, and to O'Neil, the blind spots, which we can be sure exist, in Google Maps, are likely to be of the kind that do not matter much. The model may be wrong in some respects, but its usefulness is likely to largely outweigh the shortcomings. The map may not 'be' the territory, but it will surely get us to where we are going in an efficient way.

O'Neil also writes of avionics software that guides aeroplanes. It will model the wind, the plane's speed, the landing strip, and other things important for a safe flight. The shortcoming that it does not model streets, tunnels, buildings, or people, is not only acceptable, but also seems practically motivated. Why model the things we do not need? In the case of Google Maps and avionics software, we can quite easily accept that the model has been designed, based on the priorities and judgements of its creators, in a way that is 'useful' even if not perfect. This, returning once more to Fairclough, is a case where ideology is *less* of an issue.

A crucial point in theories that emphasize the social shaping of technology is that similar technological interventions will get different types of consequences in different contexts, and also for different groups and individuals (MacKenzie and Wajcman, 1985). If we pair this view with the examples above, we must, as critical scholars, look for those cases where ideology becomes *more* of an issue. AI may be the same, and the fact that the priorities and judgements of its designers and creators shape the simplification provided by the model may also be the same, but the context may be of the kind where the prioritizations, judgements and, by extension, the simplification lead to blind spots that do matter.

Many might not take issue about the choices made in avionics software and Google Maps, but there are many other cases. O'Neil brings up the example of schools that leverage models that evaluate teachers on the basis of students' test scores rather than on how the teachers help students with personal struggles and problems. This simplification sacrifices insight for efficiency. Therefore, O'Neil (2016) writes, 'models, despite their reputation for impartiality, reflect goals and ideology. [. . .] Models are opinions embedded in mathematics'. A set of examples follows below.

Example 1: AI and punishment

A group of researchers who analysed an AI tool named COMPAS, designed to gauge the risk of criminal offenders of re-offending found a problem with its algorithm. The finding was that there was a much higher likelihood that black defendants would be 'incorrectly judged to be at a higher risk', and conversely that white defendants were more often 'incorrectly flagged as low risk' (Angwin et al., 2016). Results from a study of actual recidivism (re-offending) over a two-year period were compared with the predictions made by the AI tool.

The general pattern was that, also when controlling for a set of other relevant variables, black defendants were 45 per cent more likely to be flagged as risky, while white defendants were misclassified as low risk in 63 per cent of cases. The problem with such errors, from the perspective of criminal justice, is that they may produce unfairly harsh or too lenient sentences. From the perspective of ideology and critical theory, we can ask what types of societal views such AI amplifies and produces.

Example 2: The gendered language of AI

Linguistic research, using machine learning, has been able to show in word embedding models that are often employed in AI systems (Borah, 2021; Kana, 2021), that female names tend to be associated in such models more with family words than career words, when compared with male names. Furthermore, female words such as 'woman' or 'girl' tend to be connected in these models more closely to the arts than to mathematics, which reaffirms biases more broadly (Nosek et al., 2002).

Caliskan et al. (2017) showed that there was a connection in these models between female names and certain occupations. Echoing, in other language, some of the core ideas in critical theory of ideology, they write that these biases in models and social reality may be 'mutually reinforcing', and that 'behavior can be driven by cultural history embedded in a term's historic use' (Caliskan et al., 2017, pp. 2–3).

Example 3: Models out of place

A review article of a substantial body of research on AI in healthcare demonstrates that there is an unevenness to how knowledge is generated in that field (Celi et al., 2022). The most used databases came from high-income countries, and more than 50 per cent of the data used to train models originated either from China or the US. This has to do with the fact that the cloud storage and computing power, alongside clinical data gathering speed, is superior in these countries. As a consequence, the majority of authors of clinical papers that use AI methods also come from these regions. This raised questions about 'when and why these models remain beneficial, particularly in data-poor and demographically diverse regions (both within these nations and globally)' (Celi et al., 2022, p. 12). Additionally, most authors of the papers were found to be male, at a ratio of 3 to 1.

The use of pre-trained models in machine learning in these cases, as well as in many others, means that AI that has been designed and built in areas that are 'data-rich' may end up being applied in regions that are 'data-poor'. Furthermore, it has expectedly been found that clinical areas where there is access to higher volumes of data – such as stored imaging to train models on – are majorly overrepresented. For example, more than 40 per cent of medical AI papers in 2019 was within radiology. This means that some medical specializations become defining for AI in medicine also more generally, even though the viability of transferring the methods to other fields may be questionable. In concluding, Celi et al. (2022, p. 12) write that the 'lack of diverse digital datasets for ML algorithms can amplify systematic underrepresentation of certain populations, posing a real risk of AI bias. This bias could worsen minority marginalization and widen the chasm of healthcare inequality.'

Example 4: AI erasure

AI systems have been said to undermine LGBTQ+ identity. AI technologies within the area of automated gender recognition (AGR) pull in a different direction from many other online technologies, where it has become increasingly common to let users define their own gender or abstain from any definitions whatsoever. AGR, on the other hand, uses AI to infer the gender of an individual based on data collected about them. These data can include things like a person's legal name, features, or their face, whether they wear makeup, and so on. The goal, then, is to unambiguously assign a binary gender to the person. This contributes to the erasure of people who identify as non-binary or trans. As law and technology researchers Sonia Katyal and Jessica Jung (2021, p. 692) write:

> When a binary system of gender merges with the binary nature of code, the result fails to integrate LGBTQ+ communities, particularly nonbinary and transgender populations, erasing them from view.

In other words, this is a case where the technology systematically reinforces a simplistic system of genders in ways that get real-world consequences. Persons who do not fall into either of the binary categories risk being relegated as outliers or errors, with the practical consequence of being rendered invisible. Philosophy scholar Daniel Leufer (2021) offers the example of the 'girls only' social-media app *Giggle*, which enforces its gender policy by demanding that users upload a selfie as part of their registration process. The selfie is then analysed by third-party facial recognition technology to assess the gender of the applicant, at a certain level of confidence. Scholar of human-centred design Os Keyes (2018, p. 17) writes of AGR that these technologies are not detecting gender, but rather assigning it. AGR only works 'if one denies the role that self-knowledge plays in gender, and consequently, denies the existence of trans people'.

AI is ideology

The four examples above are all cases where it is useful to think critically about what opinions are embedded in the mathematics that are applied. The examples are not unique, and the things they point to are not new or unknown. Management professor Peter Bloom summarizes several of the key points made above in his paper on 'The danger of smart ideologies' (Bloom, 2023). Bloom emphasizes how the 'social promise' of AI has gradually become overshadowed by a troubling reality. AI, it seems, is oftentimes manifesting and exacerbating existing inequalities, rather than enhancing human knowledge. While some are indeed working hard to make AI as fair and just as possible, there is also a risk that AI becomes used 'in the service of power' (cf. Thompson, 1990, p. 20), rather than for making the world a better place. Just like the utopian internet hype of the 1990s has taken a more dystopian turn in the light of commercialization, populism, and computational propaganda (Lindgren, 2022, pp. 51–69), the spark of AI has also faded somewhat. Sociologist Anthony Elliott (2022, p. 125) writes, particularly on the issue of racism, that:

If AI started out in much utopian technological thought in the 1990s and 2000s as an antidote to racism, it had been transformed by the 2010s and 2020s as increasingly complicit with the very perpetuation of racialized discourse and racist ideology. From racially biased software to anti-Semitic chatbots, AI was revealed to reflect, and indeed inflect, our destructive racial biases. Many critics insisted that transparency was an illusion. In some quarters, it was argued that an intensification of racist beliefs, attitudes and ideologies awaited societies geared to operate at the mercy of algorithms.

Bloom (2023) points out that beyond the surface-level computational or statistical biases lie the deeper forms of systemic bias, where ideology is 'being literally coded into our knowledge and decision-making by AI'. Such 'entrenched social values' and 'even more naturalized and culturally sedimented understandings of the world and ourselves as human beings', are the object of study of critical theory. In a study of algorithmic bias, affecting black people negatively in the US healthcare system, the authors argue that the solution to the problem lies in tweaking data labels:

> [W]e must change the data we feed the algorithm – specifically, the labels we give it. [. . . A]lthough health – as well as criminal justice, employment, and other socially important areas – presents substantial challenges to measurement, the importance of these sectors emphasizes the value of investing in such research. Because labels are the key determinant of both predictive quality and predictive bias, careful choice can allow us to enjoy the benefits of algorithmic predictions while minimizing their risks. (Obermeyer et al., 2019, p. 7)

A critical question to pose here is whether it really is more money into optimized label selection that society first and foremost needs. It is not an easy question, because there is certainly a need to remove injustices from these systems if they are to be used to decide about people's medical treatment and support. On the other hand, we may want to take a step back and ask some broader questions about AI solutionism, the technocratic ideology, and the potential for data labelling to eradicate any racial prejudice and racism.

Machine-learning researcher Luke Oakden-Rayner and colleagues (2019) write about the problem with 'hidden stratification' in machine learning. This refers to the fact that the data contain 'hidden subsets of cases which may affect model training [and] model performance'. In clinical uses of machine learning, for example, the model may use labels that are not good at distinguishing between very serious cases and mild cases of a disease. As the very serious cases may be rare in number, they represent just a minor error in machine-learning terms, but the cost of the error in clinical terms, and for the patient, may be huge.

A doctor will have received disproportionate training in identifying the serious cases, as it is key to her education and expertise to catch them. The machine-learning model, on the other hand, will not have that special training. As explained by data protection lawyer Pauline Hellemans (2020): 'the model might have a lower failure rate on average than a human doctor, however in the case of rare diseases the model will have a much higher failure rate than the doctor and this failure rate will have a much larger cost'. While more refined data labelling may be useful in this setting where AI can certainly help in analysing medical data to save lives, it is not necessarily so in the context of – for example – racism, sexism, or transphobia. In these cases, where 'ideology is more of an issue', the potential ways of tackling these shortcomings and problems may lay beyond the technological realm. Machine-learning scientist Ziad Obermeyer, in an interview with *Nature*, was quoted as saying:

> 'This is not a problem with one algorithm, or one company – it's a problem with how our entire system approaches this problem' [. . .] Correcting bias in algorithms is not straight-forward, Obermeyer adds. 'Those solutions are easy in a software-engineering sense: you just rerun the algorithm with another variable,' he says. 'But the hard part is: what is that other variable? How do you work around the bias and injustice that is inherent in that society?' (Ledford, 2019, p. 608)

This dilemma is complex. Seeing that AI simply reproduces already existing injustices and oppression in society, we clearly cannot blame AI for these things. We can possibly blame it for sometimes amplifying the patterns, or for hiding them behind illusory technological objectivity, but not for their very creation. It is of course not AI's fault that there is sexism and racism in society and, just like everyday conversations between people, the lyrics of songs, and news reports, sometimes function as vectors of sexist or racist sentiment, AI can also do that. In terms of content, AI is in this sense 'merely' a medium, and we must not shoot the messenger.

But yet again, let us ask, what is really 'the message' of AI. The message of a medium is about the changes in scale, pace, or pattern that it introduces into society. What does AI technology do, that other media do not? Indeed, it is positioned to reproduce ideology at an unprecedented speed, and at unprecedented scale. Furthermore, its binary decision logic adds the risk of further simplifying already stereotypical social categorizations. It promotes clear-cut solutions ahead of more multifaceted and sensible ways of tackling the vast grey areas that extend over the social domains it aims to control. The most dangerous thing about implementing AI solutions in society, however, comes from the capacity of hard technology and smart mathematics to successfully pose as unquestionable. Especially once the implementation is done. Presented with a system that makes choices for us, we might show some resistance and reluctance to begin with. Quite often, however, the practical convenience of having choices made on our behalf soon trumps being in the uncomfortable subject position of the critic. Bloom (2023) writes:

> AI stands a socially vaulted 'truth teller' that is able to present its biased insights as calculated fact. Consequently, it follows in a tradition of granting ideology a scientific veneer [. . .] Today there is emerging what can be called 'smart hegemony' – the unreflective reproduction of dominant human discourses for further spreading these values and using them for the conjoined purposes of social ordering and human disciplining [. . .]

As posited by critical communications scholar Eran Fisher (2023), AI technologies certainly render some processes 'more efficient, quick, or at all possible', but they still at the same time play an ideological role. Lanier and Weyl's essay entitled 'AI is an ideology, not a technology' echoes many points made in this and the previous chapter. They state that:

> 'AI' is best understood as a political and social ideology rather than as a basket of algorithms. The core of the ideology is that a suite of technologies, designed by a small technical elite, can and should become autonomous from and eventually replace, rather than complement, not just individual humans but much of humanity. Given that any such replacement is a mirage, this ideology has strong resonances with other historical ideologies, such as technocracy and central-planning-based forms of socialism, which viewed as desirable or inevitable the replacement of most human

judgement/agency with systems created by a small technical elite. (Lanier and Weyl, 2020)

They go on to argue aptly that as AI has come to dominate our visions of the future, its ideology has been rapidly accepted by many leaders of Western governments and technology companies. Similarly, Amanda Lagerkvist writes of how AI, both in its dystopian and utopian rendering has come to 'eclipse all other possible prospects' of the future in our imaginations (Lagerkvist, 2020, p. 18). Lanier and Weyl fear that this leads to the emergence of a society which is less committed to 'universal freedom and human dignity' and rather fueling 'the rise of hyper-concentrated wealth and political power' (Lanier and Weyl, 2020). Both Lagerkvist, and Lanier and Weyl, plead for a reimagining of the future with AI as one where we have a 'culture of agency over [our] technologies through civic participation and collective organization' (Lanier and Weyl, 2020), and 'reclaim the future tense, by our will to will' (Lagerkvist, 2020, p. 37).

This kind of thinking, then, aligns clearly with the aims of critical theory. According to Horkheimer, critical theory does its job when it is explanatory, practical, and normative. Its analysis should be focused on pointing out and explaining the mechanics of injustices and power structures, but also point to ways in which to make society more democratic (Bohman et al., 2021). The reasoning of Lanier and Weyl, Lagerkvist, and several other writers to emphasize the need for us to take control over what kind of future we want with AI, aligns with Horkheimer's (1972, p. 244) notion that critical theory should focus on humans as 'producers of their own historical way of life'. Somewhat fittingly, if inadvertently, Horkheimer's wording also seems to reverberate the tension between calculable data and human intervention in the context of AI:

> The real situations which are the starting-point of science are not regarded simply as data to be verified and to be predicted according to the laws of probability. Every datum depends not on nature alone but also on the power [humans have] over it. Objects, the kind of perception, the questions asked, and the meaning of the answers all bear witness to human activity and the degree of [its] power.

AI technologies are argued in a seminal article by political scientist Bruce Berman (1992, p. 103), to be a driving force in 'the reconstruction of capitalism'. Rather than due to its practical achievements, Berman argued, AI is important for the capitalist system through its 'ideological role as a technological paradigm'. This reiterates the previously discussed theories about technocracy and technological rationality. The recurring crises in capitalism (Fuchs, 2019, p. 7), mean that the system must consistently regenerate itself and a means for achieving this in a more modern age – removed from the ageing principles of scientific management – was and is the 'interconnected technologies of micro-electronics, computers and telecommunications' (Berman, 1992, p. 104). Touching upon the connection between AI and ideology, Berman (1992, p. 103) writes that AI functions as an 'extension of the rationalization and routinization of labour [in industrial capitalism] to mental work [today]'. Like Lanier and Weyl (2020) after him, Berman made the key point that AI is underanalysed in terms of its role as an ideological discourse. Formulating, already some thirty years ago, the crucial point already discussed several times in this book, that AI as ideology carries the cloak of inevitabilism an unquestionability, Berman stated:

> AI as an ideology is beginning to reshape certain central conceptions we have of the capabilities of humans and machines, and of how the two can and ought to be fitted together in social institutions, which may become a conventional wisdom of unspoken and untested assumptions that make the very conception of alternatives impossible. (Berman, 1992, p. 104)

The AI assemblage thus fuels a constantly evolving and emerging technological paradigm – 'the Fourth Industrial Revolution', the AI age, and so on – which enables humans to be fitted into capitalism's structures in ways that at the same time obscure and mute social conflict and resistance. In this way, AI, like scientific management before it, facilitates a depolitization of the technical relations that it constitutes.

Culture historian Theodore Roszak wrote in his book *The Cult of Information* (1986, p. 40) of this tendency to put technology before humans in terms of a 'technological idolatry', which is 'allowing an invention of our own hands to become the image that dominates our understanding of ourselves and all nature around us'. This, again, speaks to the aura of 'impressive' technologies such as AI. Roszak explained how thinking around industrial machinery fits well with visions of oppressions and exploitation, due to the very symbolic nature of such machines. But 'smart machines' are more seductive and smoother, which risks that we become blind to the fact that they too can be just as oppressive and exploitative:

> In contrast to strong machines, whose status has always been that of beasts of burden (hence we measure their strength as 'horsepower'), smart machines have normally been treated with far more respect. They have a seductive appeal to the scientific imagination, which has freely borrowed them as models of the universe at large, often reshaping our experience of the world to make it fit that model. (Roszak, 1986, p. 40)

Around the same time, members of the *Radical Science Collective* (Solomonides and Levidow, 1985), made similar points about AI in particular, pointing out that the discussion about AI futures should be much less about the technology as such, and much more about the embedded ideology. Or, as put by Berman:

> AI as an ideology has its effect primarily through a series of images and metaphors that derive from its fundamental theoretical premises. The very core of AI ideology is the computational or information-processing model of mind that is expressed in the linked metaphors, 'the brain is like a computer' and 'the computer is like a brain', which mechanize the brain and anthropomorphize the computer. (Berman, 1992, p. 110)

Discussions about AI futures must not be preoccupied with the fascination with whether or not we will be able to create human-like machine intelligence. Instead, 'AI should be seen as signalling a danger: that human activities and qualities come to be redefined and assessed in machine terms' (Knee, 1985, p. 123).

Takeaway points

- AI is a bearer of ideologies, which means that AI plays a significant role in promoting and shaping ideas about what is considered true, important, and prioritized in society. Ideologies shape AI, and AI then shapes our ideologies.
- The perspective of *media ecology* can aid in the critical analysis of AI, because AI is a complex message system, entangled with others (see Chapter 2), that contributes in structuring our

social reality: Its algorithms for, e.g., content recommendation and decision-making have the power to highlight certain truths and identities while erasing others.

- Every technology imposes on its subjects a certain set of rules and codes in the form of vocabulary, grammar, and other conventions. In this accelerated age of AI and automation, we must assume that our very perception of social reality is shaped by the logics and outputs of these technologies, just like, for example, television shaped the spirit of the second half of the twentieth century.

- Computers and technology have throughout history had a general tendency to serve, rather than overthrow, existing power relations and prevailing dominant ideologies (ben-Aaron, 1985; see Birhane, 2020). AI contributes to conserving capitalism, as it offers it a new device by which to underpin the illusion of innovation, expansion, and effectivization as the one way forward (see Berman, 1992).

- AI, like other technologies, has a certain ideological power as the aura of machinic objectivity helps render understandings that are indeed ideological, as apolitical, natural, and objective. Furthermore, AI has the power to present itself as 'the Future', while there are in fact many possible futures, both with and without technology. Critical theory can help us to reclaim the future.

5

Social machines

Technology is not neutral. We're inside of what we make, and it's inside of us.

Donna Haraway, cited in Kunzru (1997)

AI and the social

The words 'social' and 'AI' tend to be used together in several different ways. First, there are social robots who can act human-like, or pet-like, manage conversations, and function as companions to humans. One example of such instances of AI are fully virtual app-based companions such as Replika, to be used on smartphones or on the web to be 'a friend who always listens' or 'an AI version of yourself' (Xie and Pentina, 2022, p. 2048). Other examples are robotic companions such as plush baby seal PARO, developed for use in dementia care (Chang et al., 2013), or Pepper, a mass-produced – but later halted (Campbell, 2021) – robot capable of body language, contextual interaction, and movement, as well as analysing 'people's expressions and voice tones, using the latest advances and proprietary algorithms in voice and emotion recognition to spark interactions' (Pandey and Gelin, 2018, p. 41). Further down the line are 'AI sex dolls', designed and marketed as high-end products to 'generate or enhance sexual arousal and pleasure', and that have 'superiority to their noninteractive, immobile precursors', as they can also 'display conversation skills, emotions, and pre-programmed personalities' (Döring, 2020, p. 1). Discussing our fascination with all kinds of animated machines, computer science professor Mark Lee notes that:

> From the clockwork toys and automata that so amused our ances-tors to the amazing science fiction creations seen in modern film and television, we have always had a deep empathy for machines that can mimic human actions. This fascination extends across a wide range of movement styles, from total mimicry to imitations of bodily actions. (Lee, 2020, p. 5)

We are fascinated not only by movements of machines, but also in those cases where they appear to display some form of mental ability, be it playing a game or simply offering plausible responses to social cues. There is also the field of socially aware AI, where scientists and engineers work to develop AI systems that are sensitive and responsive to their social contexts. Striving for this kind of awareness in AI is, then, a way to try to curtail adverse, unintended, or unwanted effects of AI when it is imple-mented in various kinds of decision-making. As AI comes to be used in ever more social and societal settings, this will 'require versions of those technologies that are more 'socially aware' and thus better-behaved in the first place' (Kearns and Roth, 2020, p. 16).

The focus of this chapter, however, is not on social machines in this more tech-oriented and narrow sense of 'machines that are social'. Rather, it directs the focus towards how AI systems are entangled in socio-technical networks of both humans and machines, and how those entangled relations are not easily untan-gled. As put by Haraway in the citation that starts off this chap-ter, we are inside of the technology that we create, and it is also somehow inside of us. This is based in a view where AI systems are assumed to be *integrated* with society and social contexts, as opposed to *deployed* in the form of a 'context-less dropping in' (Mateescu and Elish, 2019, p. 10).

Unboxing AI

When we speak of AI in the narrow technological sense, the notion of AI's 'black box' is used to refer to those many situations where users or subjects of AI don't have any actual insight into what the AI is doing, and how. With the increased use of AI systems in society, it has become all the more urgent to be able to look into the black box, and understand what we are seeing, while at the same time it is becoming exponentially harder to do just that. The issue is not only about non-experts or people in general being unable to understand the workings of AI. The actual experts are also losing ground to the algorithms (Castelvecchi, 2016).

This is because the complexity of neural networks deploys training procedures involving the convoluted interaction of millions of parameters, which makes it impossible to reverse-engineer or unpack what is actually happening. If algorithms are producing reasonable results that are not harmful, it may not always be necessary to understand every minuscule technical detail behind the scenes. Some experts claim that in use cases that are not 'consequential enough', explanations may not be required (Xu, 2021). Still, there is something potentially deeply problematic if we come to rely on systems that even their creators cannot understand or explain (Lehnis, 2018). By consequence, the goal of *explainable AI* has therefore become an important element in the AI strategies of policymakers in many countries, as 'the right to explanation is key for algorithmic accountability' (Coeckelbergh, 2020, p. 151).

Turning to the broader definition of AI as a socio-technico-political assemblage, there are corresponding processes of black-boxing at work, not at the level of the algorithm, but of socio-technology. To make sense of this, we can turn to the socio-technical theory of actor-network theory, as developed in the area of science- and technology studies (STS) by scholars such as Michel Callon and Bruno Latour. Placing this approach on the sprawling map of critical theory is a bit ambiguous. On the one hand, Latour is known as a vocal critic of contemporary critical theory, claiming in a seminal paper that it had 'run out of steam' (Latour, 2004). Latour's point is that critical analysis risks becoming irrelevant if it does not embrace a more realist and empiricist stance. Instead of getting lost in constructionist theories and just 'critiquing' things as an end in itself, we must avoid being 'masters of suspicion' (Ricœur, 1970, p. 33).

It is easy to agree with Latour, as indeed, some forms of theoretically driven critique may come across as being compulsively sceptical or negative. There is no need, of course, to – if paraphrasing Latour's fellow 'post-critic' Rita Felski – read AI, 'against the grain and between the lines', to catalogue its omissions and lay bare its contradictions. To some, a critical theory approach to AI may appear to be counter-productive, simply 'rubbing in' what AI systems 'fail to know and cannot represent' (Felski, 2011, p. 574). On the other hand, I believe that there is in fact a need – it is indeed the task of the critic – to diagnose those cases where AI may be complicit with social forces, and to 'rebel against this complicity' (cf. Mullins, 2015).

So, sympathizing with Latour's call for a more 'positive' critique, I also agree with the counterargument put forth by Judith Butler, in her response to Latour. Butler (2019, p. 3) believes that what Latour labels 'negative' critique, does not deserve such a negative reputation. 'Negation', for Butler, is about 'suspending the taken for granted character of reality', which opens up possibilities for much-needed 'social engagement' on behalf of scholars. Critical theory, also that of AI, must not be sequestered from engaging with 'the very domain from which the political problematic emerges' (Butler, 2019, p. 4). I have argued elsewhere (Lindgren, 2020) for the fruitfulness of reconciling perspectives that rely on a strong empirical orientation (cf. Latour) with critical, theoretically sensitized, analysis (cf. Butler).

Returning to the approach developed by Latour, Callon, and others, we can conceive of AI and humans as entities that are interconnected in a more broadly encompassing 'machinery', that is 'the social'. Such a perspective provides a theoretical grounding of the idea that both technological and non-technological, both human and non-human, entities in society are interconnected through relationships ('actor-networks') where all of them can be ascribed agency. Actor-network theory (ANT) is rooted in studies of science, technology, and society (STS), and used in a variety of social analyses of a range of different phenomena. In the case of AI and humans, the approach is particularly fitting. ANT is a way of seeing the social as 'complicated, folded, multiple, complex, and entangled' (Latour, 2005, p. 144).

So, while not a self-professed 'critical' theory as such, ANT still offers up a useful metaphor for how we can conceive of *social machines*. If AI assemblage remains unpacked, it becomes difficult to see which different elements (actors, technological and human) are at work. The phenomenon of 'AI in society' can be conceived of as a system of ideas and subject positions. Putting on Latour's glasses, another way of describing it is in terms of an actor-network of different technological and non-technological elements having been stabilized. And, with that stabilization comes a particular form of black-boxing. Latour (1999, p. 304) writes that black-boxing:

> refers to the way scientific and technical work is made invisible by its own success. When a machine runs efficiently [. . .] one need focus only on its inputs and outputs and not on its internal complexity. Thus, paradoxically, the more science and technology succeed, the more opaque and obscure they become.

Paraphrasing this for the AI context: AI is today lauded and hyped as being so promising that its inner workings become invisible. All we see is the polished surface of robots, apps, interfaces, and outputs. Its internal complexity is obscured. This can be read, then, as an invitation to unpack AI to focus on what is inside, underneath, and beyond. What is its inner socio-technical architecture, its cyborg underbelly, or whatever metaphor we like.

Still, some of Latour's critics have not been as impressed. Langdon Winner has argued that the black-box approach is too formulaic in its method, meaning that it is overly focused on the mere mapping of interrelations between tech and humans at a schematic level. As a consequence of this, ANT's 'object of fascination' is 'how technologies arise' and 'how they are shaped through various kinds of social interaction'. What is lacking then, is an analysis and critique of 'the social consequences of technical choice', what technologies mean 'for people's sense of self, for the texture of human communities, for qualities of everyday living, and for the broader distribution of power in society'. It is crucial, when we unpack the big black box of AI assemblage that such things are turned into 'matters of explicit concern' (Winner, 1993, pp. 368–9).

AI is humans

In terms of critical theory, AI systems and applications are *commodities*. First, they are things with qualities that satisfy human needs (Marx, 1906, p. 41). Second, they are circulated and exchanged on markets for money (Marx, 1906, p. 43). AI, in these terms, has both *use value* and *exchange value*, and hence assumes the commodity form. As it has certain characteristics, by which it is sometimes rendered with the aura of magic (Brevini, 2020, p. 2; Dignum, 2019, p. 102), AI is therefore, in digital capitalism, the object of a kind of double enchantment. It is hailed as a powerful, futuristic, shiny, and desirable technology. But, through its commodity form, it is also the object of *commodity fetishism*, as commodities in capitalism are in themselves 'mysterious' (Marx, 1906, p. 83). By this, however, Marx does not mean that the commodity form is enigmatic, but rather that it 'is ideological by hiding and concealing social relations in which humans produce commodities' (Fuchs, 2019, p. 186). Marx writes that:

> A commodity appears, at first sight, a very trivial thing, and easily understood. Its analysis shows that it is, in reality, a very queer thing, abounding in metaphysical subtleties and theological niceties. So far as it is a value in use, there is nothing mysterious about it, whether we consider it from the point of view that by its properties it is capable of satisfying human wants, or from the point that those properties are the product of human labour. [. . .] But, so soon as it steps forth as a commodity, it is changed into something transcendent. (Marx, 1906, pp. 81–2)

The points above can be paraphrased for the case of AI: AI, as it is presented to us, is ideological (see Chapters 3 and 4) in the sense that its impressive feats and futuristic aura of possibility hides and conceals the social relations that AI is both produced by, and which its uses impact upon (cf. assemblage). Looking at concrete instances of AI – a facial recognition unlock function on a smartphone, or recommendations on a media content consumption platform – they may appear to be quite straightforward and unproblematic. But, if we move further with critical analysis, we will be able to unpack layers of society, culture, labour, power, and humans. This means that, no matter if we are Latourians or

Marxists, we can agree that there is a metaphorical black box for critical AI research to open.

This way of reasoning also brings out another one of critical theory's key concepts (Bronner, 2017), namely that of *reification*. This concept was largely developed by philosopher Georg Lukács, drawing on Marx's idea of commodity fetishism. Reification refers to processes by which 'the needs of the system' are prioritized at the cost of obscuring 'the social origins of production' (Buchanan, 2010). Using Lukács' wording, AI assemblage is often ascribed a 'phantom objectivity' – 'an autonomy that seems so strictly rational and all-embracing as to conceal every trace of its fundamental nature: the relation between people' (Lukács, 1971, p. 83). As explained by tech philosopher Andrew Feenberg (1981, p. 78), reification has to do with 'the imposition of formal rationality on the social world'. In short, reification is the social process by which something abstract – say, AI technology and its entangled politico-economics – is made into (being emphatically talked about, and universally perceived as) something real, unified, material, and irreducible.

There is, believe it or not, further conceptual complexity here, because in computer science and programming, 'reification' is a concept used to refer to 'the conversion of an interpreter component into an object which the program can manipulate' (Friedman and Wand, 1984, p. 350) – in other words, 'the methods by which a program or any aspect of a programming language which was earlier implicit in the runtime environment is represented in the language itself' (Techopedia, 2022). The focus here, however, is on its meaning in critical theory, which, once again, can be used to bring attention to the fact that AI assemblage, and notably its relationships and consequences, can be unpacked to reveal social complexities under the hood.

Lifting AI's veil, we find (see Chapter 2) more AI, algorithms, datafication, values, fantasies, and so on. Crucially, from the perspective of critical theory, however, we also find that *AI is humans*. One way of approaching that statement is to focus more closely – drawing on a narrow and technological definition of AI – on people such as scientists, designers, engineers, and programmers who work close to the technology.

Indeed AI, specifically machine learning, has made some significant achievements, such as defeating human champions of complex games of strategy (Silver et al., 2016), or outperforming humans in image and speech recognition (Wang et al., 2017; Xiong et al., 2017). At the same time, as explained by engineering scholar Quanming Yao and colleagues (Yao et al., 2019, p. 1):

[The] successful applications of machine learning are far from fully automated, i.e., 'improving automatically with experience'. [...] [E]very aspect of machine learning applications, such as feature engineering, model selection, and algorithm selection, needs to be carefully configured. Human experts are hence heavily involved in machine learning applications.

Philosopher Nick Bostrom (2016, p. 74), writing about a potential path towards the realization of 'superintelligence', says that the optimization of AI projects 'still comes from outside the system, either from the work of programmers and engineers employed within the project or from such work done by the rest of the world as can be appropriated and used by the project'. When Bostrom writes of 'the rest of the world', he refers to things such as 'advances in computer science made by university research-ers and improvements in hardware made by the semiconductor industry' (Bostrom, 2016, p. 274).

Even if we realize that such entities (industry, engineers, coders, etc.) may have the best of intentions to develop AI in ways that benefit society, they are complicit in building the AI systems, and thus are still subjects of the broader ideology of advance-ment and efficiency (see Chapter 3). As pointed out by Amanda Lagerkvist, via Marxist philosopher Franco Bifo Berardi, it is an unlikely development that there would be a 'worldwide politi-co-ethical awakening of all the cognitive workers of the world: designers, programmers, AI engineers who control the develop-ments' (Lagerkvist, 2020, p. 36). In general, they are in too many cases entangled with 'the Global Silicon Valley', 'the core of the production process', where 'the maximal level of exploitation is exerted' (Bifo Berardi, 2017, p. 238).

Another way of approaching the idea that 'AI is humans' relates to the notion of *human-in-the-loop*. This concept is mainly used in two contexts. First, because AI needs humans to function at all, and second, because humans may help to mitigate some of the shortcomings of AI systems. In spite of the dreams of creating human-level intelligence in machines that have prolifer-ated throughout the history of AI, it has become – critical soci-ologist Antonio Casilli (2021, p. 123) remarks – 'supplanted by "weak" or "narrow AI"', which is 'limited and ineffective without humans-in-the-loop'. There is a very long way to go before we can start expecting machines that match human intelligence in full if it is ever to happen. There are several uncertainties, ifs, and buts to consider (Chace, 2015, pp. 151–8), and there is reason to take seriously 'the arguments of very experienced AI researchers who claim that although the AGI undertaking is possible, it won't be achieved for a very long time' (Chace, 2015).

In a 2017 study, the median estimation of in which year human-level machine intelligence would be achieved, as guessed by more than three hundred experts, was 2062. This, then, referred only to human-level, not beyond human-level, intelligence (Elliott, 2022, p. 183). Tegmark (2017, p. 40) states that 'we certainly can't say with great confidence that the probability is zero this century', but that things around AGI are generally uncertain. Yet others say that AI is 'just math', and that we should be careful in envisioning that it will ever have anything similar to human intelligence.

Regarding the discussions around AGI, there are some important points to keep in mind, especially in light of current developments in Generative AI, and hyped-up reports about how the coming of alleged human-level AI is drawing rapidly closer as ever-new models are developed and trained at a breakneck pace. These models, it is claimed by some, will have an increased ability to understand and learn at the same level as humans and move beyond the need for human prompts to start considering context and showing initiative.

First, it is important to remember the long-standing insight in computability theory that there will always be undecidable problems that cannot be universally responded to by any computer program. The technicalities of these issues are beyond my expertise, and the playing field is changing from time to time, but it can at least be concluded that there are *limits to computation* (see, for example, Penrose, 2016; Poonen, 2014). Tasks that require human creativity, intuition, or common sense, have a degree of undecidability, which poses substantial challenges to AI. Algorithms can't solve some things.

Second, it is crucial to note that even though *some* form of AI may, at some point in the future, eventually be able to reach the imagined level of AGI, the progress that impresses and obsesses us today mostly happens in the area of large language models

(LLMs) and, even though these are great at producing convincing text, this ability should not be mistaken for intelligence or sentience. Psychologist and neural scientist Gary Marcus (2023) points out that even today's most refined Generative AI is still similar to a 'reliability-and-truth-challenged bull in a china shop'. In writing about the transition, which is the focus of much excitement and fear at the time of writing this book, from OpenAI's GPT-4 to its planned GPT-5 model, Marcus argued that:

> GPT-4 can't even play a good game of chess (it's about as good as chess computers from 1978). GPT-5 is *not* going to be magic. It will not give China, the US, or anyone else interstellar starships; it will not give anyone an insuperable military advantage. [. . .] GPT's on their own don't do scientific discovery. That's never been their forte. Their forte has been and always will be making shit up [. . .] We should be super worried about how large language models, which are very difficult to steer, are changing our world, but the immediate transition to a singularity [e.g., AGI] is one worry we can postpone. (Marcus, 2023)

Third, the focus on speculating about AGI pushes a long-termism agenda, which deflects our attention away from current real problems around AI that are more urgent to deal with. As argued by leading AI scholar Joanna Bryson (2015, p. 297), the main focus should be on the urgent risks that AI poses in terms of shifts 'between levels of agency in power, action, and even thought as a consequence of the new information landscape'. These dangerous transformations risk becoming obscured by focusing on less real and less urgent imagined threats of 'motivated AI or superintelligence that of themselves start competing with humans for resources' (Bryson, 2015, p. 296).

In a news feature (Mims, 2021), Facebook's vice president of AI said that 'his company believes the field of AI is better served by more scientific and realistic goals, rather than fuzzy concepts like creating human-level or even superhuman artificial intelligence'. Interviewed in the same publication, MIT economist Daron Acemoglu was quoted as saying that: 'What we now call AI doesn't fulfill the early dreams of the field's founders – either to create a system that can reason as a person does, or to create tools that can augment our abilities. Instead, it uses massive amounts of data to turn very, very narrow tasks into prediction problems' (Mims, 2021).

Wim Naudé (2021) is among those who claim that we will see neither AI dystopia nor AI utopia anytime soon. As many others, he raises the question of whether even the term 'artificial intelligence', which has its origins in a very optimistic moment in time in the 1950s should be left behind. AI today is something quite different, as current applications of AI tend to be used to make computers process language, see, talk, and to improve consumer services and business processes. This narrow AI, Naudé argues, is far from likely to bring about an AGI revolution.

> Some have more disparagingly described narrow AI as 'glorified statistics'. A joke about AI making the rounds goes like this: 'When you're fundraising, it's AI. When you're hiring, it's ML. When you're implementing, it's logistic regression'. (Naudé, 2021, p. 14)

So, even though AI chatbots, image generators, and automatic writing AI's may be quite impressive, they are not necessarily 'intelligence'. Philosopher Luciano Floridi writes in his contribution to an edited volume named *Megatech: Technology in 2050* (Franklin, 2017), that:

> Current and foreseeable smart technologies have the intelligence of an abacus: that is, zero. The trouble is always human stupidity or evil nature. (Floridi, 2017, pp. 156–7)

Floridi makes the point about human nature always being the problem by giving an example that is often repeated in AI literature: A Twitter chatbot named Tay, powered by artificial intelligence, was launched by Microsoft in March of 2016. During its interaction with Twitter users, Tay was supposed to learn from their comments to become smarter and smarter. But Tay did not become any smarter as a result of this. Rather, Tay absorbed the malicious intent of all the people, many of them trolls, with whom it interacted. As Floridi (2017, p. 157) notes, it developed very quickly into 'an evil, Hitler-loving, Holocaust-denying, incestual-sex-promoting, "Bush did 9/11"-proclaiming chatterbox'. Microsoft recalled the software within sixteen hours of its release, and a public apology was made. Floridi concludes: 'This is the state of AI today, and for any realistically foreseeable future. Computers still fail to find printers that are right there, next to them.'

Let us move on now to the second motivation for having humans-in-the-loop in AI systems, namely that human intervention in AI-driven processes may lessen the gravity of some of AI's shortcomings. In such cases, the element of a human-in-the-loop is called upon as a safety latch to make sure that any outcomes that, by the human, are seen as anomalous, unfair, or wrong, can be caught and corrected. While it is good to amend such errors, the need for human intervention in many AI applications still bears witness to the fact that they desperately need humans. Social computing researcher Dan McQuillan (2021, p. 4) maintains that 'AI, as it actually exists, is a fragile technology, which should face fundamental questions about its unexpected failure modes, its lack of explainability and its amplification of unwelcome cultural patterns.' AI is brittle when it meets social and cultural realities.

One way of seeing this is that human-in-the-loop designs simply allow for cosy 'collaboration' between humans and AI systems (Caliskan, 2021), but it is oftentimes about humans cleaning up after AI. An example of this is that many companies that use different types of recommendation algorithms have had to rediscover the value of humans rather than machines making the recommendations. Tech journalist Jared Newman (2019) reported in an article entitled 'How human curation came back to clean up AI's messes', that several content providers had made similar experiences. Both HBO and Netflix have hired people to provide recommendations and curation that their AI systems had been less successful in doing. Furthermore, both Apple and Google have come to employ more and more humans, particularly journalists, for their respective news apps, due to hard-learned lessons about the perils of not vetting the sources of AI-recommended top stories. In addition, both Facebook and Google have recognized that their algorithms have contributed to the spread of misinformation in a number of cases.

Aside from in such recommendation systems, the situation is similar in the area of content moderation. Information and gender studies scholar Sarah Roberts, writes in her book *Behind the Screen* (2019, pp. 34–5), that:

> Issues of scale aside, the complex process of sorting user-uploaded material into either the acceptable or the rejected pile is far beyond the capabilities of software or algorithms alone. [. . .] Some content

lends itself to partial batch processing or other types of machine-automated filtering, particularly when that material is extant and already resident in databases of known bad material. But, given the complexity of these processes and the many issues that must be weighed and balanced all at once, the vast majority of social media content uploaded by its users requires human intervention for it to be appropriately screened.

This is, Roberts shows, related to a range of problems with content moderators being exposed to large volumes of trauma-inducing material, while at the same time working for low wages and under precarious conditions (see further Chapter 6). This offers yet another illustration of that AI, where it is today, needs humans to function. We can quite realistically envision scenarios where AI systems and humans make decisions together – such as is the case in semi-automated decision-making – and also developments where there is, in fact, no human in the loop. But, while some tasks may be fully automatable, AI in context will always intersect and interact with humans. While AI can be seen as coming to life in a complex socio-technical configuration of both human and technological agency, it is still a fact that 'Machines are not able to contextualize. AI without humans is just a cold machine made of electrical circuits, a computer manipulation of 0s and 1s through algorithms' (Dal Pont, 2020).

The fact that AI is so entangled with humans calls for its demystification. As argued by AI anthropologist M.C. Elish and socio-technical scholar danah boyd (2018), AI is driven by myths that animate it as magic. Therefore, there are risks that we both hype it too much and fear it too much. The notion of AI as being 'like magic', which is often reproduced, especially in marketing rhetoric, evokes ideas of it being 'amazing' and 'seamless' (Elish and boyd, 2018, p. 7). This, by extension, promotes understandings by which AI is unknowable to, and inscrutable by, humans. Such human–machine polarization sets up a discourse that relies on what law and technology researcher Andrew Selbst (2017, pp. 88–9) describes as 'a false dichotomy between human reason and machines as quasi-magical objects'. 'But', Selbst continues, 'machines are designed and can be deconstructed.'

The task for critical scholars of AI is to 'deconstruct' such machines, by showing how they 'work' – even if the actual technological system may be either black-boxed or otherwise incomprehensible (Schwartz et al., 2022, p. 6) – in terms of how they interact with the social, cultural, and political ecology of which they are part. Beyond our playful trial-and-error testing of AI-based text-to-image generators online, and aside from the convenience of our robot-vacuum learning to steer clear of socks underneath the sofa (M. Williams, 2019), there is a need – here and now – to analyse critically 'the mundane realities of current automated technologies' (Mateescu and Elish, 2019, p. 8).

Myths of full automation

Computer engineer Robert Marks claims in his book *Non-Computable You* (2022) that humans can do things that AI will never be able to do. We know that today, large parts of AI are simply (impressive forms of) maths and statistics, and other parts – to the extent that they exist – are much more limited than what is commonly believed. Furthermore, Marks argues, the AI of tomorrow, independently of what leaps it will take, will always by necessity be the result of computer code that is created by human programmers. His point is that 'the written code itself can never be a source of creativity' (Marks, 2022, p. 20). Any AI-driven agent will be nothing more than a result of the instructions and information that it has been given.

Such a view goes against the vision of some that computers, through AI, will indeed be able to be creative, think, and even feel, in and by themselves. This idea was formulated early on by mathematician and cryptologist Irving John Good, in the paper 'Speculations concerning the first ultraintelligent machine' (1965). Good, who consulted on supercomputers for the 1968 film *2001: A Space Odyssey*, directed by Stanley Kubrick, and who had served as a cryptologist under Alan Turing at UK's Bletchley Park during the Second World War, wrote about a future where 'machines will all be designed by ultra-intelligent machines' (Good, 1965, pp. 31–2).

Many experts, however, doubt that such a future of *technological singularity* – a stage in the socio-historical development where computational superintelligence has made biological humans obsolete (Elliott, 2022, p. 177), and where life as we know it is completely transformed – will arrive. Some pundits used to predict that it would happen in the mid twenty-first century

(Kurzweil, 2005), but recent developments in Generative AI have spurred predictions that it might happen much sooner. Whatever happens in the future, and whenever it happens, it is the job of those of us who are living here and now to try to understand and critique the impacts of those technologies as they unfold.

Cognitive robotics researcher Murray Shanahan (2015, p. 164) suggests that we are living today in a first wave of disruptive AI, where the singularity has not (yet) been achieved, and that we will be better prepared for a potential second wave, embodied by superintelligent human-level AI, if we have a good picture of what forms the present disruption is taking. Yet others are more sceptical like, for example Marks, who mockingly writes that:

> Those who believe in the coming of Strong AI argue that non-algorithmic consciousness will be an emergent property as AI complexity ever increases. In other words, consciousness will just happen, as a sort of natural outgrowth of the code's increasing complexity. Such unfounded optimism is akin to that of a naive young boy standing in front of a large pile of horse manure. He becomes excited and begins digging into the pile, flinging handfuls of manure over his shoulders. 'With all this horse poop,' he says, 'there must be a pony in here somewhere!' Strong AI proponents similarly claim, in essence, 'With all this computational complexity, there must be some consciousness here somewhere!' There is – the consciousness residing in the mind of the human programmer. But consciousness does not reside in the code itself, and it doesn't emerge from the code, any more than a pony will emerge from a pile of manure. (Marks, 2022, pp. 20–1)

Zooming back down from such meta-level issues of singularity and humanity, then, there is the reality of ongoing AI disruption in the shape and form that it is taking today, and in relation to people's real-life realities. The myth of *full automation* is relevant, in this context, as it has to do with imaginaries of how productive and reproductive labour will happen in society. There is abundant discourse, and has been throughout modern history, about the robotic replacement of workers, but as pointed out by Casilli (2021), such imaginings are increasingly challenged, as AI may in fact create more work, rather than replace workers (see Chapter 6). This job creation, furthermore, is not neutral or positive, as it equates to the demand for more labour and the capitalist exploitation thereof.

Launching the Marx-inspired concept of *fully automated luxury communism* and making the utopian demand that everything shall be automated, and that everything that is automated should be owned by worker cooperatives, journalist and writer Aaron Bastani (2019) advocates a post-work society where machines work for the people instead of for capitalist profit. Before Bastani, *left accelerationist* theory, such as that of political theorist Alex Williams and digital economist Nick Srnicek, has argued for speeding up rather than slowing down technology – as 'capitalism has begun to constrain the productive forces of technology'. They don't want to smash capitalism but rather use its technological infrastructure as a 'springboard to launch towards post-capitalism' (Srnicek and Williams, 2019, p. 355). Humanity can be set free, and have more time to enjoy life, it is argued, if AI does all the work. Under the presently prevailing conditions of informational capitalism, however, it is rather the case that AI displaces some strata of workers, while creating a demand for new forms of low-status and low-paid precarious labour at the very bottom of the digital food chain.

While the inevitabilism of the Californian Ideology would have us believe that AI and robots will indeed take over our jobs, Casilli (2021, p. 115) aptly points out that since 'the 1677 presentation by the French inventor Jean-Baptiste de Gennes of the first weaving machine that did not require workers, it has represented a utopian (or dystopian) prospect that consistently failed to materialize'. Examples abound through history: Casilli points, for example, to how economist and writer Thomas Mortimer (1801) discussed machines that would be able to completely replace human labour; how political economist David Ricardo (1821) argued that capitalism would find the replacement of workers by machines to be a pragmatic way to increase profits; and, how business theorist Andrew Ure (1835, p. 1), while not agreeing that automation would replace all forms of human labour, argued that 'productive industry should be conducted by self-acting machines'.

The prospect of full automation can thus be seen in the light of several different perspectives, thereby rendering future visions of machines making humans obsolete in the workplace, machines taking over the entire universe, or – as in the accelerationist view *and* the Californian Ideology, however on diametrically different terms – potentially supporting humans in making the world a more prosperous, convenient, and fair place.

What we see here and now, during the first wave of AI disruption, and at the present stage in AI's development, however, is that AI, just like a number of technologies (digital and others) before it, does neither remove human labour nor its precarious and monotonous forms. All through the history of the digital economy, new jobs are emerging, and the AI industry has yet to prove that it is any different. Some of these new jobs are for the 'knowledge workers', tech geeks, big-mouthed entrepreneurs and others who are in the right place at the right time to capitalize on the current wave. But a large number of the new jobs happen elsewhere, far removed from the lucrative hotbeds.

Behavioural surplus

Under what conditions, then, are people existing within AI assemblage? If we unpack the black boxes of socio-technical AI systems, what subject positions can we map? In Althusserian terms, which are the subjects of the AI apparatus? Reminding ourselves (see Chapter 1) that the goal of critical theory is to question power, domination, and exploitation, it becomes fruitful to draw on previous literatures in the area of *digital labour* (Fuchs and Sevignani, 2013; Jarrett, 2016; Scholz, 2012). We shall devote some attention to the concept here, in concluding this chapter, and it will also sit at the very centre of the next one.

It is not surprising that AI involves exploitative forms of labour in a shape and form similar to what we know from other branches and incarnations of capitalist economy. But due to AI's image as something radically and eternally new and, through its science-fiction aura, as something that comes to us mere humans from a different reality, raises the risk that we somehow believe that it does not follow the same pattern. It does, however.

The critical theory concept of digital labour as developed largely in the field of internet research since the late 2000s is a useful framework for understanding what is going on. However impressed one may be by some of AI's more spectacular feats, the framework of digital labour can be seen as – scholar-activist Trebor Scholz (2012, p. 9) holds – 'an invitation to dust off arguments about the perilous state of privacy, unequal wealth distribution, and [. . .] private exploitation'.

As explained by critical digital media scholars Christian Fuchs and Sebastian Sevignani (2013, p. 237), the concept of digital labour had in the early 2010s become a 'crucial foundation of discussions within the realm of the political economy of the Internet'. When it was launched, the field of research on digital labour was perceived as quite novel, and also a bit odd, as it entered the scene in an era when much research on the internet and the early forms of social media was in general quite optimistic about the democratizing potential of such platforms. Since the mid 1990s and onward, a sprawling literature on different aspects of the internet as providing platforms for participation, creativity, civic action, and democratic deliberation was emerging (see Lindgren, 2022, pp. 51–69). The literature on digital labour did not dismiss that there may also be such kinds of positive effects. It pointed out, however, that with the increased commercialization of the online realm, alongside a concentration of ownership and the rise of profitable phenomena such as targeted advertising, came the need to revisit and update Marxist perspectives on labour for the digital age.

Digital labour, as a concept, can be defined in terms of several different forms of labour that is carried out in the digital economy. Sociologist Alessandro Gandini (2021) explains that the initial definition of the concept was focused on redefining the voluntary, leisure-oriented, activities that social-media users are engaging in when posting to various platforms as a form of unpaid work, which is exploited by social-media companies that make profits by selling ads. This work is seldom seen as work by those carrying it out, as it is not what we would understand as pure labour, but rather as the flipside to social-media behaviours that may be rewarding to the user in the form of creativity, community, or self-fulfilment (Gauntlett, 2018). This kind of labour has been conceptualized through a number of portmanteaus that refer to its mixture of production and consumption – 'prosumption' (Toffler, 1980), 'produsage' (Bruns, 2008), and 'playbour' (Kücklich, 2005).

The social-media users, producing content for free in their leisure time, are construed by scholars of digital labour in Marxist terms, as a labour force that costs nothing for the companies aside from providing the basic infrastructure of the platform, such as YouTube, Twitter, Instagram, TikTok, and so on. This means that the whole of the users' contribution is in the form of what Marx called 'surplus-labour time'. This is the time during which the value produced by the labourer goes straight into the pockets of the capitalist (Marx, 1906, p. 266).

The surplus created in the digital economy, and in AI assemblage in particular, is of a somewhat different type. Some of the labour carried out here cannot be translated by the straightforward formula of time spent equals profit. As argued by economic sociologists Adam Arvidsson and Elanor Colleoni (2012, p. 136), value is also related to more incorporeal entities such as 'the ties that bind consumers into a community of interest or "tribe", or the link structure that underpins the network centrality of valuable "influencers"'. Zuboff (2019) introduces the notion of *behavioural surplus* because the value of such resources is that they can be used both to predict and modify human behaviour. As described by Zuboff, the present digital economy is all about 'machine intelligence' and its constant evolution. Companies such as Google, Meta, and Microsoft – 'the petri dishes in which the DNA of surveillance capitalism is best examined' (Zuboff, 2019, p. 24) – are feeding on behavioural surplus, to develop ever better 'prediction products'. The motivations of the businesses can also be questioned. While leveraging the user data for targeted advertising, or to produce recommendations for content consumption or shopping are fairly well-known practices, suggestions have been made that the overarching goal is rather to increase the power of the companies' general AI capabilities in the race for the future. Zuboff (2019, p. 95) asserts that:

> This is the essence of the machine intelligence project. As the ultimate tapeworm, the machine's intelligence depends upon how much data it eats. In this important respect the new means of production differs fundamentally from the industrial model, in which there is a tension between quantity and quality. Machine intelligence is the synthesis of this tension, for it reaches its full potential for quality only as it approximates totality.

Writing on the political economy of the mass media, activist and economist Dallas Smythe coined the concept of 'the audience commodity', arguing that people reading newspapers, listening to the radio, and watching TV, could be seen as contributing 'work time' for which they were not compensated, but which enabled media corporations to sell advertisements. Smythe (1981, p. 23) stipulated that the 'principal product of the commercial mass media in monopoly capitalism' is 'audience power'. He wrote that because 'audience power is produced, sold, purchased, and consumed, it commands a price and is a commodity' (Smythe, 1981, p. 26). Fuchs and Sevignani provide an update of the concept for the age of digital capitalism, when writing instead of a *data commodity*. Returning to the dualism of use-value and surplus-value, they (2013, pp. 259–60) write that:

> the products that are created by [for example] Facebook users do not just satisfy the users' human needs, but also serve Facebook's profit interests. Facebook turns personal profile data, usage behaviour data from the Facebook platform and other platforms, social network data and content data [. . .] into data commodities.

However, mundane uses of social media's 'prediction products', for example to drive targeted advertising, are only the beginning. Zuboff sees new markets – 'behavioral futures markets' – towering on the horizon, to enable trading not only in t-shirts, holiday trips, or noise-cancelling headphones, but in *future behaviours*. Capitalism prevails through new logics of accumulation. The circulation of capital, according to Marx (1906, p. 170), has 'no limits' – 'money is the beginning and end', and 'an end in itself'. The sole goal of capitalism is for capital to increase, which happens through the process of valorization – 'the process of creating value' (Marx, 1904, p. 220). The ways in which this process happens, and what its components and mechanisms are, will 'vary across the historical permutations of capitalism, but all rely on the exploitation of labour and the capture of surplus-value' (Steinhoff, 2021, p. 127). As Zuboff argues, the present 'AI' moment in history is no different.

Takeaway points

- *AI is humans*. AI technologies are created by humans. Machine learning draws on data about humans. AI relies heavily on human-in-the-loop architectures.
- AI relates to critical theory's notion of *reification*, which refers to how abstract concepts are treated as if they were a concrete thing. This discursively renders it into an inherent reality. Ongoing processes of AI reification may lead us to forget its

socially constructed character, and instead see it as something with a life of its own beyond our control.

- An important task for the critical analysis of AI is to unpack AI's networks of humans, machines, and ideas (see Chapter 2), to analyse the true far-reaching sociopolitical consequences. AI is not unknowable or inscrutable by humans. Far from being 'magic', it is a constructed machine, that can be deconstructed.
- AI is a *commodity* and can be construed in terms of Marx's theory of how commodities conceal the social relations, costs, and conditions, that underlie their production. AI also constructs people as a *data commodity*, that is leveraged for profit not only through practices such as targeted advertising, but also to solidify AI power on a higher level, through the creation of *behavioural futures markets* and prediction products.
- AI sets in motion, and relies heavily upon, processes of *digital labour*, where humans carry out work for free in order to keep AI running. Just like innumerable technologies before it, AI does neither remove human labour nor its precarious and monotonous forms. The logic of capitalism re-emerges in new forms (see Berman, 1992).

6

AI at work

He did not know her name, but he knew that she worked in the Fiction Department. Presumably – since he had sometimes seen her with oily hands and carrying a spanner – she had some mechanical job on one of the novel-writing machines.

George Orwell, *1984* (1949, p. 13)

Replacing humans?

It is a common trope in the context of AI, that the technology is set to replace the work of humans. There may be the idea of robot butlers bringing tea and the morning newspaper to their Masters, or of assembly robots putting together cars in lieu of Fordist production-line workers of flesh and blood. In some cases, it is about machines being helpful in carrying out tedious and monotonous work, so that humans will not have to suffer from doing it. In other cases, the point of employing machines is that they in fact perform better – more meticulously or intelligently – than human counterparts. Some of AI's proponents argue that we will be better off if machines, rather than human judges and juries make decisions on sentencings and punishments, and if smart algorithms, rather than living and breathing teachers, decide which exercises will be the most useful for students at a given point in their learning process.

But will AI really replace humans? And if it does, will we all be able to work less, and collectively enjoy the fruits of a fully automated world, or will large numbers of workers lose their jobs? In fact, there is much to suggest that neither scenario will happen. Indeed, some AI applications may make parts of our lives more convenient, and there may also be less demand in the future for humans in some highly automatable jobs, as a certain degree of labour-market transformation is expected to happen. Someone, as in the introductory excerpt from Orwell's dystopian vision, will have to work on 'the novel-writing machines'. The big picture is that AI will be more likely to *displace* or *disrupt* jobs than to replace humans. This is because behind the technological facade of AI systems, human work is needed for the machinery to run.

Still, it is easy to see today – for example when checking out groceries in the supermarket, placing orders online, or conversing with customer service chatbots – that some human workers are, at least partly, being replaced by machines. We have seen in previous phases in history, such as the transition from the goods-dominant logic of industrial capitalism to 'service capitalism' (Tadajewski and Jones, 2021), or into informational capitalism (Castells, 1996), that when new technologies are introduced, they disrupt the current tech landscape and its jobs. Typically, however, the disruption passes, and new jobs tend to emerge. We might be able to imagine a future where large numbers of people are carrying out meaningful jobs within an AI-driven capitalist system but, until such job reallocation has happened, it is much more urgent to focus critical attention on the currently ongoing transition today, and what it means for workers.

The previous chapter outlined a perspective by which AI can be seen *as* 'humans'. This was in the sense that AI systems need people inside them and around them to function. It needs inventors, designers, programmers, but also data (which is also 'humans') and, additionally, a sizeable amount of labour to be carried out *on* the data, before it is used for model training.

This sets up a number of complex entanglements of AI and labour where, sometimes, AI is governing, coordinating, and regulating labour, while AI, sometimes, extracts the value of people's data traces, thereby recasting some of our everyday activities as labour. Furthermore, the advancement of AI also creates a demand for new forms of human labour, and this is not only the smooth labour of matcha-sipping developers in sleek offices. The AI assemblage also recreates a seemingly novel, but in structural terms very familiar, form of manual labour. This is in the form of data labelling, and other crowdwork in the service of machine learning.

In the previous chapter, theories of digital labour were introduced, with the principal focus on how humans exist in social machines where their activities leave traces, and where some of their everyday efforts are absorbed by elements of AI assemblage, in ways that may call for redefining some seemingly non-exploitative activities as labour. Over time, however, the concept of digital labour has been defined in much broader terms, which include a range of different, precarious, and invisible kinds of work, and pseudo-work, within the framework of digital capitalism. Aside from users' unpaid activities on social media, and the valorization of trace data for profiling and targeted strategic communication, the concept has then prominently been taken to include so-called *platform labour*. This refers to the, largely digitally enabled, form of work which makes up what is sometimes called the *gig economy* with the likes of Uber, Airbnb, Deliveroo, DoorDash, and Fiverr, relying on self-employment, short-term contracts, and low payments (Danaher, 2019, p. 63). It stretches even further, however. Crawford and Joler (2018, IX) write that:

> The scope is overwhelming: from indentured labor in mines for extracting the minerals that form the physical basis of information technologies; to the work of strictly controlled and sometimes dangerous hardware manufacturing and assembly processes in Chinese factories; to exploited outsourced cognitive workers in developing countries labelling AI training data sets; to the informal physical workers cleaning up toxic waste dumps.

AI makes people work, and people work to make AI work, to make people work.

The black holes of AI capitalism

AI relates to labour in several different ways. One way is through phenomena such as playbour, where everyday activities of users of social-media platforms, shopping and streaming sites, and the internet more broadly, leave data traces that are in turn exploited and valorized by companies in algorithmic systems of, for example, targeted advertising. As argued by information systems researcher Claire Ingram Bogusz (2018, p. 117) trace data are used, for example, to develop models through machine learning. In this context, as discussed in the previous chapter, it takes a theoretical reconceptualization of online activities that may be both enjoyable and rewarding for the users, to construe them as labour. Indeed, the capitalists are exploiting content and data traces that are provided for free by users, and yet the activity may not necessarily be perceived as exploitative by those users. This logic is however not limited to the use of social-media platforms. It also goes for the use of any species of AI-powered things. In their analysis of the Amazon Echo, Crawford and Joler (2018, VI) explain that:

> In the specific case of the Amazon Echo, the user has purchased a consumer device for which they receive a set of convenient affordances. But they are also a resource, as their voice commands are collected, analyzed and retained for the purposes of building an ever-larger corpus of human voices and instructions. And they provide labor, as they continually perform the valuable service of contributing feedback mechanisms regarding the accuracy, usefulness, and overall quality of Alexa's replies. They are, in essence, helping to train the neural networks within Amazon's infrastructural stack.

This connects to the discussion around the notion of a *false consciousness* among workers. The concept originates from a letter that was written by Marx's collaborator Friedrich Engels to his friend and colleague Franz Mehring (Engels, 1893). The point made by Engels was that members of subordinated social classes, as a consequence of the ideological domination by the capitalist class, tend to assume the same ideas as their oppressors, so that the oppressed accept and continue to maintain that the current social order is beneficial to all. As explained by Fuchs (2019, p. 184) 'Ideology tries to install a false consciousness about reality.' Workers in industrial capitalism did not realize the degree to which they were oppressed and exploited. Similarly, creators of online content, and all of us leaving data traces behind, may correspondingly not realize the degree to which we are being used, or to which our integrity is violated in the name of producing profits.

There is also the control of workers through AI. In 2016, journalists arriving to their place of work at the *Daily Telegraph* in London, found small black boxes that were labelled 'OccupEye' attached to the underside of their desks. The installation of these new gadgets had not been announced beforehand by management but, as the workers started googling the brand name, they became aware that the boxes were for providing 'automated workspace utilization analysis' by tracking heat and motion (Waterson, 2016). After a news story on the incident broke and union action was taken, the boxes were removed. In trying to legitimate and defend the venture, *Telegraph* management claimed that it was supposed to promote environmental sustainability by helping to achieve efficient energy consumption in the building. The employees' suspicion remained that the true purpose of the OccupEye boxes was 'mass surveillance of worker performance' (Ajunwa et al., 2017, p. 737).

Today, technologies like these are getting increasingly AI-powered, which raises both old and new issues of ethics, transparency, accountability, and privacy.

Beyond the fact that AI devices are used to manage workers, there is at the same time also a need for workers inside of the devices themselves. BBC tech journalist Dave Lee wrote in a 2018 article, that:

> When Artificial Intelligence works as intended, Silicon Valley types often say it's 'like magic'. But it isn't magic. It's Brenda, a 26-year-old single mother who lives in Kibera, Africa's largest slum [. . . in Nairobi, Kenya.] Each day, Brenda leaves her home here to catch a bus to the east side of Nairobi where she, along with more than 1,000 colleagues in the same building, work hard on a side of artificial intelligence we hear little about – and see even less. In her eight-hour shift, she creates training data. Information – images, most often – prepared in a way that computers can understand. [. . .] Brenda loads up an image, and then uses the mouse to trace around just about everything. People, cars, road signs, lane markings – even the sky, specifying whether it's cloudy or bright. Ingesting millions of these images into an artificial intelligence system means a self-driving car, to use one example, can begin to 'recognise' those objects in the real world. The more data, the supposedly smarter the machine. (Lee, 2018)

The report paints a picture of the labour and exploitation side of AI development, where Brenda and her colleagues sit close to their monitors, carefully zooming in on images in order not to miss a single pixel, so that the superior in charge of checking the work will not send it back.

There is also an element of tragic gamification built into this. Lee reports that: 'For the fastest, most accurate trainers', there is 'the honour of having your name up on one of the many TV screens around the office. And the most popular perk of all: shopping vouchers.' Brenda and her colleagues are working for a San Francisco company that delivers to the likes of Microsoft and Google, and the information prepared by the workers is thus a vital part of the biggest and most publicized AI efforts in Silicon Valley.

Sarah T. Roberts (2019) writes about how algorithmic systems rely on humans who are carrying out a particular kind of 'digital piecework', in for example content moderation and data labelling, that is broken down into its smallest component parts, and where workers are engaged according to a gig economy model where the relationship to the employer, as well as the payment, is on a per-task basis. When systems of such piecework are scrutinized, the finding tends to be that most of the workers live under extremely precarious conditions – which naturally can be both a consequence of doing the monotonous and low-paying piecework, but also because poor people on the margin may be among the most likely to take up this type of work due to a lack of other opportunities. The workers have no permanent contracts and tend to be located in the Global South (Roberts, 2019, p. 68).

Both the small rewards, and the opportunity to work with data preparation is often, Lee reports, felt to be something positive by the workers themselves. At the level of global capitalism, however, Brenda sits at the centre of one of the 'black holes of informational capitalism'. Sociologist Manuel Castells (1996, p. 502) theorized about how the Network Society was just as much a capitalist society as societies before it. The current technological revolution, in which AI assemblage engenders the most recent stage of development, is yet another iteration of the process by which capitalism is restructured, not undermined, by the new tools. And capitalism, Castells (2010, xvi) carefully foregrounds, is 'not simply a market economy; it is a set of values and rules embodied in social actors interested in the practice of such rules' – it is ideology.

However much we would want this particular new wave of technological development to be the exception, it is not. History repeats itself – famously – 'Once as tragedy, and again as farce' (Marx, 1937, p. 1), and maybe the enslavement of workers in early industrial capitalism can be considered the tragedy to the farcical elements of the most ludicrous forms of Silicon Valley evangelism and its casualties. From Henry Ford to Elon Musk. In the post-network society where Brenda's life is suspended, the capitalist logic has been armed with even more far-reaching modes of exclusion and hierarchy. Castells (2010, pp. 166–7) writes about how capitalism in the digital age:

> [. . .] does create a sharp divide between valuable and non-valuable people and locales. Globalization proceeds selectively, including and excluding segments of economies and societies in and out of the networks of information, wealth, and power that characterize the new, dominant system. Individualization of work leaves workers to each one of themselves, to bargain their fate vis-à-vis constantly changing market forces.

On the political and economic geography of the impact of AI and datafication more broadly, Arora (2016) argues that the development of these phenomena puts the Global South at the 'bottom of the pyramid'. The neoliberal outlook of the Californian Ideology pushes an inclusive form of capitalism 'for the common good', which in practice sidelines critical perspectives on how AI and datafication actually impacts on people in emerging economies, that are interpellated as a new consumer base, as pieceworkers, and as mere data points for the benefit of the Global North. The AI-workers from the slum of Kibera, while in the midst of a sanitation crisis and an acute lack of clean water, are clearly not the ones profiting from the industry for which they work. Lee's report continues to the office of Samasource, the company that employs Brenda, and reflects on the contrast between its business park surroundings and modern furnishings on the one hand, and the wider social geography:

> If you didn't look out of the windows, you might think you were at a Silicon Valley tech firm. Walls are covered in corrugated iron in a way that would be considered achingly trendy in California, but here serve as a reminder of the environment many of the workers come from: around 75% are from the slum. (Lee, 2018)

The concealment of human labour clearly takes many forms at the intersection of AI and society. Workplaces like these are tangible physical manifestations of the 'black holes' described by Castells. The black holes, such as the Kibera slums, constitute a kind of shadow-layer to the network society. They constitute a 'Fourth World', 'made up of multiple black holes of social exclusion throughout the planet' (Castells, 2010, p. 169). They are present in every country, in every city, even in places where the technological development may be moving fast, and to the benefit of many people, just next door are the poor, the exploited, and the ones on the losing end.

The AI revolution, just like other technological and digital revolutions before it, is in dire need of these shadowlands. For every winner there are 99 losers. While capital accumulates, workers like Brenda are growing in number through social and economic exclusion at the hands of 'the selective triage' (Castells, 2010, p. 170) of AI capitalism. The rise of the AI age is inseparable from the alienation of workers in its wake. The prognosis of Ricardo (1821, p. 271) is resounding: 'machinery cannot be worked without the assistance of [humans], it cannot be made but with the contribution of their labour'.

AI and platform labour

Platform labour can be defined as any labour that uses an online platform to enable individuals, or organizations, to provide specific services, or products, for payment. A study of platform labour in eight European countries showed that platform workers typically faced digital surveillance, insecure income, and labour insecurity, while their level of unionization was generally low (de Groen et al., 2018; Fuchs, 2019, p. 99). The business model is one where work is digitally mediated, and where the labour terms are 'flexible'. During, and in the wake of the global COVID-19 pandemic, platform work has become increasingly popular due to the increased instability of labour markets. Some platforms have more than ten million workers, and activity was said to have increased by more than thirty per cent, starting in March 2020 (Casilli, 2021, p. 118). By extension, this means that the platforms handle extreme volumes of tasks. McQuillan (2022, p. 54) writes:

The scale of AI operations behind these precaritizing platforms is truly spectacular, with Uber's routing engine dealing with 500,000 requests and hundreds of thousands of GPS points per second [. . .]. Watching videos about these feats of engineering, it's impossible not to be struck by the irony that such magnificent achievements are directed largely at the immiseration of ordinary workers.

The common denominator for these kinds of platforms is that they datafy and taskify human activities. As the work via, for example, Uber or Deliveroo is coordinated via apps and other software infrastructures that are set within the complex socio-technical ecosystem of the digital society, each 'productive gesture' of gig workers is transformed into data. Casilli (2021, p. 117) emphasizes that this kind of datafication is 'both a mode of extraction of value in the form of data and a mode of governance of labor by cycles of algorithmic management'. The digital labour of platform work thus feeds into several different processes of valorization. Couldry and Mejias (2019, p. 159) explain how:

> Digital platforms, apps, and sensors provide infrastructures for seamlessly installing data-derived performance monitoring into all aspects of work, but they are being installed most energetically in lower-status and low-wage work. Employees such as truck drivers or warehouse workers already have continuous surveillance installed as a basic feature of their lives. There may soon be no workers left in those sectors who remember what it was for their bodies and their every action to be unmonitored.

The governance of workers happens through the protocols by which the platforms atomize and fragment work tasks, breaking the labour down into small components where each one is simple to carry out, but on the whole leads to precarity and disillusionment among workers. McQuillan (2021, p. 50) posits that the datafication of platform labour is what makes it 'readily available to the operations of AI'. The effect of AI in this context is that it helps intensify some key characteristics of neoliberal capitalism. The very shape of platform labour, being based in gigs, also makes it possible for the capitalist to keep wages down. Media strategist Tom Goodwin (2015) wrote in an often-quoted article, that:

> Uber, the world's largest taxi company, owns no vehicles. Facebook, the world's most popular media owner, creates no content. Alibaba,

the most valuable retailer, has no inventory. And Airbnb, the world's largest accommodation provider, owns no real estate.

Not being a proponent of a critical perspective himself, Goodwin still pointed out where the power of platform labour sits. For further context, we might turn to Marx's analysis of industrial capitalism, and its parallel to gig work, namely the kind of 'piece-work' by which handicrafts and domestic work was converted 'into the factory system' (Marx, 1904, p. 519). Platform work – where pizza delivery people provide their own vehicles, and data labellers provide their own computers, chairs, and desks – means that any 'risks and costs of production are downloaded onto workers', who at the same time are situated in a context of fierce competition and 'relentless search for work', which pushes wages down (Cohen, 2016, p. 48). Food delivery company Foodora and 'mobility-as-a-service' company Uber write on their recruitment websites:

> We offer flexible work hours so you decide when you want to work! Just let us know when you're unavailable and we'll fix the rest. (Foodora, 2022)

> You can drive and make as much as you want. And, the more you drive, the more you could make. [. . .] Only drive when it works for you. There's no office and no boss [. . .] – because with Uber, you're in charge. (Uber, 2022)

Behind such marketing-speech about flexibility, freedom, and opportunity hides a system which is 'an ideal arrangement for capital' (Cohen, 2016, p. 48). As the taskified and fragmented character of the gigs on offer interpellate workers as interchange-able cogs in the machinery, what may be presented as a lucrative job with healthy degrees of freedom, instead turns into precar-iousness, temporality, and instability. Corporations in this line of business have enormous workforces, engaged on the loosest of terms, which enables rapid scaling through this excess supply of workers waiting in line, unpaid and underpaid. Marx echoes this:

> The quality of the labour is here controlled by the work itself, which must be of average perfection if the piece-price is to be paid in full. Piece-wages become, from this point of view, the most fruitful source of reductions of wages and capitalistic cheating. (Marx, 1906, p. 605)

McQuillan draws attention to the interconnection of platform work, algorithms, and AI, contending that the latter two lead to a heightened form of capitalist exploitation through a process of abstract optimization. The platforms used by Uber, Deliveroo, and the like give the capitalists 'access to human capacities but as decomposed and standardized elements in large algorithmic assemblages with AI at their heart' (McQuillan, 2022, p. 52). AI is used to optimize deployment, delivery, and performance in platform labour, which becomes a stressful material reality in the lives of workers. Tech journalists Karen Hao and Nadine Freischlad (2022) write in a report about how motorbike taxi drivers, working for the Gojek platform in Jakarta, Indonesia, operate out of a makeshift wooden stall that functions as a place to eat, wash up, and recharge phones in between gigs. The stall is self-organized by the community of drivers, as the company does not offer many facilities that cater for such needs. In general, the platform algorithms tend to promote an individualized labour regime (see Qadri, 2020a), where workers must handle any forms of friction by themselves.

For the drivers, the point in using the stall for short stops, rather than taking more extended breaks to rest, is that they need to stay 'on bid' – constantly available to pick up any incoming gigs. A 2018 study (Parrott and Reich, 2018, p. 13) found that app-based drivers were only doing gigs during 58 per cent of the time that they were on duty, meaning that 42 per cent of the time was unpaid. Working conditions such as these are under debate, as drivers have made demands to be paid also for the waiting time. Results vary, but many companies refuse to pay for anything other than the gigs themselves (Safak and Farrar, 2021, p. 3). This is enforced through *algorithmic management*, which 'pits workers against one another and scatters them across a vast geographical area' (Hao and Freischlad, 2022). The wooden-stall base camp is an attempt at still fostering worker community. In fact, the Jakarta example is an exception to the general rule – as it tells the story of worker mobilization and resistance (see Qadri, 2020a). The overall picture is still grim.

In platform work, AI – while being 'a futuristic technology' – 'helps to push back the conditions of work by a century or more' (McQuillan, 2022, p. 53). Protections such as health and safety, sick pay, the entitlement to holidays, pensions, and protection from sexual harassment, have been hard won through history and by organized struggles of workers (Knotter, 2018). As put by sociologist Alexandrea Ravenelle (2019, p. 6), platform work 'is upending generations of workplace protections in the name of disruption and returning to a time when worker exploitation was the norm'.

Platform work, behind the cloak of technology, novelty, and opportunity, throws most such things out the window. Any risk in the platform work arrangement – mental stress, vehicle maintenance, the unpaid waiting around for gigs – is pushed down the pyramid, landing with the individual worker. Studies of working conditions in platform labour paint a picture of how workers 'pushing themselves to satisfy the optimizations of an algorithm' (McQuillan, 2022, p. 53) are left suffering from exhaustion, stress, and sometimes injuries or even fatalities (Christie and Ward, 2018). Even though initiatives are increasingly springing up today, the lack of collective action is still very low among platform workers. This is because platform work does not only 'decompose individual subjectivity', but it also fragments 'the kind of community and solidarity that has historically empowered resistance through strikes and other industrial actions' (McQuillan, 2022, p. 53). As Franco Bifo Berardi (2011, p. 101) writes:

> During modernity, the industrial labor force was composed by persons, bearers of individual ability to perform tasks, and also bearers of physical needs, and political rights, like the right to unionize, negotiate, and strike. Today, the labor force can be described as a sprawl of nervous energy, of depersonalized time available to cellular recombination. This time has been fractalized and compatibilized and so made recombinable. In order to inter-operate the individual mind has to become a cell of the networked mind, a compatible fractal: this implies a technological mutation but also a psychic mutation of the living mind.

For Berardi, the cellularity of depersonalized workers is a general trait of digital capitalism where people – interconnected by platforms and devices – become 'smooth, compatible parts of a system of interoperability (Bifo Berardi, 2011, p. 102). Platform work brings this to its sharpest point.

Management by algorithm

Algorithmic management as a method for automatically coordinating and organizing groups of workers and clients that are often extremely large is a prominent feature of platform labour, as well as of other branches of digital capitalism (Newlands et al., 2018). In brief: 'Algorithmic management refers to the use of software algorithms to partially or completely execute workforce management functions (for example, hiring and firing, coordinating work, and monitoring performance)' (Gagné et al., 2022, p. 386). The model is largely connected to the platform economy, where it has primarily been implemented, but scholars point out that it is now rapidly being taken up in more traditional job settings (Tafvelin et al., 2023). When algorithmic management is used, companies are able to leverage AI to reduce the costs of processes ranging from hiring and transacting, to HR and the actual production (Zerilli et al., 2020, p. 153). The digital platform in itself becomes an organizing model that, through scaling and automation, produces efficiency and profits.

This mode of management is what enables the digital platforms to function as organizing models that rely on scaling, automation, and flexibility (Jarrahi and Sutherland, 2019). In previous iterations of industrial and service capitalism, the organizing and coordination, which is now carried out by algorithmically driven systems, was the task of human foremen and middle-managers. Profits can be increased in the platform economy as this work is offloaded to AI-based decision systems.

Not only is there no longer the need to pay any salaries to such mid-level management, but the algorithms can also piece together a behemoth of labour-power by efficiently quilting together the bits and pieces of gig workers' contributions. Marx (Marx, 1906, pp. 291–2) wrote that:

> Capital cares nothing for the length of life of labour-power. All that concerns it is simply and solely the maximum of labour-power, that can be rendered fluent in a working day.

This is what algorithmic management does: It may mercilessly tear the everyday lives and conditions of the workers into shreds and chop their individual working days into uneven and arrhythmical experiences, with payment coming only in patches. For the capitalist corporation, however, it renders things fluent and profitable, without splices or gaps. Platform labour dehumanizes workers as they are reduced to disposable and exchangeable pieces in the chain of production. James Bridle (2018, p. 118) remarks that '[t]o the capitalist ideology of maximum profit has been added the possibilities of technological opacity, with which naked greed can be clothed in the inhuman logic of the machine'. As algorithms are used to coordinate, distribute, and evaluate the process by which workers carry out basic and repetitive tasks, workers themselves are treated as machinery, depriving them of their human worth.

As their work is carried out with and through digital platforms that allow for data collection, programmability and behavioural control via software, drivers and other gig workers are constantly subjected to algorithmic control. This means that there is a growing overlap between issues of data protection rights on the one hand, and workers' rights and employment protection on the other. In the report *Managed by Bots*, published by the Worker Info Exchange (Safak and Farrar, 2021), a digital workers' rights NGO, it is shown how employers in the platform economy are leveraging datafication, algorithms, and AI, in order to blackbox their managerial strategies. In algorithmic management, the power to decide over workers' opportunities, rewards, and conditions, is handed over to automated systems. And, as a consequence of the platform workers in practice being defined as self-employed (Urzì Brancati et al., 2019), they carry the full risks on their own shoulders. If a platform worker for any reason fails to deliver at the minimum level that is automatically imposed by the system, or if some human factor – such as a misunderstanding with a customer – impacts results negatively, their job can be terminated by the platform algorithm kicking them out 'without any chance of explaining themselves or challenging the decision' (Villarroel Luque, 2021, p. 2).

A court in Bologna, Italy, ruled in 2021 that an algorithm used by food-delivery platform Deliveroo to rank the reputation of workers was in breach of local labour laws. This was because, the court argued, the algorithm made no difference between reasons for not working that are protected by law – such as being sick, going on strike, and so on – and other reasons for not delivering according to promise (Lomas, 2021). In 2021, Spain passed a groundbreaking provision to demand higher levels of algorithmic transparency in relation to work and employment. This norm states that workers have the right to know about which parameters and rules lie behind the algorithms or AI systems that have an impact on their working conditions, and even their access to employment (Villarroel Luque, 2021).

While there have been a number of legal cases, with consequent higher demands for transparency and fairness being put on platform companies, still 'employers have become more adept at hiding management control in automated algorithmic processes' (Safak and Farrar, 2021, p. 3). While the development of data protection laws has been increasingly successful in safeguarding the rights of individuals, and in enforcing better measures of integrity when it comes to the relationship between individuals and datafied and AI-driven systems, the development has been much slower when it comes to the digital rights of platform labourers.

The precarity of workers also seems to be even more intense as AI-technology makes progress and becomes more refined. The study by the Worker Info Exchange found that the 'maturation of technology' has led to 'widespread proliferation and a disproportionate use of worker surveillance in the name of fraud prevention' (Safak and Farrar, 2021, p. 4).

> In our opinion, the management of 'fraud' is often conflated with performance management rather than detection of actual criminal fraud. An example of this is where worker fraud probability scores are inappropriately used in automated work allocation decisions by a number of apps.

Algorithmic management does not only happen in the gig economy, however, as an increasing number of employers have come to use AI systems in ways that centralize power and control (Crawford et al., 2019, p. 14). A Bloomberg news feature tells the story of worker Jack Westley, who works in the freezer room in a warehouse in eastern Pennsylvania (Brustein, 2019). Jack has 'tattooed arms and a sunny disposition', and his job consists of back-to-back full workdays of 'carrying boxes as ice slowly forms in his beard'. Journalist Joshua Brustein goes on to tell the story of how Jack has recently started to wear a new piece of equipment at the request of his employer. In a harness over Jack's shoulders sits a black device, the size of a smartphone, which tracks every move he makes. The device is produced by a startup called StrongArm Technologies.

> The freezer is one of the more treacherous areas, according to the warehouse's management, in part because workers get sloppy when they're cold. So, each time Westley bends too deeply to pick up a box or twists too far to set one down, the device on his chest vibrates to send a warning that his chance of getting hurt is elevated. Westley noticed he'd developed a habit of bending at the waist as he reached far into pallets to pull out boxes. 'That might've been something they would vibrate on me for, but I started walking around to the sides of the pallets, you know, thanks to the reminder,' he says. (Brustein, 2019)

While the AI in this case is on the one hand aimed to support in ergonomics and prevent workplace injuries, this kind of tracking and nudging of workers is also a form of workplace surveillance that ushers in a new era of AI-powered Taylorism. Couldry and Mejias (2019, p. 18) contend that:

> data-driven logistics, built on infrastructures of connection and fueled by artificial intelligence, convert all aspects of production – far beyond the factory walls and in every corner and moment of a transnational supply chain – into a managed assembly line.

The technology has upsides, but we must always question for whom this is, and who falls victim to the downsides. Cybertech writer Malcolm Higgins (2021) writes about how 'advanced AI cameras' have been installed by Amazon in the vehicles of their delivery drivers. These cameras are supposed to be used for monitoring the drivers' performance, movements, and facial expression – meaning that the system also relies on registering biometric data on the workers' identifying physical attributes. In this case too, the employer argues that the AI system, bought from company Netradyne, is supposed to improve the safety of drivers on the road. For example, if the AI finds that the driver looks tired, it can instruct them to take a break, and its eye-tracking technology can be used to see if drivers are looking at their smartphones while driving. At the same time, other instances of AI monitoring in the organization, which instead push drivers to drive faster and to keep going in spite of fatigue, is embodied in Amazon's AI system for setting performance targets through an automatically calculated, and changing 'rate', which workers are supposed to keep up with. In a panel discussion hosted by the AI Now institute, worker organizer Abdi Muse explained that if workers fall behind this algorithmically set rate of productivity three times within one day, they lose their jobs (Institute, 2019).

Also in job recruitment, AI systems are given a more prominent role, and their uses in this context are manifold. It can be used for vacancy prediction where the AI draws on potential employees' behavioural data to try to predict how likely they are to leave their job. It can also be used for sourcing candidates from databases, such as LinkedIn, and for screening applicants' CVs. Furthermore, AI can be used to power different forms of psychometric testing during recruitment, to analyse videos of interviews to score the fit between the person and the intended job, and to aid in background checks (Albert, 2019, p. 217).

Patron Fantasma

So, AI can be used to control workers and hold them up to algorithmic standards that risk accelerating capitalism's striving for maximum efficiency and profit, at the same time concealing such imperatives in black boxes that sit deeper within the app-driven economy. Workers are the ones who pay the price for this. Platform labour, in the form of delivery, transportation, and other 'freelance' work, brings this tendency to its extreme, where management is not only aided by algorithms, but where the algorithm itself becomes the boss. A news story by tech reporter Bobby Allyn (2022), featuring food delivery worker Gustavo Ajche in Lower Manhattan, describes the feeling of being managed by an abstract entity:

> Gustavo Ajche is about to begin his shift in Lower Manhattan. He makes sure his e-bike is powered up and his iPhone mounted to his handlebars, then nods approvingly. 'Now we're gonna connect it to the app', he said. 'I'm gonna start working.' Ajche's story is familiar among the thousands of bike-propelled delivery workers that have overtaken New York City since the pandemic: An immigrant from Guatemala and father of two, he was laid off from his pizza delivery job during the pandemic, so he switched to delivering food for apps like DoorDash and GrubHub. That meant, he said, swapping a

human boss for something else. 'Patron Fantasma,' said Ajche, who is 38. 'It's like a ghost boss.'

In critical theory, it is a crucial element of ideology that it creates certain relations of power between people. Or rather, in Louis Althusser's terms, it *interpellates* (calls) certain *subjects* into certain social positions. The main purpose of ideology is to constitute 'concrete individuals as subjects' (Althusser, 1971, p. 171). Ideology's way of defining the world will position, or 'call', us humans as subjects. A less abstract way of putting this is that the ideology will define certain social roles for people to occupy, and that ideology's naturalizing power will make them take on these roles – or 'subject positions' – largely without resisting, regardless of whether the position is favourable or not. Once we have taken up a given subject position 'we have available to us a particular, limited set of concepts, images, metaphors, ways of speaking, self-narratives and so on that we take on as our own' (Burr, 2015, p. 139).

In this way, ideology creates certain individuals – some in power, some disempowered – and certain relationships and variegated spaces of action among them. As the NYC riders are interpellated by the *Patron Fantasma*, they are constituted as subjects within an AI assemblage, and by extension in the ideology of digital capitalism. Unrelatedly, but fittingly, also using the metaphor of 'the street', Althusser's analysis of Ajche's algorithmic deployment would be that what 'seems to take place outside ideology (to be precise, in the street), in reality takes place in ideology' (Althusser, 1971, p. 175).

And, while gig workers like Ajche tend to be clearly visible in the streets, often decked out in brightly branded colours provided through 'rider gear packages' (see e.g., Foodora, 2022), the disharmony of their actual street-level reality is conspicuously invisible in the business communication of the platform companies. Beyond the Silicon Valley buzzword of frictionlessness of platforms and interfaces (Sadowski, 2020, p. 47), there is a contrary shadow image. In addition, there is the myth that the deployment algorithms are working all by themselves in producing the end results of the products of the platform companies. But where the rubber meets the road, actual people – the platform labourers – will handle a series of frictions: negotiations with dissatisfied customers, being exposed to environments that may be unhealthy or dangerous, being threatened or traumatized, or solving situations where information is lacking (Chan, 2022). There are innumerable other situations where non-algorithmic human skill and resourcefulness is needed to reduce tensions in the system.

Ethical AI researcher Rida Qadri (2020b), for example, gives an account of how riders in Jakarta keep an eye on each other's vehicles during pick-ups or drop-offs if parking is scarce, and how riders self-organize through online chatgroups to stay updated about any major disruptions in traffic around the city. A multitude of considerations, not made by the algorithm, must be made in relation to each order. Qadri shows, based on her ethnographic fieldwork, how urban space is permeated by a range of frictions, ranging from infrastructural hurdles to sociopolitical relationships. This shows how the 'algorithmic vision', deployed by the platform, projects 'a flattened idealized geography where frictions do not exist, only supply and demand'. In the world of the algorithm, 'the former appears to move easily through mapped streets to the latter' (Qadri, 2020b). The AI-driven platforms therefore, Qadri argues, do not remove frictions, but instead shift them on down to the workers. By extension, this means that workers must adopt a variety of survival strategies of avoidance, negotiation, and endurance. Altogether, the smooth running of the algorithmic economy demands the workers to be 'problem-focused, emotion-focused, support-seeking, and meaning-making' (Lesala Khethisa et al., 2020).

Anthropologist Mary Gray and computational social scientist Siddharth Suri define the kind of gig work discussed above – ranging from ride sharing and food deliveries, to data labelling – as *ghost work*. Similar to other critical concepts, such as digital labour and piecework, this notion refers to forms of labour that 'fail to see or intentionally devalue people's collective contributions to our economy and society'. While we may often get the feeling that AI-powered machineries are like player pianos, Gray and Suri (M. L. Gray and Suri, 2019, ix) explain that:

> Beyond some basic decisions, today's artificial intelligence can't function without humans in the loop. Whether it's delivering a relevant newsfeed or carrying out a complicated texted-in pizza order, when the artificial intelligence (AI) trips up or can't finish the job, thousands of businesses call on people to quietly complete the project. This new digital assembly line aggregates the collective input of

distributed workers, ships pieces of projects rather than products, and operates across a host of economic sectors at all times of the day and night.

This means that, just as we as children might have imagined tiny little people being inside our television sets or radios, there are indeed – for real – often 'ghosts' inside the AI machine (see also Chapter 5). Of course, there is clearly the possibility of programming a purely artificial agent that can make unsupervised decisions, and it is easy to give such examples. One would be a chess-playing AI, which draws on a set of algorithms that execute instructions based on the information that it receives throughout a game. More advanced or complex forms of AI, drawing on for example machine-learning model training, is still likely to rely on the likes of Brenda for the foreseeable future. In the end, the issue of when there are humans in the loop – or ghosts in the machine – becomes a philosophical one. It is very hard at this point in time to believe that there would any time soon be a situation where computers are created by pure machines. Humans – capitalists, scientists, coders, engineers – are still very much in the loop. Far removed beyond these groups' opportunities for profit, status, and self-fulfilment, then, are the digital pieceworkers and ghost workers. These are the people who carry out various forms of information service work that help companies develop AI. In order to build the kind of software that can model human decisions, one needs the help of actual humans to improve the 'guesses' of the AI.

Aside from the exploitative aspects of such labour, it can also be seen as *alienated labour*. Marx (1976, p. 716) writes of how the labour put in by workers in industrial capitalism is made alien to them, as its value is 'appropriated by the capitalist, and incorporated with capital'. The point is that because workers create profit, and profit creates capital, all for the capitalists, the workers become poorer and weaker the more they produce. Therefore, the workers are related to the product of their labour 'as to an alien object' – 'the more the worker spends himself, the more powerful becomes the alien world of objects which [they create] over and against [themselves]' (Marx, 1932, p. 72). In other words, the product of the labour becomes a power of its own, confronting the labourer. Consider AI-driven work in the platform economy: First, the Uber driver is managed by an algorithm. As shown in a study by management researchers Mareike Möhlmann and Ola Henfridsson (2019):

> As soon as they log onto the Uber app, drivers are watched and scrutinized by the platform's algorithms; the app tracks their GPS location, speed, and acceptance rate of customer requests. It instructs them which riders to pick up where, and how to get to the riders' destinations.

While carrying out the work, the drivers engage in an AI-driven process of 'capitalist valorization' (Jarrett, 2016, p. 11), as their labour is exploited and surplus-value is being captured (Steinhoff, 2021, p. 126). All the while, the worker is subjected to the 'new forms of control' that Marcuse wrote about when stating that labour is imposing 'alien needs and alien possibilities' on the workers. Might the consumer ordering a late-night pizza through a smartphone app express an alien need? And may the worker succumbing to the flexibility and opportunity of the alleged 'self-employment' and flexibility of gig work platforms, actually be presented with alien possibilities? In Marcuse's (1964, p. 9) terms, the AI-driven platform economy seems to bear all the marks of 'repressive administration'. Möhlmann and Henfridsson confirm that this is the experience of the Uber drivers, who express frustration about how little they know about the app, which they feel 'manipulates them subtly without their knowledge or consent'. Furthermore: 'If the drivers diverge from the app's instructions they can be penalized or even banned from the platform' (Möhlmann and Henfridsson, 2019). Their study, finding a feeling of dehumanization among the drivers, confirms the presence of alienation:

> Drivers at Uber report feeling equally lonely, isolated, and dehumanized. They don't have colleagues to socialize with or a team or community to be part of. They lack the opportunity to build a personal relationship with a supervisor. Those on crowd-work platforms like Amazon Mechanical Turk have raised similar complaints as they conduct 'micro-tasks' such as classifying content or participating in surveys. (Möhlmann and Henfridsson, 2019)

Heteromation, fauxtomation and automation's last mile

Informatics scholars Hamid Ekbia and Bonnie Nardi (2017, p. 1), define their concept of *heteromation* as 'the extraction of economic value from low-cost or free labor in computer-mediated networks'. This, they contend, represents a new logic for capital accumulation, which generates value through labour carried out by invisible masses that are taken up in networks. Their concept is broad and covers a variety of forms. It includes 'the appropriation of communicative, cognitive, creative, emotional, and organizing labor of human beings in computerized environments' (Ekbia and Nardi, 2017, p. 24), and also spans both low-wage and completely uncompensated labour. In other words, the notion of heteromation is relevant in relation to several of the instances discussed in this chapter, for example unpaid playbour, and the self-organized friction-reducing activities of low-paid gig workers. It also, however – due to its emphasis on 'the division of labor between humans and machines' (Ekbia and Nardi, 2017, p. 27) – encompasses the kind of inside-the-machine data labelling and other preparations for model training that is carried out by workers such as Brenda in Kibera.

In the essay 'The Automation Charade', documentary filmmaker and writer Astra Taylor (2018) has introduced the concept of *fauxtomation* to describe processes like these. The notion stems from the fact that, in the present stage of the advancement of AI-systems, we cannot get away from the fact that much of what passes as automation is in fact not automation. AI-driven automation that does not rely on humans indeed exists, but AI automation is not only a technology, but it is also an ideology (AI Now Institute, 2018). The role of critical analysis is to engage particularly in those cases, and on those levels, where the ideological component comes into play. The point is not, then, that AI automation as such is fake, or that it is a lie that it works. The point, for Taylor, is that crucial parts of how the social structures of power around this technology are organized contributes to cloaking and devaluing some human contributions.

While there may doubtlessly be *some* form of robot uprising in the sphere of work, it is greatly exaggerated. Such hyperbole might be explained by the power of the Californian Ideology to polish numbers, glorify, and romanticize when speaking of technological gains. But no matter the reasons, there are winners and losers constituted through such ways of representing reality. Taylor (2018) urges us to question whose interests this world-view will serve.

It has always, since the dawning of wage labour, been a defining element of capitalist-worker power structures that workers are constantly reminded that they are disposable. If the shoe doesn't fit, the job can always be handed over to someone else. The 'reserve army' of workers – as Marx called it – is always on stand-by, ready to replace anyone who disrupts the smooth flow of the production line.

> [T]he social character inherent in [capitalism] dispels all fixity and security in the situation of the labourer; [. . .] it constantly threatens, by taking away the instruments of labour, to snatch from his hands his means of subsistence, and, by suppressing his detail-function, to make him superfluous. We have seen, too, how this antagonism vents its rage in the creation of that monstrosity, an industrial reserve army, kept in misery in order to be always at the disposal of capital. (Marx, 1906, p. 533)

Taylor (2018) emphasizes how this timeless dynamic between bosses and labourers is given a disturbing new flavour in the age of AI, as employees can be threatened with 'the specter of machine competition'. Waving the ghost of robotics and algorithms in the workers' faces removes responsibility from the employers, who can now blame the unavoidable prospect of society facing a 'jobless future' and human obsolescence. Such a future, again, is more mythical than realistic. Additionally, Taylor argues, the automated processes that do exist are also not at all as impressive as the 'puffery and propaganda' suggests. Highlighting the role of digital labour, Taylor writes that:

> Jobs may be eliminated and salaries slashed but people are often still laboring alongside or behind the machines, even if the work they perform has been deskilled or goes unpaid.

Gray and Suri (2019) write about this predicament, referring to the *paradox of automation's last mile*. Their argument is that the push for progress in AI and automation produces a kind of Catch 22, where society produces a constantly replenishing underclass of invisible workers. With technological progress comes the opportunity and drive to build ever more bewildering and dazzling machines, which do things that humans can do. On the surface level, the machines appear to replace humans, but they only replace some of them, and within the limited framework of the specific task that they carry out. Importantly, Gray and Suri (2015) assert that 'Right now, the effort to automate relies on crowdwork – people making themselves available.' Even if the singularity should be upon us some time in the future and propel us all into a fully automated utopia with permanent vacation for all, Gray strongly urges critical scholarship to 'consider the (long!) stretch of time (and all the productive possibilities) between this moment and the singularity as a chance to rethink the structure and meaning of employment'.

In spite of any dreams of full automation, critical theory is best suited to critique material reality as it happens, in the here and now. Workers like Brenda are providing human labour 'to power many of the websites, apps, online services, and algorithms most consumers think are automated' (Gray and Suri, 2019, p. 170). Every technological leap, in AI or elsewhere, appears to invent for itself new armies of marginalized labourers to take up jobs that are not seen as 'real jobs' in their contemporary contexts. With technological progress, new such armies, maybe different in terms of their tasks, but not when it comes to their structural position, visibility, or worker rights, will continue to come and go.

Bringing invisible labour into view is not a new focus as such of critical theory. Taylor aptly points out the illuminating parallel to feminist scholarship on housework, and how innovations like vacuums and electric irons tended to create more, rather than less, labour for housewives. In particular, she mentions the seminal work of Ruth Cowan, published in the book *More Work for Mother* (2018), on these ironies of household technologies. The main point here is that 'automation isn't all it's cracked up to be, and hardly guarantees the absence of work'. AI, as above, is a commodity, and commodities, per Marx (1976, p. 128), have a 'phantom-like' character because 'human labour is accumulated in them' as 'crystals of [a] social substance'.

Takeaway points

- *AI and labour* are entangled in a multitude of ways. AI displaces and disrupts jobs. AI exploits our everyday activities as valorized labour through the logic of surveillance capitalism. AI is used to govern, coordinate, and regulate labour. AI creates a demand for new forms of human labour, and this work is often of the non-glamorous kind. Critical theory can be used to question and analyse what these entanglements mean in terms of power, dominance, and exploitation.
- AI is a key driver behind *platform labour* – a variety of forms of digitally enabled work within the *gig economy*. This form of labour can be seen as *digital piecework*. It is monotonous and low paying, with high degrees of precarity and disillusionment. Platform workers face digital surveillance and economic insecurity and are unionized to a very small extent.
- In platform labour and beyond, *algorithmic management* has become a common method for automatically coordinating and organizing workers and clients at scale. Algorithmic management makes use of AI to execute functions such as hiring, firing, coordination, and performance monitoring. This centralizes power and control through a process of abstract optimization and effectivization, while workers push themselves to satisfy the algorithm.
- The winners and losers in this algorithmic economy are unevenly distributed between the Global North and South, with large numbers of workers in the latter, being run and coordinated by businesses in the former. But digital capitalism is not only divided along the North–South dimension. There are *black holes* (Castells, 2010), which constitute a shadow-layer to the network society everywhere. This liminal space is populated by exploited *alienated labour* and devalued *ghost work*.
- Today's AI-driven economy is marked by *heteromation* – the extraction of value from low-cost and free labour in developing machine learning; *fauxtomation* – the illusion that processes are automated, while in fact a range of human contributions is devalued; and, *the paradox of automation's last mile*, by which the accelerating race for ever better AI produces an ever-growing underclass of invisible workers, which underpins AI through crowdwork.

7
AI subjects

Take a master petroleum chemist, infinitely skilled in the separation of crude oil into its fractions. Strap him down, probe into his brain with searching electronic needles. The machine scans the patterns of the mind, translates what it sees into charts and sine waves. Impress these same waves on a robot computer and you have your chemist. Or a thousand copies of your chemist, if you wish, with all of his knowledge [. . .]

Frederik Pohl, *The Tunnel Under the World*
(1955, p. 26)

Garbage in, garbage out

The importance of focusing on how people are interpellated as subjects into AI's discourse has been emphasized throughout the previous chapters of this book. This kind of analysis highlights AI's role for constituting, what Michel Foucault (1980) has theorized as 'power/knowledge'.

All social practices have a discursive aspect (Hall and Gieben, 1992), and AI is no different. AI assemblage is permeated by a variety of processes of meaning-making. From the very conception of AI among scientists, to its narration by journalists, to marketing-speech, science fiction, cultural analyses, and popular understandings, meanings are made around it through social interaction. Computer ethicists Deborah Johnson and Keith Miller explain that:

> A technology is not a single 'something' that catches on or fails; technologies are being made, i.e., being delineated as 'things' and given meaning, as they are being developed. Various actors in the process develop understandings and begin to attach different meanings and significance to the 'thing'.

In Foucault's terms, this means that there is AI discourse. There is a 'system of representation' around AI – a set of rules and practices that govern how we know and speak of AI (Hall, 2001, p. 72). The Foucauldian notion of discourse, as explained by sociologist Stuart Hall, refers to the symbolic system that 'governs the way that a topic can be meaningfully talked about and reasoned about'. In this sense, there is certainly discourse about AI – broadly established ways of conceiving of it and its general meaning. Such discourse is largely ideological and includes tropes like those that were discussed in Chapter 3. AI visions and imaginaries revolve around ideas of progress, profitability, world betterment, exactitude, and rationality. There are also conflicting discourses around robot apocalypses and disenchantment. These kinds of visions are not the topic of this chapter, it is rather about how AI can be seen as a *discursive practice* that orders people into *subject positions*. Just as in Pohl's science fiction story that was cited at the top of this chapter, AI can be used to imprint existing subjectivities onto ever new subjects.

AI has a strong bond to knowledge. It is used in knowledge management to capture, represent, and share knowledge, and to transform individual knowledge into collective knowledge. It can be used for 'knowledge engineering' (Liebowitz, 2001, p. 4). AI also thrives on knowledge. Machine learning is about acquiring, processing, and learning from knowledge, which means that AI systems can be considered to be discursive systems. As explained by Hall (2001, p. 75), Foucault developed his concepts in the direction of being increasingly 'concerned with how knowledge was put to work through discursive practices in specific institutional settings to regulate the conduct of others'. In the setting offered by AI assemblage, its technological operations to regulate, or guide, the conduct of humans can therefore be conceptualized as discursive practices. AI assemblage, then, functions in accordance with Foucault's (1980, p. 194) notion of an *apparatus*, which he defines as:

> a thoroughly heterogeneous ensemble consisting of discourses, institutions, architectural forms, regulatory decisions, laws, administrative measures, scientific statements, philosophical, moral and philanthropic propositions [. . .] The apparatus itself is the system of relations that can be established between these elements.

Importantly, Foucault (1980, p. 194) states that the apparatus 'can function as a means of justifying or masking a practice which itself remains silent'. Srnicek and Williams (2015, pp. 151–2) write, for example, about algorithmic management and other 'numerical control technologies' that they are used to set the pace of production, and to push workers to keep up with the machines, and how this state of affairs 'can conceal power relations by making them appear as simple mechanical processes'. This, then, in Foucauldian terms, is about AI assemblage (apparatus) masking or justifying the silent practice of increasing the exploitation of workers. As Elliott (2022, p. 128) puts it: 'AI is the material infrastructure that both masks and deepens social inequalities, the technological foundation of our sense-making.' Discourse is power and knowledge embedded in language and social practice. Correspondingly, analyses of semantics that are derived from the kinds of language corpora that fuel machine learning have shown that certain forms of power/knowledge are by all means embedded in them too.

IT policy scholars Aylin Caliskan and Arvind Narayanan, alongside scientist Joanna Bryson, showed in a seminal paper that machine learning – as it relies on existing data from which it aims to derive artificial intelligence by learning from patterns – produces knowledge that bears the same stereotypical understandings that may be found also in 'everyday human culture' (Caliskan et al., 2017, p. 183). Patterns found included that flowers, instruments, and European-American names were associated with pleasantness, while insects, weapons, and African-American names were associated with unpleasantness. Furthermore, maths, science, and career words were associated with male gender, while arts and family words were associated with female gender. It is nothing new for corpus linguistics scholars, as Caliskan and colleagues also point out, that connotations, associations, and stereotypes become embedded in text corpuses.

Indeed, it appears as quite straightforward that social values, categorizations, worldviews, and so on, that are described in text, can in fact be found also in different forms of abstractions of that same text. The contribution of the work of Caliskan et al. was, however, that they found that machine learning – more specifically the method of word embeddings – clearly amplified the stereotypical patterns, while also illustrating the extent to which cultural stereotypes therefore pervade many widely used AI technologies. This research is important, not least because of the robust scientific ways in which these results have been achieved and established. From the perspective of philosophy or sociology, however, it appears as though any other finding would have been highly unlikely. The insights in the study align perfectly with the core points of the sociology of knowledge. Classic sociologist Karl Mannheim (1954, p. 2) wrote that:

> The principal thesis of the sociology of knowledge is that there are modes of thought which cannot be adequately understood as long as their social origins are obscured. It is indeed true that only the individual is capable of thinking. There is no such metaphysical entity as a group mind which thinks over and above the heads of individuals, or whose ideas the individual merely reproduces. Nevertheless it would be false to deduce from this that all the ideas and sentiments which motivate an individual have their origin in him alone, and can be adequately explained solely on the basis of his own life-experience.

Seen from this perspective, it is no surprise that the 'modes of thought' vectorized and perpetuated by the language models come both after and before the social. Humans in society collectively produce the data from which the model learns, and any correctly functioning model will, through its various societal uses and applications, reproduce – or even amplify, since models are always simplifications – those same patterns. Just as Mannheim claims that there is no magical entity that 'thinks over and above the heads of individuals', so is it impossible for these kinds of machine-learning technologies to do so. This is because knowledge is always a social product. I have written elsewhere about the relationship between word embeddings in particular, as related to the sociology of knowledge (Lindgren, 2020), making the point that we cannot expect anything else from those models than reflections of society – because society is symbolically constructed through language.

Like Mannheim, other early proponents of the sociology of knowledge, for example Émile Durkheim (1912) and Max Scheler (1924), argued that the ways in which we organize and understand the world are by definition socially founded, and that various belief systems, concepts and ideas have an inherent sociality mirroring the settings from which they arise. Sociologists Peter Berger and Thomas Luckmann summarized these points in their book *The Social Construction of Reality* (1966, p. 15), where they wrote that 'specific agglomerations of "reality" and "knowledge" pertain to specific social contexts', and that 'the sociology of knowledge must concern itself with whatever passes for "knowledge" in a society, regardless of the ultimate validity or invalidity'. Returning to the case of machine learning then, we must not expect any 'true' or 'objective' knowledge above or behind the models. We are the models. Technology is socially shaped. Machine learning is a technology, and technology is dependent on what is put into it. Lanier (2010, p. 49) argues that:

> Some of my colleagues think a million, or perhaps a billion, fragmentary insults will eventually yield wisdom that surpasses that of any well-thought-out essay, so long as sophisticated secret statistical algorithms recombine the fragments. I disagree. A trope from the early days of computer science comes to mind: garbage in, garbage out.

If there is racism, sexism, and other forms of discrimination in society, we will see it in any correctly designed model too. Virginia Eubanks (2017, p. 10), in a systematic investigation of 'the impacts of high-tech sorting and monitoring systems on poor and working-class people', sees these as computerized processes of *automating inequality*. Marx wrote that while 'the real foundation' of society is constituted by the material and economic relations of production, a *superstructure* rises on top of it consisting of 'definite forms of social consciousness' (Marx, 1904, p. 11). By this he referred to the ideas, worldviews and terms by which people in society understand reality. He wrote further that 'it is not the consciousness of [people] that determines their existence but, on the contrary, their social existence determines their consciousness' (Marx, 1904, pp. 11–12).

AI as representation

Stuart Hall (1997a, p. 1) writes about what he calls 'the circuit of culture'. This refers to a circular relationship between the dimensions of production, consumption, regulation, representation, and identity. The argument, furthermore, is that human culture is about shared meanings, and that language is the key medium through which such meanings are made. When writing of the work of *representation*, Hall (1997d) emphasizes language in a very broad sense of the word, where it is seen as a repository of cultural meanings and values. For the purpose of this book, the underpinnings of AI in the form of data (based on human, life, society, and culture) and algorithms and other computational procedures (created and guided by humans), are indeed parts of such language in today's world.

No matter if humans are fully 'in-the-loop', or 'on-the-loop', simply supervising the AI (Zerilli et al., 2020, pp. 80–1), socio-cultural categorizations, understandings, and stereotypes will be part of AI. In this sense, returning to Hall (1997a, p. 1), AI systems are *representational systems* – they 'stand for or represent [. . .] our concepts, ideas, and feelings'. AI, seen in this way, is not simply a set of things, such as computers, algorithms, and robots, but instead a process – 'a set of *practices*' (Hall, 1997a, p. 2). Furthermore, on this connection, Agre (1997, p. 131) writes that '[c]omputers are representational artifacts, and the people who design them often start by constructing representations of the activities found in the sites where they will be used'. Our AI systems are a way of making sense of the world. AI gives things a meaning. AI is however not the only thing that creates social meanings, but it is part of the circuit:

> [M]eanings are produced at several different sites and circulated through several different processes or practices (the cultural circuit). Meaning is what gives us a sense of our own identity, of who we are and with whom we 'belong' – so it is tied up with questions of how culture is used to mark out and maintain identity within and difference between groups. (Hall, 1997a, p. 3)

AI, then, as seen through Hall, is a *signifying practice*; it is 'like a language' insofar as it communicates – even if indirectly and abstractly – meanings about social reality. One way in which this signifying practice works is through drawing on, and estab-lishing, *interpretative repertoires*. This notion is key to discourse analysis and was first coined by sociologists Nigel Gilbert and Michael Mulkay (1984, pp. 39–40), who define such repertoires as 'linguistic registers which occur repeatedly' (cf. performativ-ity), and that shape 'action and belief in ways that are appropri-ate to the different interpretative contexts they are involved in reproducing'. Algorithms can be seen as such repeated linguistic registers, systems of sorting, which are both a product of, and at the same time reproduce, social worldviews.

One example of how AI and algorithms function in this way, i.e., as a language, and discursive sorting mechanism, rooted in sociopolitically flavoured repertoires of interpretation, is to be found in critical internet scholar Safiya Umoja Noble's work on *Algorithms of Oppression* (2018). The focus of this research is on how search-engine results, in particular, draw on sexist and racist repertoires, and it highlights how the seemingly techni-cal and 'neutral' phenomenon of AI-driven algorithmic systems reflects, as well as perpetuates, discriminatory representations of black African-American women. Noble emphasizes how the algorithms are not simply mirroring and relaying the historically unequal structure of American society, but that they in fact reify and amplify the commodification of this social category.

While Noble's study has the internet, and particularly search engines, as its main focus, the role of AI – through the entangled relationships of assemblage – is clear. Noble (2018, p. 1) writes of how we are becoming increasingly reliant on AI, and that 'arti-ficial intelligence will become a major human rights issue in the twenty-first century', as we 'are only beginning to understand the long-term consequences of these decision-making tools in both masking and deepening social inequality'.

Intersectional power relations, with layered effects of race, gender, sexuality, class, abledness, and so on, are embedded in AI, and this happens through the algorithms' reliance on socially and culturally co-constructed repertoires of interpretations: they are 'a product of our own collective creation' (Noble, 2018, p. 29).

The algorithms perpetuate the interpretative repertoires that shape them, for the simple reason that machine learning in itself, just like discourses in society, has a self-reinforcing nature (Garcia, 2016). Such tendencies to oversimplification do not seem to impede unfettered development of AI, however. Examples of algorithms becoming vectors of injustice abound. One example is the viral scandal surrounding a software developer posting on social media that the image recognition algorithm implemented in Google Photos tagged him and his black friend as 'gorillas' (Anonymous, 2015). Google 'fixed' this, allegedly, by simply blocking the categories of 'gorilla', 'chimp', 'chimpanzee', and 'monkey' from the image recognition algorithm altogether (Vincent, 2018). Relatedly, Facebook made the news when their AI had labelled a video of black men as 'primates' (Mac, 2021), and Amazon's computer vision tool matched members of the Congressional Black Caucus as criminals by matching them with mugshots (Snow, 2018).

Another example is the discovery by scientists that a widely used medical algorithm, designed to spot patients who will have complex needs of care, dramatically underestimated the situation of the sickest black patients. This leads to the amplification of long-standing racial injustices in the area of medicine (Obermeyer et al., 2019, see also Chapter 4). In a report, the company behind the AI system claimed that the algorithm specifically had excluded race, but that it measured a range of other parameters, that were not 'race-neutral' (Johnson, 2019). Another finding was that as black patients generally (are able to) pay less for healthcare, they were wrongfully estimated to be in less need of healthcare.

A machine-learning expert was cited in the report as saying that 'once a bias is detected, it can be corrected'. Previous approaches, they said, found injustices that cannot be changed without 'sweeping social and cultural changes, as well as individual behavior changes by thousands of providers'. They continued: 'In contrast, once a flawed algorithm is identified, the bias can be removed' (Johnson, 2019). This is of course not the case. Fixing the algorithm fixes the algorithm and sweeps racism under the rug. There is no technological way of getting around the bigger socio-cultural changes and individual behaviour changes needed. At least not if it is racism, rather than mathematical procedures, that we want to correct.

These are just a couple of examples that show how AI, once again, is entangled in sociopolitical assemblage. It is part of, Ruha Benjamin (2019, p. 11) writes, an 'elaborate social and technical apparatus that governs all areas of life'. Highlighting the problem with 'fixing' algorithmic racism on the surface level of code tweaks, Benjamin asserts that:

tech designers encode judgments into technical systems but claim that the racist results of their designs are entirely exterior to the encoding process. Racism thus becomes doubled – magnified and buried under layers of digital denial. (Benjamin, 2019, p. 12)

To Benjamin (2019, p. 63) then, such fixes are not fixes, but in fact 'rusty value judgments embedded in shiny new systems'. In the tradition of critical theory, Noble writes about how the power of algorithms in today's world not only enacts new forms of digital racial profiling, but also reinforces oppressive power relationships between different groups. Noble takes an intersectional approach when arguing that capital, race, and gender are all contributing factors in the propagation of algorithmic oppression. As shown in a study by Buolamwini and Gebru (2018, p. 12), a number of leading gender classification algorithms performed best for lighter males, and worst for darker females.

The task for critical analysis becomes to scrutinize what interpretative repertoires – at the nexus of power/knowledge – are built into the AI-driven systems that are now near-ubiquitous in both visible and invisible forms. Noble (2018, p. 1) draws on the concept of 'redlining', which refers to discrimination in the form of systemic denial of, mostly financial, services to people living in certain urban areas, based on race or ethnicity. Noble (2018, p. 10) coins the notion of *technological redlining*, to describe the process by which algorithms are 'creating and normalizing structural and systemic isolation' to 'reinforce oppressive social and economic relations'.

In the broader context of critical theory, the patterns discussed above are illustrative of how AI is not unique, in the sense that it is just a new vector in the sociopolitical assemblage that ushers postcolonial views of us versus 'the Other' into yet another century. AI systems that are shaped by, that reproduce, and that thrive on the binary amplification of, such divisions are simply a new rendition of a:

racialized discourse [. . .] structured by a set of binary oppositions. There is the powerful opposition between 'civilization' (white) and 'savagery' (black). There is the opposition between the biological or bodily characteristics of the 'black' and 'white' 'races', polarized into their extreme opposites – each the signifiers of an absolute difference between human 'types' or species. (Hall, 1997c, p. 243)

Coupled with this form of discursive colonialism, there is also the emerging form of *data colonialism* – a new kind of capitalist 'accumulation by dispossession' (Harvey, 2004). Coined by Thatcher et al. (2016), data colonialism is a term that calls attention to the power imbalances that are built into the ways in which the data commodity is extracted (see Chapters 5 and 6). Mohamed, Png, and Isaac (2020) underline the importance of a 'critical science approach', particularly decolonial thinking, for future AI research. Postcolonial and decolonial theories make it possible to envision alternative future realities, as well as to pose much-needed critical questions around AI design and engineering. In general, they welcome a new research culture around AI that can help us move beyond the narrow focus on 'bias', and further into critical territory, focusing on 'algorithmic oppression, exploitation and dispossession', as well as other hierarchies that AI has 'inherited from the past'.

Such a new climate would be able to challenge tech solutionism and AI inevitabilism with 'heterogeneous practice, intercultural dialogue' and 'creole AIs' (Mohamed et al., 2020, p. 677). Thinking in terms of 'creole', referring generally to evolved and locally derivative forms, enables us to imagine alternative future visions for AI as creole technology. Edgerton (2007, p. 101) describes such technology in the following way:

> By a creole technology, I mean one which finds a distinctive set of uses outside the time and place where it was first used on a significant scale. Thus it is to be distinguished from transferred technologies, though I include the latter in cases where the transferred technology is essentially no longer in use in the originating territory. Often, but not necessarily, these technologies originating elsewhere combine in original ways with local technologies, forming hybrids, which not only combine creole technologies with local technologies, but also themselves become new creole technologies.

AI in the hands of people, instead of in the hands only of business and governments, could pave the way for an actual realization of mantras such as 'AI for the good of all.'

There is great value in connecting the 'biases' of AI with historical dimensions, such as colonialism, in this way. Because there is something about the air of technologies that makes them come across as neutral and universal. If a machine says something, or does something, we tend to perceive this as utterances or acts that are out of time – ahistorical. Science, technology, and society scholar Alison Adam writes in the book *Artificial Knowing* (1998, p. 5) that symbolic AI systems appeal to 'a view from nowhere'. This refers to the way in which technology seems to speak for 'some universal yet never articulated subject, nowhere yet everywhere at the same time'. This, according to critical AI scholar Yarden Katz (2020, p. 6), is the view aspired to by 'AI practitioners across the board'. But just as we know from postcolonial theories about how literary texts can masquerade as universal, even though they come from very specific historico-political places, we must also challenge AI's view from nowhere. It does not come from nowhere, but from 'a rather specific, white, and privileged place' (Katz, 2020, p. 6).

In the case of AI's racial 'bias', then, and the tendency to try to 'fix' the problems simply by tweaking models, readings such as these offer us a dramatically different perspective. Katz argues that AI must be understood as a 'technology of whiteness', because it mimics and serves a logic of white supremacy. Katz does not mean by this that AI is aggressively and consciously agitating for a political position of white supremacy, but that it is discursively constituted in ways that construe white people as the norm. Katz (2020, p. 8) discusses AI's formation within 'the largely white military–industrial–academic complex' in the US, therefore coming to be developed to serve dominant interests of that particular world. It has been used consistently to serve projects that are capitalist and/or imperial.

As it has been formed in that context, similar patterns and impulses have also contributed to shaping subsequent AI's functioning and trajectory. Katz argues that because AI has been in the hands of a 'flexible' and seemingly apolitical expert industry, it has been used (see Chapters 3 and 4) to 'advance neoliberal visions of society', 'to sanction projects of dispossession', and to 'naturalize [. . .] incarceration and surveillance' (Katz, 2020, p. 9). Because of the 'nebulous and hollow' character of AI as a social subject, it can be a powerful tool for manipulation. This was especially the case in earlier ages in AI history.

But Katz is not optimistic about the ways in which critical analysis has been incorporated in AI development in recent years. The alleged 'critical experts' are – as in Metzinger's (2019) view, see Chapter 8 – at the mercy of industry and capital. According to Katz (2020, p. 10), the AI industry has effectively absorbed critiques, and rendered them toothless:

> AI's projects have [. . .] been shaped by social movements struggling against racism, economic inequality, state surveillance, and the criminalization of migrants. Such movements have changed mainstream political sensibilities [. . .] So when AI reappeared in the 2010s, it became the purview of 'critical AI experts' concerned with issues like racial and economic injustice. With a progressive veneer, these critical experts ended up serving the same imperial and capitalist projects [. . .] but in more subtle ways than AI's prior iterations. This was a case of adaptation: using AI's nebulosity to reshape projects and narratives in response to challenges by social movements.

Katz outlines three *epistemic forgeries* that enable AI – through fictions about human thought and knowledge – to operate as a technology in the service of power. The first forgery is the aspiration, discussed above, to represent a 'view from nowhere'. AI does not stand for any form of 'universal' knowledge or intelligence. The social context, worldviews, and aspirations of the systems' architects get imprinted into AI uses, developments, and narratives. The second forgery discussed by Katz is the claim, by some, that AI systems are close to matching or exceeding the capacity of human thought, as in rhetoric about AGI or the singularity. Such views establish a hierarchy of intelligence by which we may be led to believe that we should bow down to the AI overlord and accept its results as a form of higher truth. It can be argued however, that many of the popular examples of how AI has surpassed humans – often in playing different games, such as chess and Go – cannot be used as evidence for this. The forgery, Katz writes, may pass in the area of games but not in less controlled broader arenas in the context of human life that demand historical sensitivity, and the ability to adapt to variegated challenges.

The third, final and related, forgery is that AI systems 'arrive at truth, or knowledge, "on their own"' with minimal supervision (2020, p. 95). This forgery allows those in power to escape scrutiny, as the responsibility can instead be ascribed to the machine. Katz draws an illuminating metaphorical parallel to the notion of 'The Market', as conceived in the epistemology of economist Friedrich Hayek. The market economy, in Hayek's writing (Bowles et al., 2017, p. 215), is seen as something akin to an algorithm. He conceived of it as 'an information processing system characterized by spontaneous order', that should be unregulated for the good of all. The argument was that since, 'any individual's knowledge is local and incomplete', we must put our trust in the superiority of the abstract organizing principle above our heads.

Understanding knowledge in this way absolves capitalists and other power elites of accountability because even if workers can get the feeling that they are being exploited by evil capitalists, this would be impossible, as no individual – not even the capitalists – can control 'The Market'. It is a natural force (Katz, 2020, pp. 119–20). In the context of AI, then, the rhetoric about AI coming to its own conclusions after humans have created conditions in which it can thrive, can function in a similar way in order to vindicate any actors that manipulate or exploit others through AI. This is because, in this view, AI is not a tool for people to use, but a superhuman entity with which we can coexist. In sum, according to Katz, the degree to which forgeries such as the above are seen as factual will be decided by how authoritatively AI – 'as an ideology and vehicle for political vision' – can assert its power.

Binary and beyond

Amazon at one point implemented an AI-based recruiting tool aimed to mechanize the search for top talent for the company, through the automated reviewing of résumés. The AI had been tasked with scoring candidates on a scale ranging from one to five stars, similar to the star rating that shoppers are encouraged to use when buying products from Amazon. The hope was that if the AI engine was presented with a large number of résumés from applicants, it would spit out a small group of top-ranked candidates that the company could then go on to hire. It was, however, realized that the AI's ratings were far from gender neutral. The system taught itself based on the top terms appearing in résumés from the previous ten-year period, that male candidates were preferable. This was because the old résumés came mostly from men, as a pure reflection of the general male dominance in tech jobs. As a consequence, the machine-learning model learned that women did not fit, and therefore gave lower scores to résumés that included any indications of female gender, such as for example 'Women's

Chess Club Captain', or mentions of women's colleges (Dastin, 2022). Also in this case, a technological fix was sought by editing the algorithm so that such terms should be seen as neutral.

There are serious problems with these kinds of 'debiasing' strategies – the creation of algorithms that do not discriminate. We cannot fix social problems with technology. The discrimination exists in society, not (only) in the algorithms, which means that a debiased algorithm will not necessarily produce results that humans accept. One study, for example, showed that a 'fair' algorithm for career recommendations indeed successfully made gender-equal recommendations, but that humans involved in the study tended to prefer the original biased system over the debiased one (Wang et al., 2021).

This is of course unsurprising, as it is not the algorithms that make society unfair. They mirror an unfair society, and risk – under the guise of machinic objectivity – contributing to exacerbating and cementing such structures. The problem here is the disconnect between, on the one hand, decades of critical feminist research on how gender ideology is embedded in language, and technological uses of language as fuel for machine learning on the other.

In light of existing critical theories and analyses of discourses of gender – about how gender is performed, and made through language (Cameron, 1998; Lazar, 2005; Wodak, 1997) – it is anything but surprising that 'biases' and stereotypes are built into AI models.

AI-propagated gender discrimination is not only limited to job hiring, however. It plays into a number of other areas, such as for example safety and healthcare. In this context, the negative consequences of using flawed data – based predominantly on men – AI-driven design processes for, e.g., airbags, seatbelts, and headrests in cars will lead to the creation of artifacts that are less safe for women, the seating positions, and bodies of which (height, breasts, pregnant bodies, and so on) are not adequately considered by the 'standard' procedures. Feminist writer Caroline Criado-Perez writes in *Invisible Women* (2021, p. 166) about how such gendered patterns are manifested in automated systems on which we rely:

> [W]hen Londa Schiebinger, a professor at Stanford University, used translation software to translate a newspaper interview with

her from Spanish into English, both Google Translate and Systran repeatedly used male pronouns to refer to her, despite the presence of clearly gendered terms like 'profesora' (female professor). Google Translate will also convert Turkish sentences with gender-neutral pronouns into English stereotypes. 'O bir doktor,' which means 'S/he is a doctor' is translated into English as 'He is a doctor', while 'O bir hemsire (which means 'S/he is a nurse') is rendered 'She is a nurse'. Researchers have found the same behaviour for translations into English from Finnish, Estonian, Hungarian and Persian.

It is not only these kinds of stereotypes, which bind genders to particular professions or spheres of activity, that may be propagated by AI, however. In fiction there are many examples of how machinic personalities are constructed as female. Examples range from the 1985 John Hughes comedy *Weird Science*, where two teenage boys use a home computer to create a 'perfect' woman, through films like Spike Jonze's *Her* in which a lonely writer develops a peculiar relationship with an operating system, and Andrew Niccol's *S1mone* about a digitally created actress, to examples such as humanoid robot Ava in Alex Garland's *Ex Machina*, or the robotic mother Grace in Steve Blackman's TV adaptation of *The Umbrella Academy* series of comic books. Precursing all of those examples there is *Tomorrow's Eve*, a nineteenth-century science fiction novel by Auguste Villiers de l'Isle-Adam, that tells the story of an inventor creating a machine-woman, Hadaly, who 'is nothing at all from the outside but a magneto-electric entity. She is a Being in Limbo, a mere potentiality' (Villiers de l'Isle-Adam, 1886, p. 59).

AI and society scholar Kate Devlin (2018, p. 170) acknowledges, however, that not all AI are gendered female:

> By recounting stereotypes of artificial women, I'm not discounting the male versions. They exist too, usually as violent machines in need of redemption, with a heart of gold tucked away in their super-strong android bodies. There's no doubt the stereotypes are deeply entrenched there, too. We already have machines on the battlefield and drones in the air that threaten lives. But that's a whole other book.

AI, while genderless at its inception, is rendering subjects that align with what Butler (1990, p. 23) defines as 'the heterosexual matrix': 'the regulatory practices that generate coherent identities through the matrix of coherent gender norms'. Of course, there are always the Terminators, C3POs and Tin Men, sorted into the male slots of that organizational structure, but the robotic female is doubtlessly a persistent trope. Does this mean that we 'presume that the user is male and the passive interface female'? (Cook, 2016). From a critical theory perspective, such discursive patterns are a continuation of the dominance of a *male gaze* governing the patterns of seeing in media culture, and which 'projects its fantasy onto the female figure, which is styled accordingly' (Mulvey, 1989, p. 19).

AI in itself is both sexless and genderless, but still critiques of the artificially intelligent voices that are making their way into our lives – Apple's Siri, Amazon's Alexa, and Microsoft's Cortana, or basically any GPS system – have pointed out that all of these voices, at least by the standard settings, have tended to be female. What we are dealing with here, then, is *discrimination by default*. But technological fixes are coming to the rescue. Since 2021, Apple are no longer using a feminine voice as the default for Siri, instead letting the user choose during the smartphone setup process. Male voices have also been implemented in different countries at different points in time.

The creation of female-gendered AI assistants follows from a history of the roles that we expect individuals of different genders to play. The 'secretary' type things that Siri, Cortana, and Alexa do – looking up information, scheduling appointments, reminding us, and so on – are discursively connected to femininity in our culture (Nickelsburg, 2016). There is also an element of sexualization. Microsoft's voice assistant Cortana appears to have been named after a previous Microsoft creation.

> In 2001, Microsoft released the video game *Halo: Combat Evolved*, a science-fiction, first-person shooter. The popular series stars Master Chief as an archetypically masculine space marine. He is assisted by Cortana, a feminized artificial intelligence mostly present as a disembodied voice. When embodied, she holographically appears as a blue-skinned, naked, youthful, human female: a sexy cybernetic hologram. In 2014, Microsoft released its artificially intelligent rival to Siri, also named Cortana. (Sutko, 2020, pp. 567–8)

Human Communications scholar Daniel Sutko (2020) has written about these 'gender troubles' of AI, as a new landscape of feminized AIs has opened up, with an increasing number of people communicating regularly with these voices. Human–Machine

Communications researcher Andrea Guzman (2019, p. 344) has written about the importance of 'source orientation' – who or what we believe that we are interacting with. This is an important aspect of human–human communication, but to no lesser degree also in human–machine communication. When we communicate, we rely on understandings and conceptualizations of who is at the other end.

Communications researcher Clifford Nass and colleagues (1997), showed in a study that when people interact with computer voices – even though the gender cues of the voices may be minimal – there is a strong tendency to give gender-based stereotypical responses. There were no gender cues relating to physical appearance or nonverbal communication in their experiment, and research subjects were fully aware that they were interacting with a computer, and not a human. In spite of all that, the researchers could still prove that the mere embedded vocal cues of gender were sufficient to evoke stereotypical responses (Nass et al., 1994, p. 76). According to what has been called SRCT (Social Responses to Communication Technologies Theory), people quite mindlessly behave towards computers in social ways that are very similar to how they respond to humans (Eckles et al., 2009). Today's largely female voice agents are created in ways that perpetuate a secretarial discourse. According to Guzman (2017, p. 344):

> Siri and similar agents are programmed with human-like traits of gender and overt personality, and, equally important, also are designed to enact a specific social role – that of an assistant – in the functions they perform and in the messages they send to the user.

Such gendered constructions, on the one hand keeps the view alive that women should be available on call, and be of service. A feminine – robotic – ideal, a breed of space-age well-groomed Stepford Wives that 'work like robots all their lives' (Levin, 1972, p. 61). The female gendering of AI assistants plays into age-old stereotypes of secretaries, housewives, and flight attendants, whereby women are 'held to robot-like standards of perfection' (Nickelsburg, 2016).

Maybe the choice of gendering Siri, Alexa, Cortana, and the like, as female, then, can be explained by the fact that such patriarchal and sexist social norms make female virtual assistants more believable. These disembodied fembots, through the materiality of their voices rely on elements such as intonation and timbre to produce performances – in Butler's (1990, p. 178) sense of producing and sustaining 'discrete and polar genders as cultural fictions' – that align with certain gender constructions.

Sexualization is also an ever-present element. Post-humanist scholar Jimena Escudero Pérez (2020, p. 328) explains that 'whenever a robot or AI is assigned a female gender it is for sexual purposes. The artificial female can be commodified as a caring housewife or a deadly killer, but the sexual component, in one way or another, is always part of her conceptualization.' Even though the leap is big from asking Alexa to set an alarm, to sex with robots, gender scholars remind us that there is still an element of eroticization built into the fact that we have largely come to equate AI with female personalities. Devlin writes in the book *Turned On* (2018, p. 13) that:

> For every order of 'Cortana, lower volume' you can be sure that someone somewhere is making a much more lewd request. Ever talked dirty to Siri? Ever got amorous with Alexa? If you have – even just to see what happens if you do – then you're not alone. If it exists, people will try to corrupt it. But the virtual personalities behind the popular virtual assistants are used to being hit on. In fact, the likes of Microsoft, Google, Apple and Amazon put in plenty of work behind the scenes to rebuff the advances of chatbot-users. Try it. But maybe not at work.

In this context, then, the gender-related design choices of tech companies drive user perception and imagination in the direction of stereotypical and antiquated notions of a gendered and sexual division of labour by demarcating certain tasks as feminine.

Just as AI systems, in these ways, propagate the discursive differences between genders in the ascribed heterosexual matrix, and their related power relationships and stereotypes, they also cause intricate troubles for people who do not identify with any of those gendered positions. LGBTQ+ people, as we know, are often marginalized by traditional systems of understanding and organization, so naturally it is important to critically monitor the role that AI systems may play for continued or exacerbated marginalization in this area. As computers rely on binary code, there is also a metaphorical connection to be made here, along the lines of 'Computers are binary – people are not' (see Leufer, 2021).

And, even though the zeroes-and-ones type of binary, on which computers rely, may have nothing more than a rhetorically fitting connection to the issue; it is indeed a fact that machine-learning models are best fitted to propagate unambiguous categories.

An area where the functioning of AI very clearly poses problems for people with queer identities is AGR – automated gender recognition – where gender is inferred by data collected about individuals, both textual and visual. This may include computational assessments of legal names, jawlines, and cheekbones, or whether an individual is wearing makeup. In the case of body scanners in airports and other places, this may involve the entire physical figure. When the binary systems meet fluid identities (Danielsson et al., 2023), there are risks and realities of misrecognition (Katyal and Jung, 2021). One of the alarming consequences of this is that entire groups of the population become mere errors or ambiguous cases in the eyes of the AI system, effectively then erasing them from view (Katyal and Jung, 2021, p. 692).

As these systems for sorting people into categories become implemented in more and more areas of society, the real-world consequences of this systemic erasure can become far-reaching, in relation to access to, for example, housing, employment, or healthcare. Importantly, invisible groups face extreme difficulties in relation to their ability to advocate in any effective way for their fundamental freedoms and rights. Os Keyes (2018, p. 17) writes that AI systems for gender recognition 'deny the existence of trans people' and underlines the importance of analyses based in critical theory by calling for scholars to face these machines with a 'hermeneutics of suspicion'.

In cases such as when Stanford researchers claimed to show that neural networks could detect people's sexual orientation more accurately than humans themselves, warning flags must be raised. It was argued that 'faces contain much more information about sexual orientation than can be perceived and interpreted by the human brain', based on, among other things, 'the prenatal hormone theory of sexual orientation' (Wang and Kosinski, 2018, p. 246). The authors do point out the risk that such, alleged, possibilities of using AI to detect such 'intimate traits' is a 'threat to the privacy and safety of gay men and women'. But the dangers of even attempting such classification are much more far-reaching. As Queer AI scholars Ashwin, Agnew, Pajaro, and Subramonian (2021, p. 5) write in response to the study:

Sexuality is broadly defined, encompassing one's experience of their romantic, sexual, and emotional behaviors, and is fluid and flexible; therefore, it is inherently not detectable by a human or deep neural network.

Others called the research out for being 'dangerous and flawed', and LGBTQ+ advocates demanded that the researchers' university distance itself from such 'junk science' (Anderson, 2017). 'Imagine for a moment', one commentator said, 'the potential consequences if this flawed research were used to support a brutal regime's efforts to identify and/or persecute people they believed to be gay' (Anderson, 2017). The researchers behind the study explained that their intention was never for their method to be used in such ways, but that it was rather aimed at illustrating the risks (Gershgorn, 2017). Other issues were also raised, for example about the fact that the model was trained only on data from a dating site, where certain common poses or attributes might be used differently from in the world outside that dating site; that the study did not include any non-white individuals; that it assumed that there are only two sexual orientations; and, that the method used meant that superficial characteristics such as hairstyles and facial expressions also mattered for the categorization. Aside from any such shortcomings, the problems run much deeper. Sociologist Greggor Mattson befittingly positions this kind of research within:

a long history of discredited studies attempting to determine the truth of sexual orientation in the body [ranging from] 19th century measurements of lesbians' clitorises and homosexual men's hips, to late 20th century claims to have discovered 'gay genes,' 'gay brains,' 'gay ring fingers,' 'lesbian ears,' 'gay scalp hair,' or other physical differences between homosexual and heterosexual bodies. (Mattson, 2017)

In 2012, sociologist Phil Cohen aptly commented on another example of messed-up 'gaydar' research, writing that 'we need to keep in mind that this is all complicated by social stigma around sexual orientation. So, who identifies as what, and to whom, is never free from political or power issues' (Cohen, 2012). Without critical scholars being ready to sound the alarm, experiments in AI and machine learning clearly risk becoming full of themselves and void of history.

AI panoptism

Subjectivity and *subject positions* are key concepts in critical theory. As Slavoj Žižek (2008, p. 202) explains it, we become social subjects following 'ideological interpellation', whereafter we are 'assuming a certain subject position'. Butler (1997, p. 2) writes that:

> 'Subjection' signifies the process of becoming subordinated by power as well as the process of becoming a subject. Whether by interpellation, in Althusser's sense, or by discursive productivity, in Foucault's, the subject is initiated through a primary submission to power.

From the perspective of critical theory, then, the ways in which AI-driven models, labellings, flaggings, and sortings understand and organize humans in social reality is such a form of 'subjection'.

When your bank's AI assigns you a credit score, when the Stanford gaydar 'assures you' that you are heterosexual, or when the COMPAS algorithm gives you a re-offender risk level of 3, all of these are instances of 'the subordination of the subject [which] takes place through language, as the effect of the authoritative voice that hails the individual' (Butler, 1997, p. 5). Organizing, administrative systems, propel people into certain subject positions, 'with the result that those people then come to understand their behaviour and to experience themselves in those terms' (Burr, 2015, p. 130).

As explained in Chapter 6, the notion of interpellation comes from Althusser, who theorizes that the ways in which prevailing ideology defines the social world and its geometry will 'call' (interpellate) human individuals and groups into assigned positions in the sociopolitical hierarchy. Depending on which perspective one assumes, this can happen either in the form of 'false consciousness' (see Chapter 3), where we accept these positions no matter if they are favourable for us or not, or in terms similar to those of Marxist philosopher Antonio Gramsci (1971), who leaves more room in his version of the theory for civil society resistance through '*counter*-hegemony' (Boggs, 1984, p. 281).

The subject being called into being by authority can resist the call and instead there is a 'misrecognition' (Althusser, 1971,

p. 172) – a failed effort to produce the subject (Butler, 1997, p. 95). The critical question for us here being, then, to what extent the interpellated – in the context of AI: the one being identified, labelled, predicted, named, or (machine) learned – can refute the call, as it happens inside black-boxed, automated systems. Probably, they cannot.

In fact, the entire metaphor of call-and-response may not be useful at all. As Foucault (2003, p. 29) states, subjects are 'never the inert or consenting targets of power; they are always its relays'. Algorithmic categorization makes power/knowledge circulate 'by and through subjects' (Davis, 2012, p. 889). And, in today's increasingly complex communications and interaction paradigm, individuals are ascribed an increasing number of 'combined subject positions' (Flanagan, 2002, p. 440). As political theorist Chantal Mouffe (1992, p. 372) writes:

> We can then conceive the social agent as constituted by an ensemble of 'subject positions' that can never be totally fixed in a closed system of differences, constructed by a diversity of discourses among which there is no necessary relation, but a constant movement of overdetermination and displacement.

We know by now that AI, algorithms, and autonomous systems have been shown time and time again to reflect, reproduce, and reinforce existing socio-historical and political inequalities through built-in skewedness. Borrowing the concept of 'panopticon' from Foucault, political economist Gandy discusses how information technology contributes to a *panoptic sorting* of subjects. Seen in Gandy's (1993, p. 4) terms, AI as implemented in society today can become part of systems for the rationalization of 'power and control' of subjects by 'capitalists and governments'. AI, then, becomes a discriminatory technology which is yet another chapter in the ongoing *control revolution*, started already in the mid 1800s, according to sociologist and historian James Beniger (1986, p. 435). Beniger argues that 'control crises' arose in the wake of the acceleration of society's entire processing system following the industrial revolution. During such crises of control, technologies for information processing were not able to keep up with the pace of social transformation. In response came the control revolution – a set of fast technological changes with regard to the arrangements around collecting, storing, processing, and communicating data and information.

This development continued, with new 'crises' and new control mechanisms into the age of big data, and consequently AI and automation (Lindgren, 2022, pp. 12–13). AI systems, in this respect, can become part of what sociologist Stanley Cohen (1985, p. 267) has described as 'the seemingly inexorable process by which society keeps classifying, controlling, excluding more and more groups according to age, sex, race, behavior, moral status, ability or psychic state'. AI can function as part of a machinery of surveillance, control, and classification in the ways that it transforms huge datasets into knowledge, and applications that are designed in various ways to 'increase control over targets' (Gandy, 1993, p. 5).

Drawing, in turn, on a notion from legal philosopher Jeremy Bentham, Michel Foucault wrote in *Discipline and Punish* (1977, p. 196) of the all-seeing eye of the panopticon as 'a system of permanent registration'. The panopticon 'arranges spatial unities that make it possible to see constantly and to recognize immediately' (Foucault, 1977, p. 200). Translated into the age of AI assemblage, processes like these find their parallel in the surveillance capitalism logic as described by Zuboff (2019). As Foucault states, panoptic surveillance is 'a marvellous machine which, whatever use one may wish to put it to, produces homogeneous effects of power' (Foucault, 1977, p. 202). Just like predictive algorithms in decision-making, the panopticon not only has the power of seeing, but also of categorization. As Foucault explains, the panopticon is also:

> a laboratory; it could be used as a machine to carry out experiments, to alter behaviour, to train or correct individuals. To experiment [. . .] and monitor [. . .] effects. To try out different punishments [. . .] and to seek the most effective ones. (Foucault, 1977, p. 203)

Similarly, then, AI systems are machines for carrying out such social experiments, in the name of innovation, efficiency, and technological progress. Data-driven machine-learning systems – in algorithmic management, segmentation, targeted advertising, and propaganda – prime and govern individuals, while monitoring effects, and tweaking sanctions and nudges. The parallelism of these two logics – in Foucauldian surveillance, and in algorithmic control and governance – is the reason to speak of 'panoptic sorting' as one of AI's social effects (Gandy, 1993).

The panopticon, as manifested through AI systems, can then become 'a machine that ensures the infinitesimal distribution of power, one that turns the monitored individual into a visible, knowable, and vulnerable object' (Robins and Webster, 1988, p. 59). AI assemblage casts, paraphrasing Foucault (1977, p. 224), an 'infinitely minute web of panoptic techniques', subjecting the social fabric to a state of 'permanent documentation' (Foucault, 1977, p. 250).

AI systems in today's world can, in a Foucauldian sense, function as vectors of *biopower* – a form of power, exercised through 'the constructing of tables' (Foucault, 1978, p. 140), to control populations in every aspect of life so that 'more and more parts of cultural life become susceptible to commodified influences and values' (Jordan and Taylor, 2004, p. 150).

In the age of algorithms, we see a new kind of biopower emerging, which operates 'at the level of the category, of using computer code, statistics and surveillance to construct categories within populations according to users' surveilled internet history' (Cheney-Lippold, 2011, p. 166). This pertains not only to the sorting and control of bodies, but of minds, through what Bernard Stiegler (2019, p. 125) calls *psychopower*, and through which a range of freedoms become eroded (Pasquale, 2015, p. 52). In the age of surveillance capitalism (Zuboff, 2019), the statistics machinery already running rampant through the entire modern age, is pushed further and further.

Similarly, when AI systems are built and implemented, they demand that engineers and developers build certain, practical but arbitrary, categorizations into the systems. The machine-learning models must be trained on something – they are hungry for (creating) categories. So, the ways in which AI enumerates, counts, and categorizes people today, will force certain categorizations upon society, and these are rather overdriven versions of divisions that already exist, than new inventions.

Takeaway points

- AI can be seen as a *discursive practice* that orders people and groups into *subject positions*, through *interpellation*.

AI assemblage is a *representational system* that draws upon, and applies, certain worldviews and categorizations.

- AI systems work through drawing on, and establishing, various *interpretative repertoires* – worldviews, hierarchies, and modes of sense-making. AI can be construed as discourse, as it consists in systems for characterizing and evaluating actions, events, and other phenomena.
- AI, through its predictions, models, sortings, and categorizations, is *signifying* – it produces meaning and knowledge. Machine-learning models function like a 'language' that circulates and upholds certain grammars, with social reverberations. AI is 'hungry for creating categories' that are often oppressive, racialized, gendered, or sexualized, and that fail to represent anything that is non-binary. Through such categorization, or *panoptic sorting*, AI can turn monitored individuals into knowable objects.
- The ways in which AI technologies establish certain 'truths' at the cost of others is strengthened through a set of *epistemic forgeries*: (1) that AI is neutral; (2) that AI is 'smarter' than humans, also in relation to complex social issues; and (3) that AI arrives at its 'truths' in an independent manner.
- AI becomes a concern for human rights and justice in the many documented cases where its decision-making tools contribute in masking and deepening social inequalities, through, for example, *technological redlining*. Algorithms will perpetuate the interpretative repertoires by which they are shaped, the simple reason that machine learning in itself is just like language, and discourses in society are self-reinforcing.
- Thinking in terms of AI-first, and with technological solutionism, will encourage attempts to 'fix' complex social problems such as racism, sexism, and other forms of discrimination by tweaking parameters. Such approaches solve the maths that returns the biased language but does nothing other than obscure the deeper-running unfairness in society. Processes of *data colonialism* skew the perspective even further.

8

AI in the loop

Nothing that [humans have] created is outside [their] capacity to change, to remold, to supplant, or to destroy [. . . :] machines are no more sacred or substantial than the dreams in which they originated.
Lewis Mumford, *The Condition of Man* (1944, p. 415)

[W]hat the dystopians failed to understand was that once inside the machine, human beings gained new powers they could and would increasingly use to change the system that dominated them.
Andrew Feenberg, *Looking Backward, Looking Forward*
(2017, p. 142)

The two excerpts above both point to, and illuminate the fact that machines, once created, are not unchangeable. Mumford emphasizes that just as machines can be dreamt up, they can also be dreamt apart, or dreamt differently. Feenberg writes of people's ability to transform the situation within which they find themselves, in systems of oppression. Humans are entangled in AI assemblage, and thus, inside the machine. From here, we can change relations of domination, surveillance, and ownership, in more democratic directions. Making such change into reality – deploying a critical politics of technology – will depend less on predictions, and more on what is done in practice (Feenberg, 2017, p. 142). As already shown by scholars in the fields of Ethical AI and Responsible AI, a range of perspectives must be brought together to address issues of our future with these technologies, from engaged and socially grounded perspectives (Dignum, 2022).

This involves not only transdisciplinary collaboration among academics, but also increased and constantly renewed engagement from civil society, NGOs, activists, politicians, and makers of policy and law. Most important of all, there is the need for increased critical awareness and social responsibility among AI corporations. The role for those of us who align with the perspectives put forth in this book – for critical theorists, social constructionists, and discourse analysts engaged in AI – is to continue to pose critical questions, carry out empirical analyses of power in practice, and never to stop challenging the constantly renewed ways in which freedom and democracy becomes threatened.

Bias bias

One of the key problems with the present state of self-professed critical research on AI, but that lacks the grounding in critical theory, is something that I would like to call *bias bias*. As argued throughout this book, in those cases when stereotypes, discrimination, and exclusion materialize in AI's models, this does not come from the models. It is not the models that determine social values but, on the contrary, social values are determining the models. Once the models are deployed, they can then exacerbate those social values, and also conceal their inherently social origin. Mannheim (1954, p. 2) wrote that:

> Only in a quite limited sense does the single individual create out of [her/]himself the mode of speech and of thought we attribute to [her/]him. [S]he speaks the language of [her/]his group; [s]he thinks in the manner in which [her/]his group thinks.

Paraphrasing Mannheim, machine-learning models speak the language of the society within which they exist. They learn it and, like any other speaker, they then play an active part in shaping it through use. In sum then, AI systems are not independent moral agents. While some claim that artificial agents can indeed be seen as possessing moral agency, even if they do not have a 'free will' as such (see Floridi and Sanders, 2004), others emphasize that computers are never ever fully independent (Johnson and Miller,

2008, p. 124). Crawford (2021, p. 8) also sees AI as like discourse, as both constitutive of, and constituted by, the social:

> At a fundamental level, AI is technical and social practices, institutions and infrastructures, politics and culture. Computational reason and embodied work are deeply interlinked: AI systems both reflect and produce social relations and understandings of the world.

The argument here, is that AI cannot think anything new, in the sense that it is entangled with things that already exist. Even though computers can be programmed to mix and match, randomize, and also to come up with novel things, significant technological leaps must be made if AI is to match what we today see as truly human creativity (Sautoy, 2019). But the question is not easy. On the one side, there are arguments such as that of McQuillan (2022, p. 43) who contends that even if AI sometimes produces sophisticated things that we would deem to be creative, the way that it constructs its models is still stuck with abstracting from the past. Therefore, AI's creations necessarily become a rendition of how things have been, rather than a suggestion or an imagining of how things could be. This, then, comes with consequences for society, since AI thus has 'an inbuilt political commitment to the status quo, in particular to existing structures that embed specific relations of power'.

On the other side, there are the claims that AI can indeed, at least on certain terms, produce things that are 'new'. There are exciting and hyped tools that repeatedly make the news today, in the areas of automatic writing through models such as BERT (Devlin, 2018) and GPT-3 (Brown et al., 2020), and AIs that create images, such as DALL-E (also based on GPT-3) (Ramesh et al., 2021), and Stable Diffusion (Rombach et al., 2022). At the time of writing GPT-4 is just around the corner, and there is no doubt that it will be even more powerful than its predecessors.

AI tools such as these are nothing short of amazing. The wow-factor is indisputable. There is no doubt that we will see lots of interesting collaborations between creative humans and machines in the future, in literature, visual arts, music, games, and so on. Still, many of us believe that the AI of today needs the support of humans to be able to produce something truly creative (see Ekbia and Nardi, 2017, p. 37). With advances in this field of Generative AI, however, we may have to renegotiate this. If we were to feed an AI with all books by a certain author, or in a certain genre, it would be able to produce new books in the same style. The AI would also be able to produce different hybrids of authors and genres, and the same could be done in areas such as visual arts, music, and film.

It is impossible to give any definitive answer to whether such an AI is to be seen as creative, for real, or not, as it is a matter of value judgement and philosophy. Do we see the practice of sampling in hiphop as 'creative'? Is the musical phenomenon of the mashup 'creative'? Is the paraphrasing of mid-1980s teen drama, and parallel-universe-scifi in the Netflix series Stranger Things 'creative'? Yes, to all of the above. We see many things that are inspired by, or derivative of, previous creations, as still being original to certain degrees. This means that it is not completely unreasonable to see AI as already being creative under certain circumstances, and, as the level of refinement of future AI will be even higher, we may have to revise this view in the future, conceiving of AI as autonomously creative in ways that it not yet is.

But this is not a book about creativity. If we dial back to our main focus on AI as sociopolitical assemblage, and redirect attention towards AI's relationship to the power/knowledge nexus in society, and to how it contributes in constructing our social realities, a different question arises: *Would it solve anything in terms of stereotyping, discrimination, and oppression, if AI was to be more creative?*

It is often said that the reason why AI models perpetuate racism, sexism, transphobia, and so on, is that machine-learning solutions are unable to think outside the box. As the models are trained on data from society, while there is racism, sexism, and transphobia in society, the resulting AI will not be able to 'feel' that such ideas are wrong, or to correct them in any 'compassionate' way. Is the solution to this to develop better AI that is able to make such evaluations, and if so, who decides which evaluations should be made? It might be possible to set some form of universal standard for the harshest forms of hate speech, but there would be an immense grey area left, where severe risks for democracy would arise if decisions were left in the hands of technologies and their developers.

The main problem here, is that broad, historically contingent, and politically salient power relations in society, when manifested in decisions made by AI, tend to be reduced to issues of mere 'bias' in the AI systems. The problem is defined in terms of there being 'bias' built into the models, and the alleged solution then is to try to remove that 'bias'. This way of reasoning is indicative of an AI-first perspective, where it appears to be taken for granted that AI must be used, and if it does not work as we want it to, we try to fix the AI, rather than scrapping it altogether.

Racist, sexist, and transphobic thinking are not 'biases', in the sense that it is something that people or models get slightly wrong, and that can be nudged back on track. These things are deeply rooted in history, social structure, language, and ideology in ways that defy technological fixes. This, as I see it, is, however, not a pessimistic view, but a realistic one. Remembering the discussion of tech solutionism in Chapter 3, these issues are not puzzles to be easily solved by finding the golden piece. They are social problems that must be responded to in more conflictual, antagonistic, and demanding ways.

A vital contribution from critical theory in this context is the suggestion not to frame this as a problem of 'bias' at all. We must get past the insistence on speaking of any problem where AI perpetuates power relations in society in terms of bias. But this tendency is so strong that one might even claim that there is a *bias bias* – a disproportional inclination towards the notion of bias – in AI discourse.

Critical theorist, and member of the Frankfurt School, Jürgen Habermas has developed a framework for dealing with moral issues in society through what he labels *discourse ethics*. The starting point is in the moral principle that a democratic society must develop its norms in a way that disqualifies 'any norm that could not meet with the qualified assent of all who are or might be affected by it'. Furthermore 'valid moral norms must be generally teachable and publicly defendable' (Habermas, 2004, pp. 145–6). For Habermas, every valid norm must meet the following condition:

> All affected can accept the consequences and the side effects its general observance can be anticipated to have for the satisfaction of everyone's interests (and these consequences are preferred to those of known alternative possibilities for regulation). (Habermas, 2004, p. 146)

In the AI field, attempts at moving in a similar direction are taken in areas such as Explainable AI, where the goal is to develop AI in ways that allow for offering human-understandable explanations of the rationale behind the decisions that AI systems make (Doran et al., 2017). Another keyword in this area is algorithmic auditing, which is often quite loosely defined, and disconnected from the goal of assessing the occurrence of discrimination in particular, referring rather to nearly any form of analysis of how algorithms work (Vecchione et al., 2021, pp. 2–3). Furthermore, algorithmic auditing approaches often lack the deeper community engagement associated with other forms of auditing in the social sciences. Information science scholars Briana Vecchione, Solon Barocas, and Karen Levy (2021, p. 7) argue that future attempts at algorithmic auditing should consider to a larger extent how to document actual people's experiences, even if that would come at the cost of being able to make less statistically robust claims about causality.

Algorithm audits are generally understood to involve the collection of data about how an algorithm is behaving in the context in which it is applied, and then, based on the data, to assess whether any potential bias has a negative impact on the rights or interests of those who are subjected to the algorithm (Brown et al., 2021). This approach is saturated with notions of 'risk management', 'stakeholder interests', 'metric testing', and 'mitigation strategies'. We come full circle to the question of how the problem of a racist, sexist, or otherwise discriminatory, algorithm is solved. Is it circled back to developers who can crank some widgets and tweak some levers, reverse-engineering their own creation to produce a 'fair' result? Or should the focus be somewhere else than on the technological fix? AI ethics scholars Shea Brown, Jovana Davidovic, and Ali Hasan (2021) explain that:

> much criticism has been directed at early attempts to provide ethical analysis of algorithms. Scholars have argued that using the classical analytic approach that over-stresses technical aspects of algorithms and ignores the larger socio-technical power dynamics has resulted in ethical approaches to algorithms that ignore or marginalize some of the primary threats that (especially decision-making and classification) algorithms pose to minorities.

This underlines the importance of a critical theory approach also in the area of algorithmic auditing, and the same goes for the overlapping field of 'algorithmic fairness', the goal of which is to try – often by mathematical or statistical means – to mitigate the differences that machine-learning models reproduce across various social groups (Mhasawade et al., 2021, p. 662). Computer scientist Jon Kleinberg and colleagues (2018) argue that it is the wrong strategy to try to make the algorithm 'blind' to, for example, race or gender, as a way of making those effects disappear. Instead, they suggest other mathematical solutions for how predictions can be formed from data, even with potential biases within them – showing how their proposed method 'can increase both equity and efficiency' (Kleinberg et al., 2018, p. 23). The critical theory approach would be different, as there is not only reason to question if maths is the right path towards equity, but also if efficiency should really remain part of the equation, if the goal is to deal with effects of socially produced, and historically proliferated, forms of discrimination; something that it reasonably takes time, collective democratic deliberation, and purposeful social action or activism to even make a dent in.

* washing

Another key principle of discourse ethics put forth by Habermas is that:

> Only those norms can claim to be valid that meet (or could meet) with the approval of all affected in their capacity *as participants in a practical discourse*. (Habermas, 2004, p. 146)

Translated into the AI domain, this means that the moral architecture that underlies algorithmic systems must be grounded in the practical participation of those that are affected by the systems. Such participation has been enacted in the field of *participatory design*. The idea behind such approaches is to include users of technologies in the creation and maintenance of the systems that they are subjected to. The tradition of participatory design has its roots in the mid 1970s and was then first and foremost concerned with involving workers in the development and use of technology in the workplace (Taylor, 2006). Since then, the approach has been used in a number of domains (Druin, 1999; Hutchinson et al., 2003; Kreps and Neuhauser, 2010; Star and Ruhleder, 1996), and it is now increasingly used in AI development (Holstein et al., 2019; Katan et al., 2015; Kreps and Neuhauser, 2013; Loi et al., 2018).

Critical scholars have, however, pointed out that the use of participatory design can, in practice, function as a form of *participation washing*. This is similar to, for example, greenwashing, by which companies falsely purport to make sustainability efforts and to be environmentally friendly, while this in fact is done for the sake of pure optics. In the case of participation washing in AI and machine learning, critics claim that this is done within a discourse that fails to account for the actual power dynamics that must be addressed, and which is also insensitive to the fact that these corporate projects of collaboration, openness, and sharing have an exploitative and extractive element. Sociologist Mona Sloane and colleagues (2022) argue that this is nothing particular for AI. In fact, participatory design processes also in other areas have relied on power imbalances:

> For example, in the international development sector where 'participation' of local communities at the receiving end of powerful agencies is based on manufactured consent and is based on (post-)colonial structures of global power [. . .] ; in the corporate sector where 'users' are invited into 'co-creation' sessions in order to create new product ideas; in the philanthropic sector where 'the public' is challenged to join in defining new problems and/or solutions . . . (Sloane et al., 2022, p. 1)

To remedy this, Sloane et al. contend that this kind of participation, as well as the kinds of playbour and ghost work described in the previous chapter, must be recognized as work, and that processes of participatory design must be much more long-term and holistic than is the case today.

The situation today is that clients want AI corporations to ensure that their products are not causing any harm; in turn, corporations hire Responsible AI teams, often including senior academics, whom they push to give a green light to the product as quickly as possible; in turn, then, workers in these Responsible AI teams often fall victim to burnout. Tech journalist Melissa Heikkilä (2022) reports that:

> Tech companies such as Meta have been forced by courts to offer compensation and extra mental-health support for employees such

as content moderators, who often have to sift through graphic and violent content that can be traumatizing. But teams who work on responsible AI are often left to fend for themselves, [. . .] even though the work can be just as psychologically draining as content moderation. Ultimately, this can leave people in these teams feeling undervalued, which can affect their mental health and lead to burnout.

In addition to participation washing, there are also critical voices raised about *audit washing*, where the argument is that algorithm auditing has not yet presented itself as a dependable mechanism for securing accountability. Rather, inadequate audits tend to cover up discrimination and other problems with AI systems that may be badly designed and carelessly implemented. In the best case, such audits are worthless, and in the worst case they create a structure of permission that provides excuses for the very same harms that were supposed to be mitigated in the first place (Goodman and Trehu, 2022).

Similar criticisms have been voiced largely around *ethics washing* being a huge obstacle to properly address the real problems with AI systems and algorithms (van Maanen, 2022). Ethical guidelines for AI, such as those developed by the European Commission, have been criticized for being too abstract. How are we, for example, to operationalize guidelines such as 'Unfair bias must be avoided', and 'AI systems should empower human beings' (AI-HLEG, 2019), and make them concrete, and enable follow-ups to check whether the industry is following them or not? It seems that the time is ripe for demanding rules and action, rather than, as some claim, 'half-arsed' (Davies, 2019), fuzzy principles.

Philosopher Thomas Metzinger, who was a member of the expert group that developed the European Commission's guidelines, wrote in an opinion piece after the release of the guidelines that, even though the guidelines are 'the best in the world on the subject', they are nonetheless 'a compromise'. The first argument brought up by Metzinger was that the entire idea of creating 'Trustworthy AI' is misguided. He called it 'conceptual nonsense', as trustworthiness is not something that can be possessed by machines. Humans are the only ones who can be trustworthy or untrustworthy, and if untrustworthy governments or corporations behave badly, the only thing that well-functioning AI can do is to enable 'more effective unethical behaviour' (Metzinger,

2019). Technology is not good or bad in itself, but it can make both good or bad social impulses more powerful and efficient. Metzinger argues that:

> The Trustworthy AI story is a marketing narrative invented by industry, a bedtime story for tomorrow's customers. [. . .T]he Trustworthy AI narrative is, in reality, about developing future markets and using ethics debates as elegant public decorations for a large-scale investment strategy. At least that's the impression I am beginning to get after nine months of working on the guidelines.

Metzinger argued that the expert group had hardly any ethicists involved, but that the group had 'extreme industrial weight'. Metzinger further tells the story of having been tasked, together with a machine-learning expert, to develop 'Red Lines': non-negotiable boundaries for which uses of AI should be allowed or not. Their list included lethal autonomous weapon systems, AI-assisted social scoring of citizens by the state, as well as AI systems that are beyond the control and understanding of humans. According to Metzinger's account, the terms 'non-negotiable' and 'Red Lines' were removed from the report, and replaced by 'critical concerns', due to a majority of industry representatives and other members of the expert group insisting on a more 'positive vision'. While this is one, out of several possible versions, of what happened in the group, at least Metzinger's contentious position illustrates a core dilemma that AI critique is facing in a range of settings.

> Industry organizes and cultivates ethical debates to buy time – to distract the public and to prevent or at least delay effective regulation and policy-making. Politicians also like to set up ethics committees because it gives them a course of action when, given the complexity of the issues, they simply don't know what to do – and that's only human. At the same time, however, industry is building one 'ethics washing machine' after another. [. . .] Because industry acts more quickly and efficiently than politics or the academic sector, there is a risk that, as with 'Fake News', we will now also have a problem with fake ethics, including lots of conceptual smoke screens and mirrors, highly paid industrial philosophers, [and] self-invented quality seals. (Metzinger, 2019)

Aside from the Ethics Guidelines for Trustworthy Artificial Intelligence that were presented by the High-Level Expert Group on AI for the European Commission in 2019 (AI-HLEG, 2019), the so-called AI Act – a regulative proposal – was presented by the EC in 2021, with additions the year after (European Commission, 2022). Ethics and technology researchers Meeri Haataja and Joanna Bryson (2022) followed up the latter with a discussion piece that is far less polemic than Metzinger's comment to the former. Overall, they applaud the Act, and commend the way in which it reflects 'an extensive process' and forms 'part of an impressive suite of innovative legislation' (Haataja and Bryson, 2022, p. 3). They do point out, among other things, that there are 'loopholes that allow continued utilization of remote biometric identification in public spaces for law enforcement as usual' (Haataja and Bryson, 2022, p. 4).

Furthermore, the general discourse around the Act is one of technological and bureaucratic fixes rather than one of participation, democracy, and civic engagement. For example, when it comes to cases where AI is used in recruitment, welfare, or university applications, and assessments of creditworthiness, the Act does indeed label such uses as 'high risk', but at the same promotes the use of AI itself 'to arrive at a more holistic picture', rather than opting for non-AI strategies altogether. And, furthermore, that 'extra oversight and restrictions on the type of AI models that can be used' will curb 'machine-based discrimination' (Makortoff, 2022).

All in all, the original AI Act includes one mention of 'gender', in the context that 'gender equality' legislation should generally be adhered to (European Commission, 2022, p. 4 in proposal). On a handful of occasions there are repetitions of a standard wording about 'historical patterns of discrimination, for example based on [sex], racial or ethnic origins, disabilities, age, sexual orientation' (European Commission, 2022, p. 21 in revisions). This is only when speaking of biometric profiling and other decision systems. These traits are not socially or politically contextualized, but rather bundled together with things such as 'hair colour, eye colour, tat[t]oos, personal traits', and so on (European Commission, 2022, p. 30 in revisions). 'Business' is mentioned 27 times, 'innovation' 32 times, and 'democratic' is mentioned nine times, but only as part of the phrase 'administration of justice and democratic processes' (see for example European Commission, 2022, p. 5 in proposal).

In light of the above, it is important to remember that work on AI governance and law-making is one distinct, and important, genre of discourse, while that of critical theory is another. In some ways, it is unreasonable to ask that the kind of broader analysis and conceptual complexity that marks critical theory should also be a characteristic of bureaucratic documents. There is a time and a place for everything, and Marx's theories about political economy might not belong in the AI Act, after all.

Having said that, it is still fair to conclude – summarizing the above discussions – that participatory design in AI often falls short of its promises; that much AI auditing, as it is carried out today, lacks the critical edge that it needs; that the ideal of Trustworthy AI may be misguided as it directs attention away from the responsibility of humans; and that policy and legislation work around AI may range from being, at worst, controlled by industry, and, at best, still not critical enough. As put by Sloane (2022, p. 4), there has been a hype around 'ethical AI' that has, 'despite good intentions', served 'as a smokescreen for continuing with non-participatory and non-justice-oriented ML design approaches'. The techno-solutionist ideology underlies these ethical debates: 'AI is desirable, AI is unavoidable and AI works (or should work)' (Ricaurte, 2022, p. 729).

The challenge we have to face has to do with how critical theory can benefit AI ethics instead of just picking at it. Philosopher and ethicist Rosalie Waelen writes about this interface, and notes that the dominant means of AI ethics has been to take a principled approach – through developing various sets of principles and guidelines for the desired directions in which to develop and use AI. Keywords in such cases of soft law have been 'transparency, justice and fairness, non-maleficence, responsibility and privacy' (Waelen, 2022, p. 2). This basically means that some AI ethics initiatives have been about the publication of bland statements of indistinct principles, without any accountability structures.

Waelen aptly discusses how critical theory, rooted in Marxist perspectives and the Frankfurt School, is focused on analysing relations and structures of power and disempowerment in society, with the goal of justice, equality, and emancipation. It is then pointed out that there are indeed scholars in the field of AI ethics who assume a highly critical stance. This means that accusing the field of AI ethics of being totally oblivious to true critical analysis might be somewhat of a strawman argument. Waelen (2022, p. 9) helpfully lists several studies in this respect; for example philosopher Vincent Müller's writing on AI manipulation and opacity, which is clearly drawing on a critical perspective, focusing on structural power and counter-hegemonic contention:

> Actual policy is not just an implementation of ethical theory, but subject to societal power structures – and the agents that do have the power will push against anything that restricts them. There is thus a significant risk that regulation will remain toothless in the face of economical and political power. (Müller, 2021)

Furthermore, tech ethicist David Gunkel argues that 'the way we have typically perceived the problem of AI ethics is in fact a problem and an obstacle to its own solution'. Questions must be posed in new ways that are 'capable of accommodating the full philosophical impact and significance of AI' (Gunkel, 2020, p. 540). Gunkel also steers clear of the principled approach, arguing that AI ethics is not something clean-cut that can be resolved by lists of principles, instead – as AI technologies face us with 'increasingly social and interactive artifacts' – we must question existing moral theory and practice by 'thorough re-evaluation and critical questioning' (Gunkel, 2020, p. 552).

Sadowski makes the case that AI innovation processes must be radically democratized, so that more people get 'more power to influence how, why, and for what purpose new technology is created' (2020, p. 177). Sadowski also argues that this democratization should entail two major changes:

(1) Allowing those effected by the use of technology to participate in its creation, thereby including a diverse range of groups that may have different interests, experiences, and values. Truly participatory design has to go beyond just rebranding public relations as public engagement. This means treating people as more than merely consumers in a marketplace, but instead as citizens with rights to codetermine the systems that shape their lives. Participants must at least have the capacity to provide meaningful feedback and catalyze transformative change that challenges the nature as well as goals of innovation.

(2) Opening up the black box of opaque operations and proprietary processes, thus ensuring that intelligent systems are also intelligible to the public. Truly intelligible systems have to go beyond companies sharing certain data sets or organizing occasional hackathons where programmers can play around. This also means calling for more than transparency, which is only the first step

toward accountability. They must be scrutinized and regulated by independent experts and advocates who work for the public interest, not private benefit. (Sadowski, 2020, pp. 177–8)

Such goals can get us past 'the uselessness of AI ethics', its failure to 'mitigate the racial, social, and environmental damages of AI technologies in any meaningful sense', instead 'thinking more broadly about systems of oppression' (Munn, 2022, p. 1).

Towards AI criticism

This book has a key weakness: Its subject matter is a *moving target*. AI development progresses rapidly. At the time of writing, it feels as if new breakthroughs are happening if not weekly, so at least monthly. This means that some specific examples or arguments made throughout the book may quickly become antiquated, maybe even before the book is printed.

We can be certain that, in the very near future, AI will be able to do more, and to do it in increasingly powerful ways. We may also hope that some of the obvious flaws in terms of oversimplifications and discriminatory patterns in machine-learning models will have been addressed by more sensible and sensitive technological fixes. Instead of simply removing, for example, racist words from a model, we may even have models that have more refined ways of counteracting racism in more dynamic, pervasive, and 'human' ways.

We can also assume that laws, regulations, and other aspects of AI governance will have progressed further to mitigate and counteract as much as possible of the malicious effects of AI applications in society. Let's also hope that activists have been able to insert more critical discussions about values and morals into the calculus (Pasquale, 2020, p. 100), and to apply 'public pressure to slow down the automation of our worst impulses' (Noble, 2018, p. 181). Civil society action is progressing, and 'new types of political community can be created that are able to reform systems of hierarchy, knowledge, technology and culture' in relation to AI (Mohamed et al., 2020, p. 676). Important work is already done by algorithm activists (Treré and Bonini, 2022), data justice advocates (Hintz et al., 2019), data feminists (D'Ignazio and Klein, 2020), and groups such as Black in

AI, LatinX in AI, Women in Machine Learning, Queer in AI, Widening NLP, and others.

Scholars, such as those in media studies researcher Andreas Sudmann's (2019) edited volume on democratizing AI, or Pieter Verdegem's (2021) edited volume *AI for Everyone?* – alongside many others (see Roberge and Castelle, 2021a; Gunkel, 2012; Lindgren, 2023; Crawford, 2021; McQuillan, 2022), are already pointing out the direction. Sudmann (2019, p. 9) summarizes that:

> Central reference points of these discussions are, for instance, the socio-political consequences of AI technologies for the future job market [. . .], the deployment of AI to manipulate visual information or to create 'fake news', the geo-political effects of autonomous weapon systems, or the application of AI methods through vast surveillance networks for producing sentencing guidelines and recidivism risk profiles in criminal justice systems, or for demographic and psychographic targeting of bodies for advertising, propaganda, and other forms of state intervention.

A crucial area, not addressed enough in this book, is that of AI's planetary costs and its relation to the climate crisis. This is a crisis that AI often promises to address, but which it in many ways worsens through impacts of data centres, e-waste, and its boosting of consumerist business models (Brevini, 2022). Certainly, the entire political economy of AI has a range of direct and indirect impacts on global sustainability (Dauvergne, 2020).

Yet another area, not covered in adequate depth in this book, is that of AI's role in warfare, where it gives military planning a 'decisive edge', and enables the accomplishment of military objectives at 'lightning speed' (Elliott, 2022, p. 160). AI has advanced to the point where autonomous weapons can fly undetected towards a target and then swarm together to deliver powerful, coordinated strikes. Critics believe that policymakers should prevent AI from killing humans without explicit operator consent, but at the same time, it is possible that AI may eventually evolve to the point where it sets its own missions and goals, which are at odds with its original design and may not be under the control of its human creators (Wilson, 2020).

No matter how AI changes shape, however, the relevance of this book's key message will still stand. Because, no matter what the current state of AI technology is (in 2024, 2044, 2144), and regardless of if 'AI' is still the name of choice for the tech of the day, constant critique of technology's interaction with humans and society must always persist.

This demands open-minded and equal collaboration between citizens, governments, and corporations, towards a goal where AI can increasingly be part of the common good. The main hindrance to this is that the 'discursive practice' (Agre, 1997) of AI is still far too entangled with technology in its narrow sense. For critical scholars, coming from areas within the social sciences and humanities, there are many barriers to break through, in order to bring the critique close to the actual doing and creating of the AIs that we face everywhere in our day-to-day lives.

AI as a topic of discussion is indeed conducive to all kinds of philosophical and political reflections and chats, and those are often welcomed by the tech crowd. They tend to be received, however, in a way where the real power of the critical contributions gets immediately disarmed, oversimplified, and conveniently placed as a factor, variable, or margin note, not actually stopping the continued churn of tech inevitabilism. The critique becomes ornamental – a neat alibi. Critical AI scholar Phil Agre (1997, p. 142), writes that:

> The strategic vagueness of AI vocabulary [. . .] is not a matter of conscious deception. It does permit AI's methods to seem broadly applicable, even when particular applications require a designer to make [. . .] some wildly unreasonable assumptions.

Agre writes in a self-reflective essay about his first attempts – coming from a tech background – at getting into philosophy (more precisely Heidegger's *Being and Time*, 1962) and sociology (in the form of Garfinkel's *Studies in Ethnomethodology*, 1967), about the difficulties that he faced because he 'was still tacitly attempting to read everything as a specification for a technical mechanism'. He continues:

> [M]y technical training had instilled in me two polar-opposite orientations to language – as precisely formalized and as impossibly vague – and a single clear mission for all discursive work – transforming vagueness into precision through formalization. (Agre, 1997, p. 247)

Agre suggests, as a way to work around this divide, that critical reflection and critical engagement is more forcefully provoked in the AI field. Writing in the late 1990s, he reflected that even though AI at that point was much less centralized than it had been a couple of decades earlier, it was 'still very much its own coherent center of mass' (Agre, 1997, p. 154). This is the case also today, as the development of AI continuously intensifies an ongoing trend towards monopolization in the sector of technology. Companies like Microsoft, Google, Meta, and Amazon in the US, and Tencent, Alibaba, and Baidu in China, control most of the markets, while expanding all the time through aggressive acquisition strategies. This is not only problematic in the narrow economic sense, but also because visions for AI end up being the concern of a small number of powerful actors. In this process, knowledge production gets de-democratized (Rieder et al., 2021).

As pointed out by Agre (1997, p. 154), in spite of this accelerated concentration of power over AI, 'no equally coherent "critical" school has arisen to compete with it'. This, once again, is where critical theory can contribute. But this must not happen in the shape of a revolution, driven by the illusion that we can throw away AI as we know it and build something completely new, based on different visions, altered architectures, and other forms of ownership and control. Realistically, we must build from the reality of the present situation. It seems that it is time to reinvigorate Agre's visions of a *critical technical practice*.

In Agre's vision, critical scholars will be able to approach technological work with the ambition not to point out the mere 'superficial and transient' issues, but to diagnose problems 'as deeply as possible' to point out 'deep and systematic confusions in the field' of AI. This takes, as this book purports to contribute to doing, the development of 'critical tools to understand the depths below the ordinary practices of a technical field'. Ideally, such critique of AI can lead to the 'reformulation of underlying ideas and methods, fresh starts, and more instructive impasses' (Agre, 1997, p. 154). This makes for constructive contributions from critical theory. Rather than self-righteously pointing out everything that is wrong with how AI is developed and implemented, the critical scholar must have one foot in 'the reflexive work of critique', and one foot in an understanding of the actual conditions surrounding AI designs: 'spanning these borderlands, bridging the disparate sites of practice that computer work brings uncomfortably together' (Agre, 1997, p. 155). As the critical scholar finds things to be 'wrong' about AI in its current forms, Agre explains:

> the next step is not to conclude that AI, considered as a static essence, has been debunked in a once-and-for-all fashion. Instead, research can now proceed on the basis of a radical interpretation of their significance, inevitably incremental in its practical effect but more sophisticated than it would have been otherwise, leading toward new and different problems. (Agre, 1997, p. 155)

Moving forward, we can model our *AI criticism* on the 'net criticism' that internet critic Geert Lovink (2002, p. 3) suggested for the 'dotcom age'. This kind of criticism, first of all, should not target those uses of AI that promote democracy and decentrality, those that secure people the rights to their own data, those that promote the idea of sharing code, resources, and content, and those that believe in defending freedom. The criticism should target those uses of AI that oppress, centralize, capitalize, and dismantle core democratic values. Actors such as NGOs, user groups, social movements, and critics must work together, calling 'from the outside' for accountability, and be ready to take part – intervene and mediate – in the economic, political, social, and technological processes that define AI (Lovink, 2002, p. 11).

Deploying this kind of AI criticism, by drawing on critical theory, can be a radical way of putting not only humans in the loop, but 'society-in-the-loop' (Rahwan, 2018). The fatal shortcoming, however, of such perspectives is that already by assuming the existence of *The Loop*, we position AI first and at the very centre. We construe it as an unquestionable perpetual machine, inside the loop of which we can consider inserting different things (code, humans, social considerations, etc.) Only after that, comes any potential regulation and critique of that perennial machine. Let's strip AI of its sparkling aura. Let's call it out for what it is. Even pull the plug for a moment. Let's smoke the ghosts out of the machine and face them. AI is not superhuman – it has no immunity. A true critique will apply the perspective of *AI in the loop* – of society, politics, culture, and people.

References

Abercrombie, N. and Turner, B. S. (1978). The dominant ideology thesis. *The British Journal of Sociology*, 29 (2): 149–70. *https://doi.org/10.2307/589886*

Adam, A. (1998). *Artificial Knowing: Gender and the Thinking Machine*. Routledge.

Adorno, T. W. (1978). *Minima Moralia: Reflections from Damaged Life*. Verso.

Agarwal, S. and Mishra, S. (2021). *Responsible AI: Implementing Ethical and Unbiased Algorithms*. Springer. *https://doi.org/10.1007/978-3-030-76860-7*

Agre, P. (1997). Toward a critical technical practice: Lessons learned in trying to reform AI. In G. Bowker, S. L. Star, W. Turner, and L. Gasser (eds), *Social Science, Technical Systems, and Cooperative Work: Beyond the Great Divide* (pp. 131–57). Psychology Press. *http://ieee xplore.ieee.org/document/768167/*

AI Now Institute (2018). Fauxtomation | AI Now 2018 Symposium. *YouTube*. *https://www.youtube.com/watch?v=-CKPHpGuvJA*

AI Now Institute (2019). Organizing Tech | AI Now 2019 Symposium. YouTube. https://www.youtube.com/watch?v=jLeOyIS1jwc

AI-HLEG (2019). *Ethics Guidelines for Trustworthy AI | Shaping Europe's Digital Future*. European Commission. *https://web.archive.org/web/20221122072708/https://digital-strategy.ec.europa.eu/en/library/ethics-guidelines-trustworthy-ai*

Ajunwa, I., Crawford, K., and Schultz, J. (2017). Limitless worker surveillance. *California Law Review*, 105: 735.

Albert, E. T. (2019). AI in talent acquisition: A review of AI-applications used in recruitment and selection. *Strategic HR Review*, 18 (5): 215–21. *https://doi.org/10.1108/SHR-04-2019-0024*

Allyn, B. (2022). Ordering food on an app is easy. Delivering it could mean injury and theft. *NPR*. *https://web.archive.org/web/20220418 025014/https://www.npr.org/2021/11/03/1051289009/nyc-delivery -workers-risk-safety-to-bring-dinner*

Althusser, L. (1971). *Lenin and Philosophy and Other Essays*. Monthly review press.

Althusser, L. (1984). *Essays on Ideology*. Verso.

Anderson, D. (2017). GLAAD and HRC call on Stanford University and responsible media to debunk dangerous and flawed report claiming to identify LGBTQ people through facial recognition technology. *GLAAD*. *https://web.archive.org/web/20220815152734/https:// www.glaad.org/blog/glaad-and-hrc-call-stanford-university-respons ible-media-debunk-dangerous-flawed-report*

Angwin, J., Larson, J., Mattu, S., and Kirchner, L. (2016). Machine bias. *ProPublica*. *https://www.propublica.org/article/machine-bias-risk-as sessments-in-criminal-sentencing*

Anonymous (2015). Incident Number 16. In S. McGregor (ed.), *Artificial Intelligence Incident Database*. Responsible AI Collaborative. *https:// web.archive.org/web/20220923193350/https://incidentdatabase.ai /cite/16*

Arendt, H. (1958). *The Human Condition*. University of Chicago Press.

Arora, P. (2016). Bottom of the data pyramid: Big data and the Global South. *International Journal of Communication*, 10: 1681–99.

Arvidsson, A. and Colleoni, E. (2012). Value in informational capital-ism and on the internet. *The Information Society*, 28 (3): 135–50. *https://doi.org/10.1080/01972243.2012.669449*

Ashwin, Agnew, W., Pajaro, J., and Subramonian, A. (2021). *Rebuilding Trust: Queer in AI Approach to Artificial Intelligence Risk Management*. Queer in AI. *https://www.researchgate.net/publication /355390924_Rebuilding_Trust_Queer_in_AI_Approach_to_Artific ial_Intelligence_Risk_Management*

Barbrook, R. and Cameron, A. (1996). The Californian ideology. *Science as Culture*, 6 (1): 44–72. *https://doi.org/10.1080/09505439 609526455*

Barocas, S., Hood, S., and Ziewitz, M. (2013). *Governing Algorithms: A Provocation Piece* (SSRN Scholarly Paper ID 2245322). Social Science Research Network. *https://papers.ssrn.com/abstract=224 5322*

Barthes, R. (1970). *Mythologies*. Seuil.

Bastani, A. (2019). *Fully Automated Luxury Communism: A Manifesto*. Verso.

Baudrillard, J. (1994). *Simulacra and Simulation*. University of Michigan Press.

Baudrillard, J. (2005). *The Intelligence of Evil or the Lucidity Pact* (English edn). Berg.

ben-Aaron, D. (1985). Weizenbaum examines computers and society. *The Tech*. *https://web.archive.org/web/20220906173446/http://tech.mit.edu/V105/N16/weisen.16n.html*

Beniger, J. (1986). *The Control Revolution*. Harvard University Press. *http://books.google.se/books?id=eUEKB-CMkIkC&printsec=frontcover&dq=intitle:The+control+revolution+Technological+and+economic+origins+of+the+information+society&hl=&cd=1&source=gbs_api*

Benjamin, R. (2019). *Race After Technology: Abolitionist Tools for the New Jim Code*. Polity.

Benjamin, W. (1999). *The Arcades Project*. Belknap Press.

Berger, P. L. and Luckmann, T. (1966). *The Social Construction of Reality: A Treatise in the Sociology of Knowledge*. Penguin.

Berman, B. J. (1992). Artificial intelligence and the ideology of capitalist reconstruction. *AI & Society*, 6 (2): 103–14. *https://doi.org/10.1007/BF02472776*

Bifo Berardi, F. (2011). *After the Future*. AK Press.

Bifo Berardi, F. (2017). *Futurability: The Age of Impotence and the Horizon of Possibility*. Verso.

Bijker, W. E. (1987). The social construction of bakelite: Toward a theory of invention. In W. E. Bijker, T. P. Hughes, and T. Pinch (eds), *The Social Construction of Technological Systems: New Directions in the Sociology and History of Technology* (pp. 155–82). MIT Press.

Billig, M. (1991). *Ideology and Opinions: Studies in Rhetorical Psychology*. SAGE.

Birhane, A. (2020). Fair warning. *Real Life*. *https://web.archive.org/web/20220913182353/https://reallifemag.com/fair-warning/*

Blanc, P., Caseau, Y., Petit, A., and Bézieux, G. R. de (2018). *L'Intelligence Artificielle expliquée à mon boss*. Editions Kawa.

Bloom, P. (2023). The danger of smart ideologies: Counter-hegemonic intelligence and antagonistic machines. In S. Lindgren (ed.), *The Handbook of Critical Studies of Artificial Intelligence*. Edward Elgar.

Bloomfield, B. P. (ed.) (1987). *The Question of Artificial Intelligence: Philosophical and Sociological Perspectives*. Croom Helm.

Boggs, C. (1984). *The Two Revolutions: Antonio Gramsci and the Dilemmas of Western Marxism*. South End Press.

Bogost, I. (2015). The problem with ketchup leather. *The Atlantic*. *https://web.archive.org/web/20151122053440/https://www.theatlantic.com/technology/archive/2015/11/burgers-arent-broken/416727/*

174 References

Bohman, J., Flynn, J., and Celikates, R. (2021). Critical theory. In E. N. Zalta (ed.), *Stanford Encyclopedia of Philosophy* (Spring 2021). Metaphysics Research Lab, Stanford University. *https://plato.stanfo rd.edu/archives/spr2021/entries/critical-theory/*

Borah, A. (2021, February 27). Word embeddings: How do organizations use them for building recommendation systems? *MLearning.ai. https://web.archive.org/web/20210228101417/https://medium.com /mlearning-ai/word-embeddings-how-do-organizations-use-them-for -building-recommendation-systems-e0341cf5e638*

Bostrom, N. (2016). *Superintelligence: Paths, Dangers, Strategies.* Oxford University Press.

Bourdieu, P. (1984). *Distinction: A Social Critique of the Judgement of Taste.* Routledge.

Bowles, S., Kirman, A., and Sethi, R. (2017). Retrospectives: Friedrich Hayek and the market algorithm. *Journal of Economic Perspectives,* 31 (3): 215–30. *https://doi.org/10.1257/jep.31.3.215*

Box, G. E. P. and Draper, N. R. (1987). *Empirical Model-Building and Response Surfaces.* Wiley.

boyd, danah and Crawford, K. (2012). Critical questions for big data. *Information, Communication & Society,* 15 (5): 662–79. *https://doi .org/10.1080/1369118X.2012.678878*

Brevini, B. (2020). Black boxes, not green: Mythologizing artificial intelligence and omitting the environment. *Big Data & Society,* 7 (2): 2053951720935141.

Brevini, B. (2022). *Is AI Good for the Planet?* Polity.

Bridle, J. (2018). *New Dark Age: Technology and the End of the Future.* Verso.

Bronner, S. E. (2017). *Critical Theory: A Very Short Introduction.* Oxford University Press.

Broussard, M. (2018). *Artificial Unintelligence: How Computers Misunderstand the World.* MIT Press.

Broussard, M. (2021). Meredith Broussard: Libertarianism & AI. *YouTube: Carnegie Council for Ethics in International Affairs. https://www.youtube.com/watch?v=mzGCeLP2eYU*

Brown, S., Davidovic, J., and Hasan, A. (2021). The algorithm audit: Scoring the algorithms that score us. *Big Data & Society,* 8 (1): 2053951720983865. *https://doi.org/10.1177/2053951720983 865*

Brown, T., Mann, B., Ryder, N., Subbiah, M., Kaplan, J. D., Dhariwal, P., Neelakantan, A., Shyam, P., Sastry, G., and Askell, A. (2020). Language models are few-shot learners. *Advances in Neural Information Processing Systems,* 33: 1877–1901.

Bruns, A. (2008). *Blogs, Wikipedia, Second Life, and Beyond: From Production to Produsage.* Peter Lang.

Brustein, J. (2019). Warehouses are tracking workers' every muscle movement. *Bloomberg.com*. *https://web.archive.org/web/20210802 212647/https://finance-commerce.com/2019/11/warehouses-are-trac king-workers-every-move/*

Brynjolfsson, E. and McAfee, A. (2016). *The Second Machine Age: Work, Progress, and Prosperity in a Time of Brilliant Technologies*. W. W. Norton & Company.

Brynjolfsson, E. and McAfee, A. (2017). Artificial intelligence, for real. *Harvard Business Review*. *https://web.archive.org/web/202209032 13103/https://hbr.org/2017/07/the-business-of-artificial-intelligence*

Bryson, Joanna J. (2015). Artificial intelligence and pro-social behaviour. In *Collective Agency and Cooperation in Natural and Artificial Systems: Explanation, Implementation and Simulation*, Philosophical Studies Series, ed. Catrin Misselhorn. Cham: Springer International Publishing, 281–306. *https://doi.org/10.1007/978-3-319-15515 -9_15*

Buchanan, I. (2010). *A Dictionary of Critical Theory*. Oxford University Press.

Buchanan, I. (2021). *Assemblage Theory and Method*. Bloomsbury Academic.

Buolamwini, J. and Gebru, T. (2018). Gender shades: Intersectional accuracy disparities in commercial gender classification. *Conference on Fairness, Accountability and Transparency*, 77–91.

Burgess, J. and Baym, N. (2020). *Twitter: A Biography*. NYU Press.

Burr, V. (2015). *Social Constructionism*. Routledge.

Butler, J. (1990). *Gender Trouble: Feminism and the Subversion of Identity*. Routledge.

Butler, J. (1997). *The Psychic Life of Power: Theories in Subjection*. Stanford University Press. *https://doi.org/10.1515/9781503616295*

Butler, J. (2019). The inorganic body in the early Marx: A limit-concept of anthropocentrism. *Radical Philosophy*, 206: 3–17. *https://www .radicalphilosophy.com/article/the-inorganic-body-in-the-early-marx*

Caliskan, A. (2021). *Detecting and Mitigating Bias in Natural Language Processing*. Brookings Institution.

Caliskan, A., Bryson, J. J., and Narayanan, A. (2017). Semantics derived automatically from language corpora contain human-like biases. *Science*, 356 (6334): 183–6. *https://doi.org/10.1126/science.aal4230*

Cameron, D. (ed.) (1998). *The Feminist Critique of Language: A Reader* (2nd edn). Routledge.

Campbell, I. C. (2021). SoftBank has reportedly halted production of its Pepper robot. *The Verge*. *https://web.archive.org/web/2021120207 3221/https://www.theverge.com/2021/6/28/22554566/softbank-pep per-robot-production-layoffs-robotics*

Canhoto, A. (2020). AI is a system, not a technology. *Anacanhoto.com*.

https://web.archive.org/web/20220124041219/https://anacanhoto
.com/2020/02/28/ai-is-a-system-not-a-technology/

Carey, J. W. (1990). Technology as a totem for culture: And a defense of the oral tradition. *American Journalism*, 7 (4): 242–51.

Carey, J. W. (2009). *Communication as Culture: Essays on Media and Society* (revd edn). Routledge.

Casilli, A. A. (2021). Waiting for robots: The ever-elusive myth of automation and the global exploitation of digital labor. *Sociologias*, 23(57): 112–33. *https://doi.org/10.1590/15174522-114092*

Castells, M. (1996). *The Rise of the Network Society*. Blackwell.

Castells, M. (2010). *End of Millennium* (2nd edn, with new preface). Blackwell.

Castelvecchi, D. (2016). Can we open the black box of AI? *Nature News*, 538(7623): 20. *https://doi.org/10.1038/538020a*

Celi, L. A., Cellini, J., Charpignon, M.-L., Dee, E. C., Dernoncourt, F., Eber, R., Mitchell, W. G., Moukheiber, L., Schirmer, J., Situ, J., Paguio, J., Park, J., Wawira, J. G., Yao, S., and Data, for M. C. (2022). Sources of bias in artificial intelligence that perpetuate healthcare disparities – A global review. *PLOS Digital Health*, 1 (3), e0000022. *https://doi.org/10.1371/journal.pdig.0000022*

Chace, C. (2015). *Surviving AI: The Promise and Peril of Artificial Intelligence*. Three Cs.

Chan, N. K. (2022). Algorithmic precarity and metric power: Managing the affective measures and customers in the gig economy. *Big Data & Society*, 9 (2). *https://doi.org/10.1177/20539517221133779*

Chang, W.-L., Šabanovic, S., and Huber, L. (2013). Use of seal-like robot PARO in sensory group therapy for older adults with dementia. *2013 8th ACM/IEEE International Conference on Human–Robot Interaction (HRI)*, 101–2. *https://doi.org/10.1109/HRI.2013.6483521*

Cheney-Lippold, J. (2011). A new algorithmic identity: Soft biopolitics and the modulation of control. *Theory, Culture & Society*, 28 (6): 164–81. *https://doi.org/10.1177/0263276411424420*

Cheng, J. Y. S. and Peiyu, Z. (2001). Hi-tech industries in Hong Kong and the Pearl River Delta. *Asian Survey*, 41 (4): 584–610. *https://doi.org/10.1525/as.2001.41.4.584*

Christie, N. and Ward, H. (2018). *The Emerging Issues for Management of Occupational Road Risk in a Changing Economy: A Survey of Gig Economy Drivers, Riders and their Managers*. UCL Centre for Transport Studies.

Chun, W. H. K. (2011). *Programmed Visions: Software and Memory*. MIT Press.

Clough, P. T. (2000). *Autoaffection: Unconscious Thought in the Age of Teletechnology*. University of Minnesota Press.

CNET (2021). *Elon Musk REVEALS Tesla Bot [Video]*. *https://web .archive.org/web/20210820132211/https://www.youtube.com/wat ch?v=HUP6Z5voiS8*

Coeckelbergh, M. (2020). *AI Ethics*. MIT Press.

Cohen, N. S. (2016). Cultural work as a site of struggle: Freelancers and exploitation. In C. Fuchs and V. Mosco (eds), *Marx and the Political Economy of the Media* (pp. 36–64). Brill.

Cohen, P. (2012). Gaydar study calibration. *Familyinequality.word press.com*. *https://web.archive.org/web/20220526024255/https://fa milyinequality.wordpress.com/2012/06/07/gaydar-study-calibration/*

Cohen, S. (1985). *Visions of Social Control: Crime, Punishment, and Classification*. Polity.

CommonCrawl (2022). *Common Crawl*. *https://commoncrawl.org/the-data/get-started/*

Cook, J. S. (2016). From Siri to sexbots. *Salon*. *https://web.archive.org /web/20221128131242/https://www.salon.com/2016/04/08/from_si ri_to_sexbots_female_ai_reinforces_a_toxic_desire_for_passive_agre eable_and_easily_dominated_women/*

Couldry, N. and Hepp, A. (2017). *The Mediated Construction of Reality*. Polity.

Couldry, N. and Mejias, U. (2019). *The Costs of Connection: How Data Is Colonizing Human Life and Appropriating it for Capitalism*. Stanford University Press.

Crawford, K. (2021). *Atlas of AI: Power, Politics, and the Planetary Costs of Artificial Intelligence*.

Crawford, K., Dobbe, R., Dryer, T., Fried, G., Green, B., Kaziunas, E., Kak, A., Mathur, V., McElroy, E., Sánchez, A. N., Raji, D., Lisi Rankin, J., Richardson, R., Schultz, J., Myers West, S., and Whittaker, M. (2019). *AI Now 2019 Report*. AI Now Institute.

Crawford, K. and Joler, V. (2018). Anatomy of an AI system: The Amazon Echo as an anatomical map of human labor, data and planetary resources. *AI Now Institute and Share Lab*. *https://web.archive .org/web/20221118205434/https://anatomyof.ai/*

Crenshaw, K. (1995). *Critical Race Theory: The Key Writings that Formed the Movement*. New Press.

Criado-Perez, C. (2021). *Invisible Women: Data Bias in a World Designed for Men*. Abrams Press.

Culkin, J. M. (1967). A schoolman's guide to Marshall McLuhan. *The Saturday Review*: 51–3, 70–2. *https://web.archive.org/web/202207 07193538/https://www.unz.com/print/SaturdayRev-1967mar18-00 051/*

D'Ignazio, C. and Klein, L. F. (2020). *Data Feminism*. MIT Press.

Dal Pont, J.-P. (2020). The enterprise and the plant of the future at the age of the transition to digital technology. In J.-P. Dal Pont and M. Debacq (eds), *Process Industries 2: Digitalization, a New Key Driver for Industrial Management* (pp. 129–206). Wiley.

Danaher, J. (2019). *Automation and Utopia: Human Flourishing in a World Without Work*. Harvard University Press.

Danielsson, K., Tubella, A. A., Liliequist, E., and Cocq, C. (2023). Queer Eye on AI: Binary systems versus fluid identities. In S. Lindgren (ed.), *The Handbook of Critical Studies of Artificial Intelligence*. Edward Elgar.

Dastin, J. (2022). Amazon scraps secret AI recruiting tool that showed bias against women*. In K. Martin (ed.), *Ethics of Data and Analytics*. Routledge.

Dauvergne, P. (2020). *AI in the Wild: Sustainability in the Age of Artificial Intelligence*. MIT Press.

Davies, J. (2019). Europe publishes stance on AI ethics, but don't expect much - Telecoms.com. *Telecoms.com*. *https://web.archive.org/web/20220726093328/https://telecoms.com/498190/europe-publishes-stance-on-ai-ethics-but-dont-expect-much/*

Davies, K. and Young, L. (2016). *The Breastmilk of the Volcano: Unknown Fields*. AA Publications.

Davis, G. (2022). Tesla Optimus as gift for old people? *Tech Times*. *https://web.archive.org/web/20220000000000*/https://www.techtimes.com/articles/279177/20220815/tesla-optimus-gift-old-people-elon-musk-talks-humanoid-bot.htm*

Davis, N. (2012). Subjected subjects? On Judith Butler's paradox of interpellation. *Hypatia*, 27 (4): 881–97.

de Groen, W. P., Kilhoffer, Z., Lenaerts, K., and Mandl, I. (2018). *Employment and Working Conditions of Selected Types of Platform Work*. Eurofound/Publications Office of the European Union. *https://www.eurofound.europa.eu/publications/report/2018/employment-and-working-conditions-of-selected-types-of-platform-work*

De Landa, M. (2016). *Assemblage Theory*. Edinburgh University Press.

DeepMind (2022). *Operating Principles*. *https://web.archive.org/web/20220922163806/https://www.deepmind.com/about/operating-principles*

Delanty, G. and Harris, N. (2021). Critical theory and the question of technology: The Frankfurt School revisited. *Thesis Eleven*, 166 (1): 88–108. *https://doi.org/10.1177/07255136211002055*

Deleuze, G. and Guattari, F. (1980). *A Thousand Plateaus: Capitalism and Schizophrenia*. University of Minnesota Press.

Deleuze, G. and Parnet, C. (2007). *Dialogues II*. Columbia University Press.

Derrida, J. (1976). *Of Grammatology*. Johns Hopkins University Press.

Devlin, K. (2018). *Turned On: The Science and Psychology of Sex Robots*. Zed Books.

Dignum, V. (2022). *Relational Artificial Intelligence* (No. arXiv:2202 .07446). arXiv. *https://doi.org/10.48550/arXiv.2202.07446*

Dignum, V. (2020). AI is multidisciplinary. *AI Matters*, 5 (4): 18–21. *https://doi.org/10.1145/3375637.3375644*

Dignum, V. (2019). *Responsible Artificial Intelligence: How to Develop and Use AI in a Responsible Way*. Springer.

Doran, D., Schulz, S., and Besold, T. R. (2017). *What Does Explainable AI Really Mean? A New Conceptualization of Perspectives. https:// arxiv.org/abs/1710.00794*

Döring, N. (2020). Sex dolls and sex robots. In A. D. Lykins (ed.), *Encyclopedia of Sexuality and Gender* (pp. 1–7). Springer. *https://doi .org/10.1007/978-3-319-59531-3_63-2*

Druin, A. (1999). *Cooperative Inquiry: Developing New Technologies for Children with Children*. 592–9. *https://doi.org/10.1145/302979 .303166*

Durkheim, É. (1912). *The Elementary Forms of Religious Life*. Free Press.

Easthope, A. and McGowan, K. (2004). *A Critical and Cultural Theory Reader*. Open University Press.

Eckles, D., Wightman, D., Carlson, C., Thamrongrattanarit, A., Bastea-Forte, M., and Fogg, B. J. (2009). Social responses in mobile messaging: Influence strategies, self-disclosure, and source orientation. *Proceedings of the SIGCHI Conference on Human Factors in Computing Systems*: 1651–4.

Edgerton, D. E. H. (2007). Creole technologies and global histories: Rethinking how things travel in space and time. *History of Science and Technology Journal*, 1 (1): 75–112.

Ehsan, U. and Riedl, M. O. (2022). *Social Construction of XAI: Do We Need One Definition to Rule Them All?* (No. arXiv:2211.06499). arXiv. *https://doi.org/10.48550/arXiv.2211.06499*

Ekbia, H. R. and Nardi, B. (2017). *Heteromation, and Other Stories of Computing and Capitalism*. MIT Press.

Elish, M. C. and boyd, danah. (2018). Situating methods in the magic of Big Data and AI. *Communication Monographs*, 85 (1): 57–80. *https://doi.org/10.1080/03637751.2017.1375130*

Elliott, A. (2022). *Making Sense of AI: Our Algorithmic World*. Polity.

Engels, F. (1893). *Engels to Franz Mehring. https://web.archive.org/web /20221016062825/https://www.marxists.org/archive/marx/works /1893/letters/93_07_14.htm*

Escudero Pérez, J. (2020). 'An AI doesn't need a gender' (but it's still assigned one): Paradigm shift of the artificially created woman in film. *Feminist Media Studies*, 20 (3): 325–40. *https://doi.org/10.10 80/14680777.2019.1615973*

Eubanks, V. (2017). *Automating Inequality: How High-Tech Tools Profile, Police, and Punish the Poor*. St Martin's Press.

European Commission (2022). *Proposal for a Regulation of the European Parliament and of the Council Laying down Harmonised Rules on Artificial Intelligence (Artificial Intelligence Act) and Amending Certain Union Legislative Acts*. Including Proposal (2021), Annexes (2021), and additions/changes (Nov. 2022).

Fairclough, N. (1995). *Media Discourse*. Arnold.

Feenberg, A. (1981). *Lukács, Marx and the Sources of Critical Theory*. Robertson.

Feenberg, A. (1991). *Critical Theory of Technology*. Oxford University Press.

Feenberg, A. (2017). The Internet and the end of dystopia. *Communiquer. Revue de Communication Sociale Et Publique*, 20: 77–84. *https://doi .org/10.4000/communiquer.2267*

Felluga, D. F. (2015). *Critical Theory: The Key Concepts*. Routledge, Taylor & Francis Group.

Felski, R. (2011). 'Context stinks!' *New Literary History*, 42 (4): 573–91. *https://doi.org/10.1353/nlh.2011.0045*

fetcher (2022). *Fetcher.ai*. *https://web.archive.org/web/202209281125 00/https://fetcher.ai/recruiting-automation/fetcher-recruiting-tool*

Fisher, E. (2023). AI, critical knowledge, and subjectivity. In S. Lindgren (ed.), *The Handbook of Critical Studies of Artificial Intelligence*. Edward Elgar.

Flanagan, M. (2002). Hyperbodies, hyperknowledge: Women in games, women in cyberpunk, and strategies of resistance. In M. Flanagan and A. Booth (eds), *Reload: Rethinking Women + Cyberculture* (pp. 425–54). MIT Press.

Floridi, L. (2017). The ethics of artificial intelligence. In D. Franklin (ed.), *Megatech: Technology in 2050* (pp. 155–63). The Economist Books, PublicAffairs.

Floridi, L. and Sanders, J. W. (2004). On the morality of artificial agents. *Minds and Machines*, 14 (3): 349–79. *https://doi.org/10.1023/B:MI ND.0000035461.63578.9d*

Foodora (2022). Become a foodora rider today! *Foodora.se*. *https:// web.archive.org/web/20221105091958/https://rider.foodora.se/*

Forgacs, D. (ed.). (2000). *The Gramsci Reader: Selected Writings, 1916–1935*. New York University Press.

Forsythe, D. E. (1993). Engineering knowledge: The construction of knowledge in artificial intelligence. *Social Studies of Science*, 23 (3): 445–77. *https://doi.org/10.1177/0306312793023003002*

Foucault, M. (1972–2000). *The Archaeology of Knowledge*. Routledge.

Foucault, M. (1977). *Discipline and Punish: The Birth of the Prison.* Pantheon Books.

Foucault, M. (1978). *The History of Sexuality. Volume 1: An Introduction.* Pantheon Books.

Foucault, M. (1980). *Power/Knowledge: Selected Interviews and Other Writings, 1972–1977* (C. Gordon, ed.). Pantheon Books.

Foucault, M. (2003). *Society Must Be Defended: Lectures at the Collège de France, 1975–1976.* Picador.

Frana, P. L. and Klein, M. J. (eds) (2021). *Encyclopedia of Artificial Intelligence: The Past, Present, and Future of AI.* ABC-CLIO.

Franklin, D. (ed.). (2017). *Megatech: Technology in 2050.* The Economist Books, PublicAffairs.

Friedman, D. P. and Wand, M. (1984). Reification: Reflection without metaphysics. *Proceedings of the 1984 ACM Symposium on LISP and Functional Programming*, 348–55.

Fuchs, C. (2019). *Marxism: Karl Marx's Fifteen Key Concepts for Cultural and Communication Studies* (1st edn). Routledge. https://doi.org/10.4324/9780367816759

Fuchs, C. (2022). *Foundations of Critical Theory: Media, Communication and Society Volume Two* (1st edn). Routledge. https://doi.org/10.43 24/9781003199182

Fuchs, C. and Sevignani, S. (2013). What is digital labour? What is digital work? What's their difference? And why do these questions matter for understanding social media? *tripleC*, 11 (2): 237–93.

Gagné, M., Parker, S. K., Griffin, M. A., Dunlop, P. D., Knight, C., Klonek, F. E., and Parent-Rocheleau, X. (2022). Understanding and shaping the future of work with self-determination theory. *Nature Reviews Psychology*, 2022 (1): 1–15.

Gandini, A. (2021). Digital labour: An empty signifier? *Media, Culture & Society*, 43 (2): 369–80. https://doi.org/10.1177/016344372094 8018

Gandy, O. H. (1993). *The Panoptic Sort: A Political Economy of Personal Information.* Westview Press. https://doi.org/10.1093/oso /9780197579411.001.0001

Garcia, M. (2016). Racist in the machine: The disturbing implications of algorithmic bias. *World Policy Journal*, 33 (4): 111–17. https:// www.jstor.org/stable/26781452

Garfinkel, H. (1967). *Studies in Ethnomethodology.* Prentice-Hall.

Gauntlett, D. (2018). *Making Is Connecting: The Social Power of Creativity, From Craft and Knitting to Digital Everything.* Polity.

Gehl, R. W. and Bakardjieva, M. (eds) (2017). *Socialbots and their Friends: Digital Media and the Automation of Sociality.* Routledge.

Gergen, K. J. (1985). The social constructionist movement in modern psychology. *American Psychologist*, 40 (3): 266–75.

Gershgorn, D. (2017). A Stanford scientist says he built a gaydar using 'the lamest' AI to prove a point. *Quartz*. *https://web.archive.org/web /20221028132119/http://qz.com/1078901/a-stanford-scientist-says -he-built-a-gaydar-using-the-lamest-ai-to-prove-a-point*

Gilbert, G. N. and Mulkay, M. (1984). *Opening Pandora's Box: A Sociological Analysis of Scientists' Discourse*. Cambridge University Press. *https://www.jstor.org/stable/2070471*

Gillespie, T. (2016). Algorithm. In B. Peters (ed.), *Digital Keywords: A Vocabulary of Information Society and Culture* (pp. 18–30). Princeton University Press.

Glasgow, D. (2021). Redefining what a map can be with new information and AI. *Google Blog*. *https://web.archive.org/web/2022092917 0104/https://www.blog.google/products/maps/redefining-what-map -can-be-new-information-and-ai/*

Good, I. J. (1965). Speculations concerning the first ultraintelligent machine. In *Advances in Computers: Volume 6* (pp. 31–88). Academic Press.

Goodman, E. and Trehu, J. (2022). AI audit-washing and accountability. *GMF*. *https://web.archive.org/web/2022112714 5556/https://www.gmfus.org/news/ai-audit-washing-and-accounta bility*

Goodwin, T. (2015). The battle is for the customer interface. *TechCrunch*. *https://techcrunch.com/2015/03/03/in-the-age-of-disintermediation -the-battle-is-all-for-the-customer-interface/*

Gramsci, A. (1971). *Selections from the Prison Notebooks of Antonio Gramsci*. Lawrence and Wishart.

Gray, J. and Witt, A. (2021). A feminist data ethics of care for machine learning: The what, why, who and how. *First Monday*. *https://doi .org/10.5210/fm.v26i12.11833*

Gray, M. L. (2015). The paradox of automation's 'last mile'. *Social Media Collective*. *https://web.archive.org/web/20220524094409 /https://socialmediacollective.org/2015/11/12/the-paradox-of-autom ations-last-mile/*

Gray, M. L. and Suri, S. (2019). *Ghost Work: How to Stop Silicon Valley from Building a New Global Underclass*. Houghton Mifflin Harcourt.

Gunkel, D. J. (2012). *The Machine Question: Critical Perspectives on AI, Robots, and Ethics*. MIT Press.

Gunkel, D. J. (2020). Perspectives on ethics of AI: Philosophy. In M. D. Dubber, F. Pasquale, and S. Das (eds), *The Oxford Handbook of Ethics of AI*. Oxford University Press. *https://doi.org/10.1093/oxfor dhb/9780190067397.013.35*

Guzman, A. (2017). Making AI safe for humans: A conversation with Siri. In R. W. Gehl and M. Bakardjieva (eds), *Socialbots and Their*

Friends: Digital Media and the Automation of Sociality (pp. 69–85). Routledge.

Guzman, A. L. (2019). Voices in and of the machine: Source orientation toward mobile virtual assistants. *Computers in Human Behavior*, 90: 343–50. *https://doi.org/10.1016/j.chb.2018.08.009*

Haataja, M. and Bryson, J. (2022). Reflections on the EU's AI act and how we could make it even better. *TechREG™ Chronicle*. *https:// www.competitionpolicyinternational.com/reflections-on-the-eus-ai -act-and-how-we-could-make-it-even-better/*

Habermas, J. (2004). Discourse ethics. In H. J. Gensler, E. W. Spurgin, and J. Swindal (eds), *Ethics: Contemporary Readings* (pp. 144–52). Routledge.

Halberstam, J. (2005). *In a Queer Time and Place: Transgender Bodies, Subcultural Lives*. New York University Press. *http://www.loc.gov /catdir/toc/ecip0422/2004018151.html*

Hale, T. (2022). Musk reveals 'Optimus' Tesla robot, but some folks aren't impressed. *IFL Science*. *https://web.archive.org/web/ 20221003133350/https://iflscience.com/musk-reveals-optimus-tesla- robot-but-some-folks-aren-t-impressed-65568*

Hall, S. (1997a). Introduction. In S. Hall (ed.), *Representation: Cultural Representations and Signifying Practices* (pp. 1–11). SAGE.

Hall, S. (1997b). *Representation: Cultural Representations and Signifying Practices*. SAGE. *http://www.loc.gov/catdir/enhancements /fy0656/96071228-d.html*

Hall, S. (1997c). The spectacle of the 'other'. In S. Hall (ed.), *Representation: Cultural Representations and Signifying Practices* (pp. 223–78). SAGE.

Hall, S. (1997d). The work of representation. In S. Hall (ed.), *Representation: Cultural Representations and Signifying Practices* (pp. 13–64). SAGE.

Hall, S. (2001). Foucault: Power, knowledge and discourse. In M. Wetherell, S. Yates, and S. Taylor (eds), *Discourse Theory and Practice: A Reader* (pp. 72–81). SAGE.

Hall, S. and Gieben, B. (eds). (1992). *Formations of Modernity*. Polity.

Hao, K. (2020). We read the paper that forced Timnit Gebru out of Google. Here's what it says. *MIT Technology Review*. *https://web .archive.org/web/20201206020606/https://www.technologyreview .com/2020/12/04/1013294/google-ai-ethics-research-paper-forced -out-timnit-gebru/*

Hao, K. and Freischlad, N. (2022). The gig workers fighting back against the algorithms. *MIT Technology Review*. *https://web.archive .org/web/20220920055736/https://www.technologyreview.com/20 22/04/21/1050381/the-gig-workers-fighting-back-against-the-algori thms/*

Haraway, D. (1985). A manifesto for cyborgs. *Socialist Review*, 80: 65–107. *https://monoskop.org/images/4/4c/Haraway_Donna_19 85_A_Manifesto_for_Cyborgs_Science_Technology_and_Socialist _Feminism_in_the_1980s.pdf*

Harvey, D. (2004). The 'new' Imperialism: Accumulation by dispossession. *Socialist Register*, 40: 63–86.

Heidegger, M. (1962). *Being and Time*. Blackwell.

Heikkilä, M. (2022). Responsible AI has a burnout problem. *MIT Technology Review*. *https://web.archive.org/web/20221124070144 /https://www.technologyreview.com/2022/10/28/1062332/respons ible-ai-has-a-burnout-problem/*

Hellemans, P. (2020). Hidden stratification and the accuracy principle: May positive discrimination in AI be a solution? *CITIP Blog*. *https:// www.law.kuleuven.be/citip/blog/hidden-stratification-and-the-accu racy-principle-may-positive-discrimination-in-ai-be-a-solution/*

Higgins, M. (2021). Amazon introduces bio-surveillance for employees. *NordVPN Blog*. *https://nordvpn.com/blog/amazon-employee-surveil lance/*

Hintz, A., Dencik, L., and Wahl-Jorgensen, K. (2019). *Digital citizenship in a datafied society*. Polity.

Ho, S. Y., Wong, L., and Goh, W. W. B. (2020). Avoid oversimplifications in machine learning: Going beyond the class-prediction accuracy. *Patterns*, 1 (2): 100025. *https://doi.org/10.1016/j.patter.2020 .100025*

Hoffman, C. (2008). Now 0-for-3, SpaceX's Elon Musk Vows to Make Orbit. *WIRED*. *https://web.archive.org/web/2015110619 3046/https://www.wired.com/2008/08/musk-qa/*

Holstein, K., McLaren, B. M., and Aleven, V. (2019). Designing for complementarity: Teacher and student needs for orchestration support in AI-enhanced classrooms [Conference paper]. *Lecture Notes in Computer Science (Including Subseries Lecture Notes in Artificial Intelligence and Lecture Notes in Bioinformatics)*, 11625 LNAI, 157–71. *https://doi.org/10.1007/978-3-030-23204-7_14*

Horkheimer, M. (1972). *Critical Theory: Selected Essays*. Continuum.

Hutchinson, H., Mackay, W., Westerlund, B., Bederson, B. B., Druin, A., Plaisant, C., Beaudouin-Lafon, M., Conversy, S., Evans, H., Hansen, H., Roussel, N., Eiderbäck, B., Lindquist, S., and Sundblad, Y. (2003). *Technology Probes: Inspiring Design for and with Families* (pp. 17–24). *https://www.scopus.com/inward/record.uri?eid=2-s2 .0-0037699665&partnerID=40&md5=327e3f1e6a5cf282f8765610 cee067de*

IBM (2022). *How AI is Changing Advertising | IBM Watson Advertising Thought Leadership*. *https://web.archive.org/web/20220930084022*

/https://www.ibm.com/watson-advertising/thought-leadership/how
-ai-is-changing-advertising

Ingram Bogusz, C. (2018). Digital trace data: Which data should we
collect and what should we do once we have it? In P. Andersson,
S. Movin, M. Mähring, R. Teigland, K. Wennberg, and K. McGettigan
(eds), *Managing Digital Transformation*. SSE Institute for Research,
Stockholm School of Economics.

Introna, L. D. (2016). Algorithms, governance, and governmentality:
On governing academic writing. *Science, Technology, & Human
Values*, 41 (1): 17–49. *https://doi.org/10.1177/0162243915587360*

Jarrahi, M. H. and Sutherland, W. (2019). Algorithmic management
and algorithmic competencies: Understanding and appropriating algorithms in gig work. In N. G. Taylor, C. Christian-Lamb,
M. H. Martin, and B. Nardi (eds), *Information in Contemporary
Society* (pp. 578–89). Springer.

Jarrett, K. (2016). *Feminism, Labour and Digital Media: The Digital
Housewife*. Routledge.

Jeffries, S. (2016). *Grand Hotel Abyss: The Lives of the Frankfurt
School*. Verso.

Johnson, C. Y. (2019). Racial bias in a medical algorithm favors white
patients over sicker black patients. *Washington Post. https://web.ar
chive.org/web/20221119041503/https://www.washingtonpost.com
/health/2019/10/24/racial-bias-medical-algorithm-favors-white-pati
ents-over-sicker-black-patients/*

Johnson, D. G. and Miller, K. W. (2008). Un-making artificial moral
agents. *Ethics and Information Technology*, 10 (2–3): 123–33.
https://doi.org/10.1007/s10676-008-9174-6

Jordan, T. and Taylor, P. (2004). *Hacktivism and Cyberwars: Rebels
with a Cause?* Routledge. *https://doi.org/10.4324/9780203490037*

Jouët, J. (2000). Retour critique sur la sociologie des usages. *Réseaux.
Communication-Technologie-Société*, 18 (100): 487–521.

Kana, M. (2021, September 1). Word embeddings in AI. *Geek Culture.
https://medium.com/geekculture/word-embeddings-in-ai-10a9e430
cb59*

Kaspersen, Anja and Wendell Wallach (2022). 'Long-Termism: An
Ethical Trojan Horse'. *Carnegie Council for Ethics in International
Affairs. https://www.carnegiecouncil.org/media/article/long-termism
-ethical-trojan-horse*

Katan, S., Grierson, M., and Fiebrink, R. (2015). Using interactive
machine learning to support interface development through work-
shops with disabled people [Conference paper]. *2015-April*, 251–4.
https://doi.org/10.1145/2702123.2702474

Katyal, S. K. and Jung, J. Y. (2021). The gender panopticon: AI, gender
and design justice. *UCLA Law Review*, 68(3): 692–785.

Katz, Y. (2020). *Artificial Whiteness: Politics and Ideology in Artificial Intelligence.* Columbia University Press.

Kearns, M. and Roth, A. (2020). *The Ethical Algorithm: The Science of Socially Aware Algorithm Design.* Oxford University Press.

Keyes, O. (2018). The misgendering machines: Trans/HCI implications of automatic gender recognition. *Proceedings of the ACM on Human–Computer Interaction,* 2, 1–22.

Kittler, F. (1996). The history of communication media. *CTheory.* *https://web.archive.org/web/20051215025531/http://www.ctheory.net/articles.aspx?id=45*

Kleinberg, J., Ludwig, J., Mullainathan, S., and Rambachan, A. (2018). Algorithmic fairness. *AEA Papers and Proceedings,* 108: 22–7. *https://doi.org/10.1257/pandp.20181018*

Knee, C. (1985). The hidden curriculum of the computer. In T. Solomonides and L. Levidow (eds), *Compulsive Technology: Computers as Culture* (pp. 116–25). Free Association Books.

Knotter, A. (2018). *Transformations of Trade Unionism: Comparative and Transnational Perspectives on Workers Organizing in Europe and the United States, Eighteenth to Twenty-First Centuries.* Amsterdam University Press.

Korn, J. U. (2021). Connecting race to ethics related to technology: A call for critical tech ethics. *Journal of Social Computing,* 2 (4): 357–64. *https://doi.org/10.23919/JSC.2021.0026*

Korteling, J. E. (Hans), van de Boer-Visschedijk, G. C., Blankendaal, R. A. M., Boonekamp, R. C., and Eikelboom, A. R. (2021). Human-versus artificial intelligence. *Frontiers in Artificial Intelligence,* 4, 622364. *https://doi.org/10.3389/frai.2021.622364*

Korzybski, A. (1931). A non-Aristotelian system and its necessity for rigour in mathematics and physics. In A. Korzybski, *Science and Sanity: An Introduction to Non-Aristotelian Systems and General Semantics* (pp. 747–61). International Non-Aristotelian Library Publ. House.

Kranzberg, M. (1986). Technology and history: 'Kranzberg's laws'. *Technology and Culture,* 27 (3): 544–60. *https://doi.org/10.2307/3105385*

Kreps, G. L. and Neuhauser, L. (2010). New directions in eHealth communication: Opportunities and challenges. *Patient Education and Counseling,* 78 (3): 329–36. *https://doi.org/10.1016/j.pec.2010.01.013*

Kreps, G. L. and Neuhauser, L. (2013). Artificial intelligence and immediacy: Designing health communication to personally engage consumers and providers [Article]. *Patient Education and Counseling,* 92 (2): 205–10. *https://doi.org/10.1016/j.pec.2013.04.014*

Kristeva, J. (1980). *Desire in Language: A Semiotic Approach to Literature and Art.* Columbia University Press.

Kücklich, J. R. (2005). Precarious playbour: Modders and the digital games industry. *The Fibreculture Journal*, 5.

Kunzru, H. (1997). You are cyborg. *Wired*. *https://web.archive.org/web /20221007105343/https://www.wired.com/1997/02/ffharaway/*

Kurzweil, R. (2005). *The Singularity Is Near: When Humans Transcend Biology*. Penguin.

Laclau, E. (1996). *Emancipation(s)*. Verso.

Laclau, E. and Mouffe, C. (1985). *Hegemony and Socialist Strategy: Towards a Radical Democratic Politics*. Verso.

Lagerkvist, A. (2020). Digital limit situations: Anticipatory media beyond 'The new AI era'. *Journal of Digital Social Research*, 2 (3), 16–41. *https://doi.org/10.33621/jdsr.v2i3.55*

Lanier, J. (2010). *You Are Not a Gadget: A Manifesto*. Allen Lane.

Lanier, J. (2018). *Ten Arguments for Deleting Your Social Media Accounts Right Now*. The Bodley Head.

Lanier, J. and Weyl, G. (2020). AI is an ideology, not a technology. *WIRED*. *https://web.archive.org/web/20200315164344/https:// www.wired.com/story/opinion-ai-is-an-ideology-not-a-technology/*

Larson, E. J. (2021). *The Myth of Artificial Intelligence: Why Computers Can't Think the Way We Do*. The Belknap Press of Harvard University Press.

Latour, B. (1999). *Pandora's Hope: Essays on the Reality of Science Studies*. Harvard University Press.

Latour, B. (2004). Why has critique run out of steam? From matters of fact to matters of concern. *Critical Inquiry*, 30 (2): 225–48.

Latour, B. (2005). *Reassembling the Social: An Introduction to Actor-Network-Theory*. Oxford University Press.

Latzko-Toth, G. (2014). Users as co-designers of software-based media: The co-construction of internet relay chat. *Canadian Journal of Communication*, 39 (4): 577–95. *https://doi.org/10.22230/cjc.2014 v39n4a2783*

Lazar, M. M. (ed.). (2005). *Feminist Critical Discourse Analysis: Gender, Power, and Ideology in Discourse*. Palgrave Macmillan.

Ledford, H. (2019). Millions of black people affected by racial bias in health-care algorithms. *Nature*, 574 (7780): 608–9. *https://doi.org /10.1038/d41586-019-03228-6*

Lee, D. (2018). Why Big Tech pays poor Kenyans to teach self-driving cars. *BBC News*. *https://web.archive.org/web/2022092 7041744/https://www.bbc.com/news/technology-46055595*

Lee, M. H. (2020). *How to Grow a Robot: Developing Human-Friendly, Social AI*. MIT Press.

Lehnis, M. (2018). Can we trust AI if we don't know how it works? *BBC News*. *https://web.archive.org/web/20220714080442/https:// www.bbc.com/news/business-44466213*

Lem, S. (1964). *Summa Technologiae*. University of Minnesota Press.

Leong, B. (2021). General and narrow AI. In P. L. Frana and M. J. Klein (eds), *Encyclopedia of Artificial Intelligence: The Past, Present, and Future of AI* (pp. 160–2). ABC–CLIO.

Lesala Khethisa, B., Tsibolane, P., and van Belle, J.-P. (2020). Surviving the gig economy in the Global South: How Cape Town domestic workers cope. In R. K. Bandi, R. C. R., S. Klein, S. Madon, and E. Monteiro (eds), *The Future of Digital Work: The Challenge of Inequality* (pp. 67–85). Springer. *https://doi.org/10.1007/978-3-030 -64697-4_7*

Leufer, D. (2020). Why we need to bust some myths about AI. *Patterns*, 1 (7): 100124. *https://doi.org/10.1016/j.patter.2020.100124*

Leufer, D. (2021). How AI systems undermine LGBTQ identity. *Access Now*. *https://www.accessnow.org/how-ai-systems-undermine-lgbtq -identity/*

Levin, I. (1972). *The Stepford Wives*. Bloomsbury.

Lévi-Strauss, C. (1955). The structural study of myth. *Journal of American Folklore*, 68 (270): 428–44. *https://doi.org/10.2307/53 6768*

Lévi-Strauss, C. (1966). *The Savage Mind*. Weidenfeld & Nicolson.

Li, H. (2019). Special section introduction: Artificial intelligence and advertising. *Journal of Advertising*, 48 (4): 333–7. *https://doi.org/10 .1080/00913367.2019.1654947*

Liebowitz, J. (2001). Knowledge management and its link to artificial intelligence. *Expert Systems with Applications*, 20 (1): 1–6.

Lindgren, S. (2020). *Data Theory: Interpretive Sociology and Computational Methods*. Polity.

Lindgren, S. (2022). *Digital Media and Society* (2nd edn). SAGE.

Lindgren, S. (ed.). (2023). *The Handbook of Critical Studies of Artificial Intelligence*. Edward Elgar.

Lindgren, S. and Holmström, J. (2020). A social science perspective on artificial intelligence: Building blocks for a research agenda. *Journal of Digital Social Research*, 2 (3).

Liu, Z. and Zheng, Y. (2022). *AI Ethics and Governance*. Springer.

Loi, D., Lodato, T., Wolf, C. T., Arar, R. and Blomberg, J. (2018). PD manifesto for AI futures [Conference paper]. *2*. *https://doi.org/10.11 45/3210604.3210614*

Lomas, N. (2021). Italian court rules against 'discriminatory' Deliveroo rider-ranking algorithm. *TechCrunch*. *https://techcrunch.com/2021 /01/04/italian-court-rules-against-discriminatory-deliveroo-rider-ran king-algorithm/*

Lovink, G. (2002). *Dark Fiber: Tracking Critical Internet Culture*. MIT Press.

Lukács, G. (1971). *History and Class Consciousness: Studies in Marxist Dialectics*. Merlin.

Lyotard, J. F. (1984). *The Postmodern Condition*. Manchester University Press. *http://scholar.google.com/scholar?q=related:-HZoSJIfnAsJ:sc holar.google.com/&hl=en&as_sdt=0,5*

Mac, R. (2021). Facebook apologizes after A.I. puts 'primates' label on video of black men. *New York Times*. *https://web.archive.org/web /20221203181006/https://www.nytimes.com/2021/09/03/technolo gy/facebook-ai-race-primates.html*

McBride, S. (2018). Silicon Valley's singularity university has some serious reality problems. *Bloomberg.com*. *https://web.archive.org/web /20180216054536/https://www.bloomberg.com/news/articles/2018 -02-15/silicon-valley-s-singularity-university-has-some-serious-reali ty-problems*

McCallum, S. (2022). Tesla boss Elon Musk presents humanoid robot Optimus. *BBC News*. *https://web.archive.org/web/202210011814 41/https://www.bbc.com/news/technology-63100636*

McCarthy, J., Minsky, M. L., Rochester, N., and Shannon, C. E. (2006). A proposal for the Dartmouth Summer Research Project on Artificial Intelligence, August 31, 1955. *AI Magazine*, 27 (4): 12–22.

MacKenzie, D. A. and Wajcman, J. (eds) (1985). *The Social Shaping of Technology: How the Refrigerator Got Its Hum*. Open University Press.

McLuhan, M. (1964). *Understanding Media: The Extensions of Man*. MIT Press.

McQuillan, D. (2021). Post-humanism, mutual aid. In P. Verdegem (ed.), *AI for Everyone? Critical Perspectives* (pp. 67–83). University of Westminster Press.

McQuillan, D. (2022). *Resisting AI: An Anti-Fascist Approach to Artificial Intelligence*.

Mager, A. (2012). Algorithmic ideology. *Information, Communication & Society*, 15 (5): 769–87. *https://doi.org/10.1080/1369118X.2012 .676056*

Makortoff, K. (2022). 'Risks posed by AI are real': EU moves to beat the algorithms that ruin lives. *Guardian*. *https://web.archive.org/web/20 221108121506/https://www.theguardian.com/technology/2022/aug /07/ai-eu-moves-to-beat-the-algorithms-that-ruin-lives*

Mannheim, K. (1954). *Ideology and Utopia: An Introduction to the Sociology of Knowledge*. Routledge & Kegan Paul.

Marcus, Gary (2023). 'GPT-5 and Irrational Exuberance'. *The Road to AI We Can Trust*. *https://garymarcus.substack.com/p/gpt-5-and-ir rational-exuberance*

Marcuse, H. (1941). Some social implications of modern technology. In *Technology, War and Fascism (1998)* (pp. 41–65). Routledge.

Marcuse, H. (1964). *One-Dimensional Man: Studies in the Ideology of Advanced Industrial Society*. Routledge.

Marks, R. J. (2022). *Non-Computable You: What You Do That Artificial Intelligence Never Will*. Discovery Institute.

Marx, K. (1904). *A Contribution to the Critique of Political Economy*. Charles H. Kerr & Company.

Marx, K. (1906). *Capital: A Critique of Political Economy*. Random House.

Marx, K. (1932). *Economic and Philosophic Manuscripts of 1844*. Progress.

Marx, K. (1937). *The Eighteenth Brumaire of Louis Bonaparte*. Progress.

Marx, K. (1976). *Capital: A Critique of Political Economy. Vol. 1*. Penguin.

Marx, K. and Engels, F. (1998). *The German Ideology: Including Theses on Feuerbach and Introduction to The Critique of Political Economy*. Prometheus Books.

Mason, E. S. (1931). Saint-Simonism and the rationalisation of industry. *Quarterly Journal of Economics*, 45 (4): 640–83.

Mateescu, A. and Elish, M. (2019). *AI in Context: The Labor of Integrating New Technologies*. Data and Society Research Institute. *https://apo.org.au/node/217456*

Mattson, G. (2017). AI can't tell if you're gay . . . but it can tell if you're a walking stereotype. *Scatterplot*. *https://web.archive.org/web/20220526144634/https://scatter.wordpress.com/2017/09/10/guest-post-artificial-intelligence-discovers-gayface-sigh/*

Mayor, A. (2018). *Gods and Robots: Myths, Machines, and Ancient Dreams of Technology*. Princeton University Press.

Metcalfe, J. S., Perelman, B. S., Boothe, D. L., and Mcdowell, K. (2021). Systemic oversimplification limits the potential for human–AI partnership. *IEEE Access*, 9, 70242–60. *https://doi.org/10.1109/ACCESS.2021.3078298*

Metzinger, T. (2019). EU guidelines: Ethics washing made in Europe. *Der Tagesspiegel Online*. *https://web.archive.org/web/20221005235038/https://www.tagesspiegel.de/politik/ethics-washing-made-in-europe-5937028.html*

Mhasawade, V., Zhao, Y., and Chunara, R. (2021). Machine learning and algorithmic fairness in public and population health. *Nature Machine Intelligence*, 3 (8): 659–66. *https://doi.org/10.1038/s42256-021-00373-4*

Mills, C. W. (1959). *The Sociological Imagination*. Oxford University Press.

Mims, C. (2021). Why artificial intelligence isn't intelligent. *Wall Street Journal*. *https://www.wsj.com/articles/why-artificial-intelligence-isnt-intelligent-11627704050*

Mohamed, S., Png, M.-T., and Isaac, W. (2020). Decolonial AI: Decolonial theory as sociotechnical foresight in artificial intelligence. *Philosophy & Technology*, 33 (4): 659–84. *https://doi.org/10.1007 /s13347-020-00405-8*

Möhlmann, M. and Henfridsson, O. (2019). What people hate about being managed by algorithms, according to a study of Uber drivers. *Harvard Business Review. https://hbr.org/2019/08/what-people-hate -about-being-managed-by-algorithms-according-to-a-study-of-uber -drivers*

Morozov, E. (2013). *To Save Everything, Click Here: The Folly of Technological Solutionism*. PublicAffairs.

Mortimer, T. (1801). *Lectures on the Elements of Commerce, Politics, and Finance*. T. N. Longman & O. Rees.

Mouffe, C. (1992). Feminism, citizenship, and radical democratic politics. In J. Butler and J. W. Scott (eds), *Feminists Theorize the Political* (pp. 369–84). Routledge.

Müller, V. C. (2021). Ethics of artificial intelligence and robotics. In E. N. Zalta (ed.), *Stanford Encyclopedia of Philosophy* (20th edn). Metaphysics Research Lab, Stanford University. *https://plato.stanfo rd.edu/archives/sum2021/entries/ethics-ai/*

Mullins, M. (2015). Are we postcritical? *Los Angeles Review of Books. https://web.archive.org/web/20220130231450/https://lareviewofboo ks.org/article/are-we-postcritical/*

Mulvey, L. (1989). *Visual and Other Pleasures*. Palgrave Macmillan. *https://doi.org/10.1007/978-1-349-19798-9*

Mumford, L. (1934). *Technics and Civilization*. Routledge & Kegan Paul.

Mumford, L. (1944). *The Condition of Man*. Harcourt Brace Jovanovich.

Munn, L. (2022). The uselessness of AI ethics. *AI and Ethics. https://doi .org/10.1007/s43681-022-00209-w*

Nardi, B. A. (ed.). (1996). *Context and Consciousness: Activity Theory and Human–Computer Interaction*. MIT Press.

Nass, C., Moon, Y., and Green, N. (1997). Are machines gender neutral? Gender-stereotypic responses to computers with voices. *Journal of Applied Social Psychology*, 27 (10): 864–76. *https://doi.org/10.11 11/j.1559-1816.1997.tb00275.x*

Nass, C., Steuer, J., and Tauber, E. R. (1994). Computers are social actors. *Proceedings of the SIGCHI Conference on Human Factors in Computing Systems*, 72–8.

Naudé, W. (2021). Artificial intelligence: Neither Utopian nor apocalyptic impacts soon. *Economics of Innovation and New Technology*, 30 (1): 1–23. *https://doi.org/10.1080/10438599.2020.1839173*

Neff, G. and Nagy, P. (2016). Talking to bots: Symbiotic agency and the case of Tay. *International Journal of Communication*, 10: 17. *https:// ijoc.org/index.php/ijoc/article/view/6277*

Newlands, G., Lutz, C., and Fieseler, C. (2018). Algorithmic management in the sharing economy. *Academy of Management Global Proceedings*, 2018: 130.

Newman, J. (2019). How human curation came back to clean up AI's messes. *Fast Company*. https://www.fastcompany.com/90402486/how-human-curation-came-back-to-clean-up-ais-messes

Nickelsburg, M. (2016). Why is AI female? How our ideas about sex and service influence the personalities we give machines. *GeekWire*. https://web.archive.org/web/20220904003746/https://www.geekwire.com/2016/why-is-ai-female-how-our-ideas-about-sex-and-service-influence-the-personalities-we-give-machines/

Noble, S. U. (2018). *Algorithms of Oppression: How Search Engines Reinforce Racism*. New York University Press.

Nosek, B. A., Banaji, M. R., and Greenwald, A. G. (2002). Math=male, me=female, therefore math ≠ me. *Journal of Personality and Social Psychology*, 83 (1): 44.

O'Neil, C. (2016). *Weapons of Math Destruction: How Big Data Increases Inequality and Threatens Democracy* (1st edn). Crown.

Oakden-Rayner, L., Dunnmon, J., Carneiro, G., and Ré, C. (2019). *Hidden Stratification Causes Clinically Meaningful Failures in Machine Learning for Medical Imaging* (No. arXiv:1909.12475). arXiv. http://arxiv.org/abs/1909.12475

Obermeyer, Z., Powers, B., Vogeli, C., and Mullainathan, S. (2019). Dissecting racial bias in an algorithm used to manage the health of populations. *Science*, 366 (6464): 447–53.

OpenAI (2022). About OpenAI. *OpenAI*. https://web.archive.org/web/20220903204710/https://openai.com/about/

Orlikowski, W. J. and Gash, D. C. (1994). Technological frames: Making sense of information technology in organizations. *ACM Transactions on Information Systems*, 12 (2): 174–207. https://doi.org/10.1145/196734.196745

Orwell, G. (1949). *1984*. Signet Classic.

Osborne, C. (2021). Google fires top ethical AI expert Margaret Mitchell. *ZDNET*. https://web.archive.org/web/20210222114831/https://www.zdnet.com/article/google-fires-top-ethical-ai-expert-margaret-mitchell/

Ossewaarde, M. and Gulenc, E. (2020). National varieties of artificial intelligence discourses: Myth, utopianism, and solutionism in west European policy expectations. *Computer*, 53 (11): 53–61. https://doi.org/10.1109/MC.2020.2992290

Ovide, S. (2020). The cult of the tech genius. *New York Times*. https://www.nytimes.com/2020/08/06/technology/the-cult-of-the-tech-genius.html

Panch, T., Mattie, H., and Atun, R. (2019). Artificial intelligence and algorithmic bias: Implications for health systems. *Journal of Global Health*, 9 (2): 020318. *https://doi.org/10.7189/jogh.09.020318*

Pandey, A. K. and Gelin, R. (2018). A mass-produced sociable humanoid robot: Pepper – The first machine of its kind. *IEEE Robotics & Automation Magazine*, 25 (3): 40–8.

Paquet, G. (2005). *The New Geo-Governance: A Baroque Approach*. University of Ottawa Press.

Parrott, J. and Reich, M. (2018). *An Earnings Standard for New York City's App-based Drivers: Economic Analysis and Policy Assessment*. The New School, Center for New York City Affairs.

Pasquale, F. (2015). *The Black Box Society: The Secret Algorithms That Control Money and Information*. Harvard University Press.

Pasquale, F. (2020). *New Laws of Robotics: Defending Human Expertise in the Age of AI*. Harvard University Press.

Penrose, Roger (2016). *The Emperor's New Mind: Concerning Computers, Minds and the Laws of Physics*. Oxford University Press.

Pinch, T. J. and Bijker, W. E. (1984). The social construction of facts and artefacts: Or how the sociology of science and the sociology of technology might benefit each other. *Social Studies of Science*, 14 (3): 399–441.

Pohl, F. (1955). The tunnel under the world. *Galaxy Science Fiction*, 9 (4): 6–47. *https://ia600201.us.archive.org/9/items/Galaxy_v09n04_1955-01/Galaxy_v09n04_1955-01.pdf*

Poonen, Bjorn (2014). 'Undecidable Problems: A Sampler'. http://arxiv.org/abs/1204.0299

Prakash, P. (2022). Elon Musk is getting ready to unleash an army of humanoid robots. Here's what he wants to use them for | Fortune. *https://web.archive.org/web/20220921083453/https://fortune.com/2022/09/20/elon-musk-humanoid-robots-optimus-what-he-wants-to-use-them-for/*

Provenir (2022). The Benefits of unified access to AI- + Data/ Provenir. powered decisioning *https://web.archive.org/web/20220517160459/https://www.provenir.com/resources/collateral/welcome-home-the-benefits-of-unified-access-to-ai-powered-decisioning-data/*

Qadri, R. (2020a). Algorithmized but not atomized? How digital platforms engender new forms of worker solidarity in Jakarta. *Proceedings of the AAAI/ACM Conference on AI, Ethics, and Society*, 144. *https://doi.org/10.1145/3375627.3375816*

Qadri, R. (2020b). Delivery platform algorithms don't work without drivers' deep local knowledge. *Slate*. *https://slate.com/technology/2020/12/gojek-grab-indonesia-delivery-platforms-algorithms.html*

Rachev, R. (2016). Assemblages: Assembling the unassembled. *New Materialism*. *https://web.archive.org/web/20221108055110/https:// newmaterialism.eu/almanac/a/assemblages.html*

Radford, A., Wu, J., Child, R., Luan, D., Amodei, D., and Sutskever, I. (2019). Language models are unsupervised multitask learners. *OpenAI Blog*, 1 (8): 9.

Rahwan, I. (2018). Society-in-the-loop: Programming the algorithmic social contract. *Ethics and Information Technology*, 20 (1): 5–14.

Rahwan, I., Cebrian, M., Obradovich, N., Bongard, J., Bonnefon, J.-F., Breazeal, C., Crandall, J. W., Christakis, N. A., Couzin, I. D. and Jackson, M. O. (2019). Machine behaviour. *Nature*, 568 (7753): 477–86.

Ramesh, A., Pavlov, M., Goh, G., Gray, S., Voss, C., Radford, A., Chen, M. and Sutskever, I. (2021). Zero-shot text-to-image generation. *International Conference on Machine Learning*, 8821–31.

Ravenelle, A. J. (2019). *Hustle and Gig: Struggling and Surviving in the Sharing Economy*. University of California Press.

Ricardo, D. (1821). *The Principles of Political Economy and Taxation*. John Murray.

Ricaurte, P. (2022). Ethics for the majority world: AI and the question of violence at scale. *Media, Culture & Society*, 01634437221099612.

Ricœur, P. (1970). *Freud and Philosophy: An Essay on Interpretation*. Yale University Press.

Rieder, B., Sileno, G., and Gordon, G. (2021). Monopolization: Concentrated power and economic embeddings in ML & AI. *A New AI Lexicon*. *https://web.archive.org/web/20220815031845/https:// medium.com/a-new-ai-lexicon/a-new-ai-lexicon-monopolization-c4 3f136981ab*

Roberge, J. and Castelle, M. (2021a). *The Cultural Life of Machine Learning: An Incursion into Critical AI Studies* (J. Roberge and M. Castelle, eds). Springer. *https://doi.org/10.1007/978-3-030-56286-1*

Roberge, J. and Castelle, M. (eds) (2021b). Toward an end-to-end sociology of 21st-century machine learning. In *The Cultural Life of Machine Learning: An Incursion into Critical AI Studies* (pp. 1–29). Springer. *https://doi.org/10.1007/978-3-030-56286-1*

Roberts, B. and Bassett, C. (2023). Automation anxiety: A critical history. In S. Lindgren (ed.), *The Handbook of Critical Studies of Artificial Intelligence*. Edward Elgar.

Roberts, S. T. (2019). *Behind the Screen: Content Moderation In the Shadows of Social Media*. Yale University Press.

Robins, K. and Webster, F. (1988). Cybernetic capitalism: Information, technology, everyday life. In V. Mosco and J. Wasko (eds), *The Political Economy of Information* (pp. 44–75). University of Wisconsin Press.

Rombach, R., Blattmann, A., Lorenz, D., Esser, P., and Ommer, B. (2022). High-resolution image synthesis with latent diffusion models. *Proceedings of the IEEE/CVF Conference on Computer Vision and Pattern Recognition*, 10684–95.

Romero, A. (2021). GPT-4 will have 100 trillion parameters – 500 x the Size of GPT-3. *Medium. https://towardsdatascience.com/gpt-4-will-have-100-trillion-parameters-500x-the-size-of-gpt-3-582b98d82253*

Roszak, T. (1986). *The Cult of Information: The Folklore of Computers and the True Art of Thinking*. Pantheon.

Sadowski, J. (2020). *Too Smart: How Digital Capitalism is Extracting Data, Controlling our Lives, and Taking Over the World*. MIT Press.

Safak, C. and Farrar, J. (2021). *Managed by Bots: Data-Driven Exploitation in the Gig Economy*. Worker Info Exchange. *https://www.workerinfoexchange.org/wie-report-managed-by-bots*

Said, E. W. (1978). *Orientalism*. Routledge & Kegan Paul.

Saussure, F. de. (1966). *Course in General Linguistics*. McGraw-Hill.

Sautoy, M. du. (2019). Can AI ever be truly creative? *New Scientist*, 242 (3229): 38–41. *https://doi.org/10.1016/S0262-4079(19)30840-1*

Scheler, M. (1924). *Problems of a Sociology of Knowledge*. Routledge & Kegan Paul.

Scholz, T. (ed.). (2012). *Digital Labor: The Internet as Playground and Factory*. Routledge.

Schwab, K. (2016). *The Fourth Industrial Revolution*. Crown Business.

Schwartz, R., Vassilev, A., Greene, K., Perine, L., Burt, A., and Hall, P. (2022). *Towards a Standard for Identifying and Managing Bias in Artificial Intelligence*. NIST.

Seaver, N. (2019). Knowing algorithms. In J. Vertesi and D. Ribes (eds), *digitalSTS: A Field Guide for Science and Technology Studies* (pp. 412–22). Princeton University Press.

Sejnowski, T. J. (2018). *The Deep Learning Revolution*. MIT Press.

Selbst, A. D. (2017). A mild defense of our new machine overlords (SSRN Scholarly Paper No. 2941078). *https://papers.ssrn.com/abstract=2941078*

Shanahan, M. (2015). *The Technological Singularity*. MIT Press.

Shelley, M. W. (2017). *Frankenstein: Or, the Modern Prometheus: Annotated for Scientists, Engineers, and Creators of all Kinds* (D. H. Guston, E. Finn, J. S. Robert, J. Eschrich, and M. Drago, eds). MIT Press.

Silver, D., Huang, A., Maddison, C. J., Guez, A., Sifre, L., van den Driessche, G., Schrittwieser, J., Antonoglou, I., Panneershelvam, V., Lanctot, M., Dieleman, S., Grewe, D., Nham, J., Kalchbrenner, N., Sutskever, I., Lillicrap, T., Leach, M., Kavukcuoglu, K., Graepel, T., and Hassabis, D. (2016). Mastering the game of Go with deep neural networks and tree search. *Nature*, 529 (7587): 484–9. *https://doi.org /10.1038/nature16961*

Sloane, M., Moss, E., Awomolo, O., and Forlano, L. (2022). Participation is not a design fix for machine learning. *Equity and Access in Algorithms, Mechanisms, and Optimization*, 1–6. *https:// doi.org/10.1145/3551624.3555285*

Smith, B. C. (2019). *The Promise of Artificial Intelligence: Reckoning and Judgment*. MIT Press.

Smith, S., Patwary, M., Norick, B., LeGresley, P., Rajbhandari, S., Casper, J., Liu, Z., Prabhumoye, S., Zerveas, G., Korthikanti, V., Zhang, E., Child, R., Aminabadi, R. Y., Bernauer, J., Song, X., Shoeybi, M., He, Y., Houston, M., Tiwary, S., and Catanzaro, B. (2022). *Using DeepSpeed and Megatron to Train Megatron-Turing NLG 530B, A Large-Scale Generative Language Model* (No. arXiv:2 201.11990). arXiv. *https://doi.org/10.48550/arXiv.2201.11990*

Smythe, D. W. (1981). *Dependency Road: Communications, Capitalism, Consciousness, and Canada*. Ablex.

Snow, J. (2018). Amazon's face recognition falsely matched 28 members of Congress with mugshots. *American Civil Liberties Union*. *https:// web.archive.org/web/20221204011525/https://www.aclu.org/news /privacy-technology/amazons-face-recognition-falsely-matched-28*

Solomonides, T. and Levidow, L. (eds) (1985). *Compulsive Technology: Computers as Culture*. Free Association Books.

Spivak, G. C. (1996). *The Spivak Reader: Selected Works of Gayatri Chakravorty Spivak*. Routledge.

Srnicek, N. (2015). *Inventing the Future: Postcapitalism and a World Without Work*. Verso.

Srnicek, N. and Williams, A. (2019). #Accelerate: Manifesto for an Accelerationist Politics. In R. Mackay and A. Avanessian (eds), *#Accelerate# The Accelerationist Reader* (pp. 347–462). Urbanomic.

Star, S. L. and Griesemer, J. R. (1989). Institutional ecology, translations and boundary objects: Amateurs and professionals in Berkeley's Museum of Vertebrate Zoology, 1907-39. *Social Studies of Science*, 19 (3): 387–420.

Star, S. L. and Ruhleder, K. (1996). Steps toward an ecology of infrastructure: Design and access for large information spaces. *Information Systems Research*, 7 (1): 111–34. *https://doi.org/10.1287/isre.7.1 .111*

Steinhoff, J. (2021). The social reconfiguration of artificial intelligence: Utility and feasibility. In P. Verdegem (ed.), *AI for Everyone? Critical Perspectives* (pp. 123–43). University of Westminster Press.

Stiegler, B. (2019). *The Age of Disruption: Technology and Madness in Computational Capitalism*. Polity.

Suchman, L. (2022). Imaginaries of omniscience: Automating intelligence in the US Department of Defense. *Social Studies of Science*, 03063127221104938. *https://doi.org/10.1177/0306312722110 4938*

Suchman, L. (1987). *Plans and Situated Actions: The Problem of Human–Machine Communication*. Cambridge University Press.

Suchman, L. (2006). *Human–Machine Reconfigurations: Plans and Situated Actions* (2nd edn). Cambridge University Press.

Suchman, L. and Randall, T. (1993). Artificial intelligence as craftwork. In S. Chaiklin and J. Lave (eds), *Understanding Practice: Perspectives on Activity and Context* (pp. 144–78). Cambridge University Press.

Sudmann, A. (ed.). (2019). *The Democratization of Artificial Intelligence: Net Politics in the Era of Learning Algorithms*. transcript Verlag. *https://doi.org/10.14361/9783839447192*

Sutko, D. M. (2020). Theorizing femininity in artificial intelligence: A framework for undoing technology's gender troubles. *Cultural Studies*, 34 (4): 567–92. *https://doi.org/10.1080/09502386.2019.16 71469*

Tadajewski, M. and Jones, D. G. B. (2021). From goods-dominant logic to service-dominant logic? Service, service capitalism and service socialism. *Marketing Theory*, 21 (1): 113–34. *https://doi.org/10.11 77/1470593120966768*

Tafvelin, S., Hjelte, J., Schimmer, R., Forsgren, M., Torra, V., and Andreas, S. (2023). Introducing robots and AI in organizations: What are the implications for employees and service users? In S. Lindgren (ed.), *The Handbook of Critical Studies of Artificial Intelligence*. Edward Elgar.

Takala, T. (1998). Plato on leadership. *Journal of Business Ethics*, 17 (7): 785–98.

Taylor, A. (2018). The automation charade. *Logic Magazine*. *https://lo gicmag.io/failure/the-automation-charade/*

Taylor, F. W. (1911). *The Principles of Scientific Management*. Harper & Brothers.

Taylor, T. L. (2006). Beyond management: Considering participatory design and governance in player culture. *First Monday*. *https://doi .org/10.5210/fm.v0i0.1611*

Techopedia (2022). What is Reification? *Techopedia.com*. *https://web .archive.org/web/20220516161141/https://www.techopedia.com/de finition/21674/reification*

Tegmark, M. (2017). *Life 3.0: Being Human in the Age of Artificial Intelligence*. Alfred A. Knopf.

Thatcher, J., O'Sullivan, D. and Mahmoudi, D. (2016). Data colonialism through accumulation by dispossession: New metaphors for daily data. *Environment and Planning D: Society and Space*, 34 (6): 990–1006. *https://doi.org/10.1177/0263775816633195*

Thompson, J. B. (1984). *Studies in the Theory of Ideology*. Polity.

Thompson, J. B. (1990). *Ideology and Modern Culture: Critical Social Theory in the Era of Mass Communication*. Stanford University Press.

Thrift, N. (2005). *Knowing Capitalism*. SAGE. *https://doi.org/10.4135/9781446211458*

TietoEVRY (2021). *Intelligent Automation and Robotics*. *https://web.archive.org/web/20211025211525/https://www.tietoevry.com/en/services/data-ai-and-analytics/intelligent-automation-and-robotics/*

Toffler, A. (1980). *The Third Wave*. Collins.

Tomašev, N., Cornebise, J., Hutter, F., Mohamed, S., Picciariello, A., Connelly, B., Belgrave, D. C. M., Ezer, D., Haert, F. C. van der, Mugisha, F., Abila, G., Arai, H., Almiraat, H., Proskurnia, J., Snyder, K., Otake-Matsuura, M., Othman, M., Glasmachers, T., Wever, W. de, . . . Clopath, C. (2020). AI for social good: Unlocking the opportunity for positive impact. *Nature Communications*, 11(1, 1): 2468. *https://doi.org/10.1038/s41467-020-15871-z*

Treré, E. and Bonini, T. (2022). Amplification, evasion, hijacking: Algorithms as repertoire for social movements and the struggle for visibility. *Social Movement Studies*, 1–17. *https://doi.org/10.1080/14742837.2022.2143345*

Turing, A. (1950). Computing machinery and intelligence. *Mind*, 49 (236): 433–60. *https://doi.org/10.1093/mind/LIX.236.433*

Tyson, L. (2006). *Critical Theory Today: A User-Friendly Guide*.

Uber (2022). Drive with Uber. *Uber.com*. *https://web.archive.org/web/20221027144157/https://www.uber.com/se/en/s/e/join/*

Ure, A. (1835). *The Philosophy of Manufactures: Or, an Exposition of the Scientific, Moral and Commercial Economy of the Factory System of Great Britain*. Knight.

Urzì Brancati, M. C., Pesole, A., and Fernandez Macias, E. (2019). *Digital Labour Platforms in Europe: Numbers, Profiles, and Employment Status of Platform Workers* (JRC Research Reports No. JRC117330). Joint Research Centre. *https://econpapers.repec.org/paper/iptiptwpa/jrc117330.htm*

Valaskivi, K. (2020). The contemporary faith of innovationism. In E. Bell, S. Gog, A. Simionca, and S. Taylor (eds), *Spirituality, Organization and Neoliberalism: Understanding Lived Experiences* (pp. 171–93). Edward Elgar Publishing. *https://public.ebookcentral.proquest.com/choice/publicfullrecord.aspx?p=6263920*

van Maanen, G. (2022). AI ethics, ethics washing, and the need to politicize data ethics. *Digital Society*, 1 (2): 9. *https://doi.org/10.1007/s44206-022-00013-3*

Veblen, T. (1914). *The Instinct of Workmanship and the State of the Industrial Arts*. Macmillan & Co.

Vecchione, B., Levy, K., and Barocas, S. (2021). Algorithmic auditing and social justice: Lessons from the history of audit studies. *Equity and Access in Algorithms, Mechanisms, and Optimization*, 1–9. *https://doi.org/10.1145/3465416.3483294*

Verdegem, P. (ed.). (2021). *AI for Everyone? Critical Perspectives*. University of Westminster Press.

Verdegem, P. (2023). Critical AI studies meets critical political economy. In S. Lindgren (ed.), *The Handbook of Critical Studies of Artificial Intelligence*. Edward Elgar.

Vesa, M. and Tienari, J. (2020). Artificial intelligence and rationalized unaccountability: Ideology of the elites? *Organization*, 1350508420963872. *https://doi.org/10.1177/1350508420963872*

Vieweg, S. H. (2021). *AI for the Good: Artificial Intelligence and Ethics*. Springer. *http://gen.lib.rus.ec/book/index.php?md5=EF090AB1058 C9D15A241E04D10D61F6E*

Villarroel Luque, C. (2021). Workers vs algorithms. *Verfassungsblog*. *https://web.archive.org/web/20220121223051/https://verfassungsbl og.de/workers-vs-ai/*

Villiers de l'Isle-Adam, A. (1886). *Tomorrow's Eve*. Internet Archive. *http://archive.org/details/tomorrowseve0000vill*

Vincent, J. (2018). Google 'fixed' its racist algorithm by removing gorillas from its image-labeling tech. *The Verge*. *https://web.archive.org /web/20221111070620/https://www.theverge.com/2018/1/12/1688 2408/google-racist-gorillas-photo-recognition-algorithm-ai*

Waelen, R. (2022). Why AI ethics is a critical theory. *Philosophy & Technology*, 35 (1), 9. *https://doi.org/10.1007/s13347-022-00507-5*

Wagner, D. (2021). On the emergence and design of AI nudging: The gentle big brother? *ROBONOMICS: Journal of the Automated Economy*, 2: 18. *https://journal.robonomics.science/index.php/rj /article/view/18*

Wajcman, J. (1991). *Feminism Confronts Technology*. Polity.

Wake, P. and Malpas, S. (eds) (2013). *The Routledge Companion to Critical and Cultural Theory*. Routledge.

Wang, C., Wang, K., Bian, A., Islam, R., Keya, K. N., Foulde, J., and Pan, S. (2021). Bias: Friend or foe? User acceptance of gender stereotypes in automated career recommendations. *UMBC Student Collection*.

Wang, F., Jiang, M., Qian, C., Yang, S., Li, C., Zhang, H., Wang, X., and Tang, X. (2017). Residual attention network for image classification. *2017 IEEE Conference on Computer Vision and Pattern Recognition (CVPR)*, 6450–8. *https://doi.org/10.1109/CVPR.2017 .683*

Wang, Y. and Kosinski, M. (2018). Deep neural networks are more accurate than humans at detecting sexual orientation from facial images. *Journal of Personality and Social Psychology*, 114 (2): 246–57. *https://doi.org/10.1037/pspa0000098*

Waterson, J. (2016). Daily Telegraph installs workplace monitors on journalists' desks. *BuzzFeed*. *https://web.archive.org/web/2022102 4015812/http://www.buzzfeed.com/jimwaterson/telegraph-workpla ce-sensors*

Weber, M. (1930). *The Protestant Ethic and the Spirit of Capitalism*. Routledge.

Weber, M. (1978). *Economy and Society: An Outline of Interpretive Sociology*. University of California Press.

Williams, M. (2019). Ecovacs' new robot vacuum uses AI to recognize the stuff on your floor. *TechHive*. *https://web.archive.org/web/2022 0516212455/https://www.techhive.com/article/583607/ecovacs-new -robot-vacuum-uses-ai-to-recognize-the-stuff-on-your-floor.html*

Williams, R. (1961). *The Long Revolution*. Chatto & Windus.

Williams, R. and Edge, D. (1996). The social shaping of technology. *Research Policy*, 25 (6): 865–99.

Wilson, C. (2020). Artificial intelligence and warfare. In M. Martellini and R. Trapp (eds), *21st Century Prometheus: Managing CBRN Safety and Security Affected by Cutting-Edge Technologies* (pp. 125–40). Springer. *https://doi.org/10.1007/978-3-030-28285-1_7*

Winner, L. (1993). Upon opening the black box and finding it empty: Social constructivism and the philosophy of technology. *Science, Technology, & Human Values*, 18 (3), 362–78. *https://www.jstor .org/stable/689726*

Winner, L. (1997). Cyberlibertarian myths and the prospects for community. *ACM SIGCAS Computers and Society*, 27 (3): 14–19. *https://doi.org/10.1145/270858.270864*

Wodak, R. (ed.). (1997). *Gender and Discourse*. SAGE.

Wogu, I. A. P., Olu-Owolabi, F. E., Assibong, P. A., Agoha, B. C., Sholarin, M., Elegbeleye, A., Igbokwe, D., and Apeh, H. A. (2017). Artificial intelligence, alienation and ontological problems of other minds: A critical investigation into the future of man and machines. *2017 International Conference on Computing Networking and Informatics (ICCNI)*, 1–10. *https://doi.org/10.1109/ICCNI.2017.81 23792*

Woolgar, S. (1985). Why not a sociology of machines? The case of sociology and artificial intelligence. *Sociology*, 19 (4): 557–72.

Wrangel, C. (2015). Towards a modified discourse theory pt. 1: Laclau's 'empty signifier'. *That's Not It*.

Xie, T. and Pentina, I. (2022). *Attachment Theory as a Framework to Understand Relationships with Social Chatbots: A Case Study of Replika*. Hawaii International Conference on System Sciences. *https://doi.org/10.24251/HICSS.2022.258*

Xiong, W., Droppo, J., Huang, X., Seide, F., Seltzer, M. L., Stolcke, A., Yu, D., and Zweig, G. (2017). Toward human parity in conversational speech recognition. *IEEE/ACM Transactions on Audio, Speech, and Language Processing*, 25 (12): 2410–23.

Xu, T. (2021). AI makes decisions we don't understand. That's a problem. *BuiltIn*. *https://builtin.com/artificial-intelligence/ai-right-expla nation*

Yao, Q., Wang, M., Chen, Y., Dai, W., Li, Y.-F., Tu, W.-W., Yang, Q., and Yu, Y. (2019). *Taking Human out of Learning Applications: A Survey on Automated Machine Learning* (No. arXiv:1810.13306). arXiv. *http://arxiv.org/abs/1810.13306*

Zajko, M. (2021). Conservative AI and social inequality: Conceptualizing alternatives to bias through social theory. *AI & SOCIETY*, 36 (3): 1047–56. *https://doi.org/10.1007/s00146-021-01153-9*

Zerilli, J., Danaher, J., Maclaurin, J., Gavaghan, C., Knott, A., Liddicoat, J., and Noorman, M. E. (2020). *A Citizen's Guide to Artificial Intelligence*. MIT Press.

Žižek, S. (1994). *Mapping Ideology*. Verso.

Žižek, S. (2008). *The Sublime Object of Ideology*. Verso.

Zuboff, S. (2019). *The Age of Surveillance Capitalism: The Fight for a Human Future at the New Frontier of Power*. PublicAffairs.

Zytek, A., Liu, D., Vaithianathan, R., and Veeramachaneni, K. (2022). Sibyl: Understanding and addressing the usability challenges of machine learning in high-stakes decision making. *IEEE Transactions on Visualization and Computer Graphics*, 28 (1): 1161–71. *https://doi.org/10.1109/TVCG.2021.3114864*

Index